Natural Computing Series

Series Editors

More information about this series at http://www.springer.com/series/4190

Nelishia Pillay · Rong Qu
Editors

Automated Design of Machine Learning and Search Algorithms

Springer

Editors
Nelishia Pillay
Department of Computer Science
University of Pretoria
Pretoria, South Africa

Rong Qu
School of Computer Science
University of Nottingham
Nottingham, UK

ISSN 1619-7127
Natural Computing Series
ISBN 978-3-030-72071-1 ISBN 978-3-030-72069-8 (eBook)
https://doi.org/10.1007/978-3-030-72069-8

This Springer imprint is published by the registered company Springer Nature Switzerland AG
The registered company address is: Gewerbestrasse 11, 6330 Cham, Switzerland

To my parents Perumal and Sinathra Manickum, thank you for believing in me and always being there.

Nelishia Pillay

To my dearest daughter Jess Xue, who makes me a happier and better person.

Rong Qu

Foreword

It is an honor for me to write the Foreword for the book entitled *Automated Design of Machine Learning and Search Algorithms* by Nelishia Pillay (University of Pretoria) and Rong Qu (University of Nottingham). Nelishia and Rong have done a wonderful job on selecting and collecting investigation on the important subject of automatically designing algorithms of great appeal to researchers in the field. Interesting themes are covered in the book coming from different techniques and perspectives such as machine learning, combinatorial optimization, theoretical analysis of hyper-heuristics, generation of robotic swarms, generation hyper-heuristics for producing constructive and perturbative heuristics, current and future trends in the automated design using hyper-heuristics, transfer learning in neural architectures and knowledge reuse, and evolution of classifiers for single and multi-class classification.

Automated generation and improving algorithms for solving a particular or a wide set of problems is not an easy task, but with the advancement on artificial intelligence and the computational power in recent years, the research has evolved to produce solid and sophisticated methods with less human intervention. However, this is still a big challenge with a long way to have the crystal ball to devise the best algorithm or tool for solving a given problem, but this book indeed contributes to close that gap, and it is a good resource that every researcher and practitioner in the area should have and read. It is an issue to come up with relevant methods by either evolving complete algorithms given some initial components, or constructing methods that take an existing algorithm and improve it or adapt it to a given domain. Defining the primitives that compose the search space is another important aspect since they should capture the knowledge of experts about useful algorithmic components and operators for allowing the generation of new algorithm variants. We need competent frameworks and architectures for integrating and combining algorithmic constituents and techniques to strive steadily towards the ultimate goal.

This book includes recent advances across automated machine learning and automated algorithm design, where the performance of techniques and algorithms has been strengthened with the support of state-of-the-art models, theories, frameworks and benchmarks. The emerging research directions in those areas present a series of challenges over multiple research communities in machine learning, bio-inspired computation and optimization. Other issues related to automated design are raised in the book and presented as future directions such as reusability, explainable automated algorithms, computational costs, theoretical aspects, automated design standardization, and semi-automated design.

My recognition goes to Nelishia and Rong, two successful female researchers in our community. I know that they have worked very hard to make possible this special collection.

Monterrey, Mexico
January 2021

Hugo Terashima-Marin

Preface

As we move into the fourth industrial revolution, the need for off-the-shelf tools for designing machine learning and search algorithms to solve real-world problems is fast-increasing. This book is comprised of chapters written by leading researchers in automated design of machine learning and search algorithms, highlighting current trends and future directions in the fast-developing area.

Chapter 1 provides an introduction to the book and overviews the area of automated design of machine learning and search algorithms, the topics covered by the subsequent chapters, and challenges experienced in the research.

Chapter 2 presents an overview of methodologies developed in automated machine learning (AutoML) within the last decade, with the definitions of components of AutoML, providing a nice introduction to the topic.

Chapter 3 provides a standardisation for search algorithms based on General Combinatorial Optimisation Problem (GCOP), a new model that defines automated design of search algorithms as an optimisation problem.

Chapter 4 focuses on the theoretical aspects of automated design, an area which has not received sufficient attention. A complexity analysis of hyper-heuristics is presented for selecting heuristics for combinatorial optimisation.

Chapter 5 presents AutoMoDe, a novel approach for the automated offline design of robot swarms by combining and configuring parametric modules of low-level behaviors to evolve high-level collective behaviors.

Chapter 6 presents a novel generation hyper-heuristic for the automated generation of constructive and perturbative heuristics for highly different optimization problems which are encoded as "intermediate" graphs.

Chapter 7 provides an overview of past, current and future trends in hyper-heuristics in the context of automated design. One of the challenges is to build widely accepted libraries in the hyper-heuristic consortium.

Chapter 8 examines methods for reducing the computational cost of neural architecture search. Transfer learning in evolutionary algorithms is an emerging area that has a lot of potential for automated design.

Chapter 9 illustrates knowledge transfer in the automated generation of heuristics by reusing useful subtrees and feature importance in genetic programming based generation hyper-heuristics.

Chapter 10 compares the performance of genetic algorithms and grammatical evolution for the automated design of genetic programming for the evolution of classifiers for binary and multiples classification.

Chapter 11 summaries current trends in the area and proposes future research directions.

We would like to thank all the authors for their excellent contributions to the book. It was a great pleasure to work with and bringing together leading researchers from multiple disciplines across artificial intelligence, evolutionary computation and optimisation research.

Pretoria, South Africa
Nottingham, UK
December 2020

Nelishia Pillay
Rong Qu

Acknowledgements

A big thank to the authors for their invaluable contributions to the book. We would also like to thank Professor Hugo Terashima-Marin for writing the foreward of the book. A final thank you to Mr. Ronan Nugent for all his guidance and assistance throughout the whole process from the preparation to publishing the book.

Contents

Contributors

Mazhar Ansari Ardeh Victoria University of Wellington, Wellington, New Zealand

Mauro Birattari Université libre de Bruxelles, Brussels, Belgium

Hugo Jair Escalante Computer Science Departments, Centro de Investigación y de Estudios Avanzados del IPN, Mexico city, Mexico;
Instituto Nacional de Astrofísica, Óptica y Electrónica, Puebla, Mexico

Gianpiero Francesca Toyota Motor Europe, Brussels, Belgium

Emma Hart Edinburgh Napier University, Edinburgh, Scotland

Yaochu Jin Department of Computer Science, University of Surrey, Guildford, UK

Antoine Ligot Université libre de Bruxelles, Brussels, Belgium

Yi Mei Victoria University of Wellington, Wellington, New Zealand

Mustafa Mısır Department of Computer Engineering, Istinye University, Zeytinburnu, Istanbul, Turkey;
Duke Kunshan University, Kunshan, Jiangsu, China

Thambo Nyathi National University of Science and Technology, Bulawayo, Zimbabwe

Pietro S. Oliveto Department of Computer Science, University of Sheffield, Sheffield, UK

Ben Paechter Edinburgh Napier University, Edinburgh, Scotland

Nelishia Pillay University of Pretoria, Pretoria, South Africa

Rong Qu University of Nottingham, Nottingham, United Kingdom

Christopher Stone University of St Andrews, St Andrews, Scotland

Mengjie Zhang Victoria University of Wellington, Wellington, New Zealand

Hangyu Zhu Department of Computer Science, University of Surrey, Guildford, UK

Acronyms

ACO	Ant Colony Optimization
AM	All Moves
AutoAD	Automated Algorithm Design
AutoDes	Automated Design
AutoML	Automated Machine Learning
BNF	Backus Naur Form
BP	Bin Packing
CBR	Case-Based Reasoning
COP	Combinatorial Optimisation Problems
EA	Evolutionary Algorithm
EC	Evolutionary Computation
FLOPs	Floating Point Operations per Second
GA	Genetic Algorithm
GCOP	General Combinatorial Optimization Problem
GE	Grammatical Evolution
GEP	Gene Expression Programming
GHH	Generation Hyper-Heuristic
GLS	Greedy Local Search
GP	Genetic Programming
GPHH	Genetic Programming-Based Hyper-Heuristic
HH	Hyper-Heuristic
ILS	Iterated Local Search
LLH	Low-Level Heuristic
MA	Move Acceptance
MeA	Memetic Algorithm
MH	Meta-Heuristic
MKP	Multidimensional Knapsack Problem
ML	Machine Learning
MOEA	Multi-objective Evolutionary Algorithm
NAS	Neural Architecture Search

NFLT	No Free Lunch Theorem
NSGA	Non-dominated Sorting Genetic Algorithm
OI	Only Improving
PAP	Population-Based Algorithm Portfolios
PSO	Particle Swarm Optimization
RL	Reinforcement Learning
RLS	Randomized Local Search
SA	Simulated Annealing
SHH	Selection Hyper-Heuristic
SMBO	Sequential Model-Based Optimisation
SR	Simple Random
SRMA	Simple Random Move Acceptance
TGP	Tree-Based Genetic Programming
TS	Tabu Search
TSP	Travelling Salesman Problem
UCARP	Uncertain Capacitated Arc Routing Problem

Chapter 1
Recent Developments of Automated Machine Learning and Search Techniques

Rong Qu

Abstract The recent successes of artificial intelligence, in particular machine learning, for solving real-world problems have motivated the advances towards automated design of algorithms and systems with less human involvement. In machine learning and meta-heuristic search algorithms, different lines of relevant research are now emerging, with findings feeding into each other. This book presents a selection of some recent advances across automated machine learning (AutoML) and automated algorithm design (AutoAD), where the effectiveness and efficiency of techniques and algorithms has been enhanced with the support of new taxonomies, models, theories, as well as frameworks and benchmarks. The emerging new lines of exciting research directions in AutoML and AutoAD present new challenges across multiple research communities in machine learning, evolutionary computation and optimisation research.

1.1 Introduction

With the recent fast developments of artificial intelligence in tackling practical problems comes an increasing demand of general tools and intelligent methods with less human involvement for solving new problems. These include automated machine learning (AutoML) and automated algorithm design (AutoAD) in a broad range of application domains. This book selects some of the latest developments across AutoML and AutoAD, and presents key challenges and research issues, calling for and encouraging further advances towards automated intelligent algorithms and systems for solving more new real-world problems.

The wide range of recent developments range from the automated design of heuristics [10, 12, 20] and control software [1] using meta-heuristics and genetic programming [8] to automated design of neural architectures [23] and classifier algorithms

R. Qu (✉)
University of Nottingham, Nottingham, United Kingdom
e-mail: rong.qu@nottingham.ac.uk

N. Pillay and R. Qu (eds.), *Automated Design of Machine Learning and Search Algorithms*, Natural Computing Series,
https://doi.org/10.1007/978-3-030-72069-8_1

[14] using evolutionary algorithms. Application problems include mainly combinatorial optimisation [8, 10, 12, 20] and classification problems [3, 14, 23].

Within the context of automated design of machine learning and meta-heuristics search algorithms discussed in Sect. 1.2, some interesting research issues are emerging, posing challenges on future advances across different disciplines of machine learning, evolutionary computation and optimisation research as discussed in Sect. 1.3. The chapter concludes in Sect. 1.4 by summarising developments and challenges, and encouraging several directions of future research.

1.2 Automated Algorithm Design and Machine Learning

Until recently, the success of most intelligent algorithms and systems heavily relies on extensive human expertise, which often highly depends on experts' skills on making various decisions. These include, at a lower level, how to fine-tune the parameters or settings of the chosen algorithms or models; and at a higher level, how to select the most appropriate algorithms or system architecture for solving the problems at hand. The algorithms or systems designed manually in an ad-hoc manner are also often problem-specific, requiring a large amount of effort adapting existing algorithms or re-designing new algorithms. These algorithms are often discarded after problem solving, wasting extensive human resources.

With the fast developments in machine learning, there is now evidence that AutoML [5] is achievable [3] in both research and practice. There exist highly effective machine learning methods ready for use for non-experts with limited knowledge. Based on the definitions of components in AutoML, the brief review in Chap. 2 on the AutoML methodologies in supervised learning provides a nice complimentary introduction to the field [3]. Of particular interest is that evolutionary computation naturally plays an important role in *Optimizer*, one of the three important components in AutoML methods. Some of the challenges identified in Chap. 2, e.g. large-scale optimisation and transfer of learning in AutoML, require further collaboration and integration of machine learning and computational search algorithms.

Chapter 8 provides an excellent example of the latest developments in AutoML integrating machine learning and evolutionary algorithms [23]. The computational expensive offline optimisation in neural architecture search (NAS) is extended to federated learning within distributed real-time systems for edge devices. With the focus on reducing computational costs, two NSGA-II-based multi-objective evolutionary algorithms have been investigated to automatic online NAS for image classification. Much more research remains to be addressed with evolutionary computation for NAS, including the model averaging aggregation for tasks of different features and security of privacy leakage.

Research in AutoAD comes along another line of developments in optimisation research. In building a standard towards automated algorithm design, Chap. 3 presents a new taxonomy to categorise relevant research into three streams, namely automated algorithm configuration, algorithm selection and algorithm composition [18]. With different decisions of parameters, algorithms and algorithm components, automated algorithm design can be defined as an optimisation problem exploring a search space of these decisions. A new model named general combinatorial optimisation problem (GCOP) is defined [19], where elementary algorithm components are considered as decision variables in the search space of algorithms. Chapter 3 also demonstrates that various meta-heuristics and selection hyper-heuristics can be defined with this unified general GCOP model.

In designing control software for robot swarms, Chap. 5 presents a modular principle in AutoMoDe to automatically assemble predefined parametric modules [1]. By exploring a search space of all possible low-level individual behaviours of robots, AutoMoDe optimises the performance of their collective high-level behaviours. This modular principle presents an interesting contrast to that of the GCOP model in Chap. 3, where the design of meta-heuristic algorithms is defined as an optimisation problem upon the search space of elementary algorithmic components [18]. AutoMoDe automatically selects, combines and fine-tunes predefined modules to design control software offline by using Iterated F-race [2], a highly successful framework for automated configuration of meta-heuristics for combinatorial optimisation problems.

Chapter 4 presents an analysis and overview of time complexity and learning in selection hyper-heuristics for function optimisation [12]. It is evidenced that mixing multiple low level heuristics and switching acceptance criteria are necessary to achieve optimal performance. Furthermore, adaptive learning is crucial in selecting low-level heuristics at different stages of hyper-heuristics. The importance of comprehension in automated selection of low-level heuristics is highlighted in Chap. 7, where powerful tools in machine learning might be of great support. Time complexity is less studied in the existing literature but is a fundamental issue to underpin algorithm design. With analysis on time and landscapes, theoretical studies can lead to more insights and knowledge on algorithm behaviour and performance.

While Chap. 4 focuses on selection hyper-heuristics [12], Chaps. 6, 9 and 10 concern generation hyper-heuristics, presenting interesting findings for both combinatorial optimisation [8, 20] and classification [14] problems. Compared to the extensively studied selection hyper-heuristics, generation hyper-heuristics are relatively less studied. They focus on automatic generation of heuristics themselves, thus removing human involvement in providing problem-specific low-level heuristics. Problem attributes need to be provided instead, in addition to a set of general operators/grammars. Genetic programming and grammatical evolution have been employed, addressing interesting research issues of common solution representation [20] in Chap. 6, knowledge transfer [8] in Chap. 9 and fitness landscape [14] in Chap. 10.

Chapter 10 concerns the automated design of classifier algorithms, where chromosomes in grammatical evolution consist of design decisions for different classification tasks [14]. In contrast to the automated search of neural architectures in Chap. 8, this presents a different perspective of integrating evolutionary computation and machine learning in AutoML. With the fitness analysis on genetic algorithm and grammatical evolution, it is also interesting to reveal the different features of the landscapes for multi-class classification and binary classification. In the literature, theoretical analysis such as fitness landscape or time complexity received less research attention, however, is crucial in sustaining the fundamentals towards effective AutoML [3] and AutoAD [18].

In Chap. 6, an "intermediate" graph-based solution representation is studied for designing constructive and perturbative heuristics for highly different combinatorial optimisation problems [20]. The research makes an important step towards further removing expert's involvement in defining solution encoding, to which the problem-specific heuristics are applied. Defining common problem encoding is often neglected in the literature, however, is highly important in AutoAD. Further advances on extending the scope of cross-domain general solution encoding is crucial in sharing and retaining knowledge of automatically designed effective algorithms addressing different problem domains of common structures.

Chapter 9 highlights the importance of knowledge transfer [8], which also receives less attention in the literature of hyper-heuristics, and also meta-heuristics. In guiding the search directions, it is shown that reusing subtrees in the initialisation is more effective than feature importance evolved automatically by genetic programming. Challenging issues remain, including the lack of understanding on truly useful subtrees and building blocks, and the handling of redundant branches (i.e. issue of bloating) in genetic programming.

Chapter 7 presents an insightful overview of hyper-heuristics within the context of autonomous problem solvers [10]. One interesting research issue discussed is on the set of low-level heuristics, which is still hand-picked by human experts for particular problems; while a set of strong problem-specific heuristics does not always warranty strong performance of hyper-heuristics. This echos the definition of a set of elementary algorithm components in GCOP in Chap. 3, which could also deliver strong performance if simple components are composed effectively [19]. The observations are also supported by the theoretical proof in Chap. 2, where multiple low-level heuristics are necessary to achieve optimal performance of hyper-heuristics.

1.3 Challenges in Automated Design of Algorithms and Machine Learning

Recent developments in AutoML have achieved great success in solving various real-world problems based on advanced research, see surveys in [5] and Chap. 4. In AutoAD, different lines of research emerge on automated configuration [21] and automated selection [5] of algorithms. Based on the new taxonomy of algorithm design, another line of research on automated algorithm composition has also been defined [18], where hyper-heuristics represent a subset of such methods. In the autonomy of algorithms and techniques in artificial intelligence, it is interesting to see that different lines of developments integrating machine learning and evolutionary computation are emerging, underpinning each other to address wider range of problems.

It is difficult to review exclusively the latest advances in AutoML and AutoAD across multiple disciplines, however, some of the key challenges and research issues can be identified based on the blend of the latest developments presented in this book. These include in particular the comprehension and interpretability of the algorithms/techniques [8, 12] and theoretical studies [3, 10, 18], which are still neglected although frequently mentioned in the literature. Research addressing these challenges all underpin further advances in AutoML and AutoAD.

Theoretical Fundamentals

Theoretical analysis is relatively less concerned in AutoAD. The overview of time complexity in Chap. 2 on selection hyper-heuristics proves the necessity of multiple low-level heuristics and acceptance criteria, as well as adaptive learning in selecting effective low-level heuristics [6]. In generation hyper-heuristics, it is highly interesting that the fitness landscapes for genetic algorithms and grammatical evolution present different ruggedness for binary and multi-class classifications [14]. Hyper-heuristics have shown to achieve to some extent free lunches [22], and are more general than some algorithms [10, 17]. More findings with rigorous theoretical analysis will further underpin the fundamentals and better understanding of AutoAD.

While well-defined models and architectures exist in AutoML, in meta-heuristic algorithms, there is a lack of common models or frameworks. Most frameworks in AutoAD are defined descriptively, lacking a fundamentally consistent structure and standard. More research is needed towards modelling and standardising algorithm design [18]; otherwise many of the research findings remain local [10] for specific problems, or are discarded in the rich but scattered literature. Some progress has been made, including the highly successful Iterated F-race framework for automated algorithm configurations [2] and the widely adapted HyFlex platform [11] and EvoHyp toolkit [13] in hyper-heuristics [15]. In [19], a new taxonomy is defined based on the decisions considered in AutoAD, to support the development of common models such as GCOP in Chap. 3 in automated design of general search algorithms.

The idea of modularity presents an interesting principle in designing both control software in Chap. 5 and meta-heuristic algorithms in Chap. 3. In the two distinctive domains, with the search spaces of behaviours and algorithmic components, respectively, the automated design of control software and search algorithms can both be defined as optimisation problems, where modules and components are automatically assembled and optimised. Existing powerful optimisation platforms and frameworks including Iterated F-Race [2] and HyFlex [11] can also be adapted to quickly implement the optimisation, and potentially sustain knowledge sharing across different disciplines and application domains.

In AutoAD, establishing general and common solution encoding presents another challenge for different combinatorial optimisation problems. In Chap. 6, a graph-based encoding shows to be successful representing multiple different problems. With common encoding, knowledge and expertise in AutoAD could be accumulated and retained in a consistent structure for comparable and transferable investigations in different domains.

Interpretability, Reusability and Generality

AutoML demands extensive search, generating a vast amount of information [3]. Extensive information also exists in AutoAD on designing or generating effective algorithms. The relatively well-structured machine learning models can support analysis on designing effective systems thus to extract reusable knowledge. However, this is not the case in search algorithms, where there is a lack of common frameworks or unified models, based on which systematic analysis could be conducted to identify explainable or reusable knowledge. In both AutoML and AutoAD, the extensive information is yet to be collected in consistent structures and analysed to extract transferable and reusable knowledge in designing effective search algorithms and machine learning systems.

While search algorithms that have been criticised for lacking theoretical support, explainability and interpretability are often known as unsolved challenges in machine learning. Some attempts have been made to transfer the information evolved in genetic programming [8, 20] into knowledge of generating heuristics. With the consistent data structures in genetic programming, potential knowledge in grammars [20], subtrees and feature importance [8] could be retained and reused in designing effective algorithms addressing similar or even different tasks or problems. More collaborative efforts across disciplines are needed in both AutoML and AutoAD to reveal new transferable knowledge thus to enhance the reusability of algorithms.

In retaining and reusing knowledge evolved automatically, the issue of common solution encoding is understudied, although the search of algorithms is highly dependant on solution representation. The scope of general encoding for multiple domains remains an interesting research issue; while the common graph-based representation in Chap. 6 presents a promising step towards reusing some general properties and knowledge in the automatically generated grammars for highly different combinatorial optimisation problems, and potentially a diverse range of other problems.

Generality of algorithms, although widely mentioned in hyper-heuristics [15], is still often neglected in the literature. Chapter 7 considers generality of algorithms at a higher level with three criteria, namely across multiple problems, distinctive heuristic sets and varying experimental conditions. Based on a new taxonomy, a four-level assessment of algorithm generality [16] has been defined upon problem domain, problems, instances and benchmark set from a multi-objective perspective. In operational research, the well-established benchmarks (e.g. the OR Library[1]) provide excellent problem sets for generality assessments in designing effective algorithms.

With further advances in interpretability, reusability and generality, the reuse of methods in AutoML and AutoAD with less human involvement will lead to enormous savings of human effort and accumulate continuous and consistent research outcomes.

Integration of Machine Learning and Optimisation Research

The integration of research outcomes across machine learning and optimisation research has enhanced the efficiency of algorithms, advances fed into each other

[1] http://people.brunel.ac.uk/~mastjjb/jeb/info.html.

to address various issues in AutoML and AutoAD. Evolutionary computation has been successfully applied in the intensive search in machine learning, enhancing the optimisation in AutoML. For example, in AutoML, powerful evolutionary algorithms have been used in federated learning to reduce computational costs to improve neural architecture search [23].

In AutoAD, feature engineering in machine learning may contribute to identifying the key attributes of search spaces or problems when designing search algorithms, e.g. genetic programming. In hyper-heuristics, the selection of low-level heuristics, parametric modules or algorithmic components can be naturally supported by offline or online learning [9]. The great success recently in machine learning means efficient models can be easily adapted in learning the knowledge in AutoAD, enhancing the comprehension of algorithm design.

Benchmarking and Competitions

As reviewed in [3], the series of AutoML challenges, from the *Prediction challenge* [4] since 2006 to the most recent *AutoDL* competition [7] in 2020, not only led to some highly effective and popular AutoML methods, but also set consistent standards, boosting advanced research in AutoML. In AutoAD, platforms and frameworks such as Iterated F-Race [2], HyFlex [11] and EvoHyp [13] have also been widely adapted by more researchers. However, significant standalone research presumably still stays local and hidden, and has made limited contributions to the literature [10] without benchmarking and standardising the outcomes.

1.4 Conclusions

With the recent successes in machine learning and optimisation research, researchers are now exploring the scope of designing effective algorithms or intelligent methods with less human involvement, towards automated machine learning (AutoML) and automated algorithm design (AutoAD). Promising findings have emerged at the interface of different disciplines, and outcomes have fed into each other, addressing a broad range of research issues and leading to new challenges in AutoML and AutoAD.

With the well-structured pipelines and models in machine learning, powerful optimisation algorithms have been successfully adapted in evolutionary computation to enhance the efficiency of search for either hyperparameters or neural architectures in AutoML. With the frameworks and large amount of datasets, outcomes can be effectively accumulated, establishing further comprehension of machine learning. Challenges in AutoML now remain to be on the interpretability of the models, which also represents a key issue of explainable AI in machine learning communities.

In AutoAD, different streams of research advances have resulted into automatically designed algorithms which outperform some manually designed algorithms.

However, there is still a lack of theoretical studies, for example, on general standards and models, as well as common problem encoding for different problems. The establishment of these fundamentals is important so that research findings are accessible across the different communities with common structures, and not remain hidden or locally. Some efforts have been made in building new taxonomies and models, although there is still a scope of further collaboration in machine learning and evolutionary computation, impacting on real-world problems.

References

1. M. Birattari, A. Ligot, G. Francesca, Automode: a modular approach to the automatic off-line design and fine-tuning of control software for robot swarms, in *Automated Design of Machine Learning and Search Algorithms*, ed. by N. Pillay, R. Qu (Springer, 2021)
2. M. Birattari, Z. Yuan, P. Balaprakash, T. Stützle, F-race and iterated F-race: an overview, in *Experimental Methods for the Analysis of Optimization Algorithms* (2010), pp. 311–336
3. H.J. Escalante, Automated machine learning - a brief review at the end of the early years, in *Automated Design of Machine Learning and Search Algorithms*, ed. by N. Pillay, R. Qu (Springer, 2021)
4. I. Guyon, A.R.S. Azar Alamdari, G. Dror, J.M. Buhmann, Performance prediction challenge, in *Proceedings of the International Joint Conference on Neural Networks (IJCNN 2006)* (Vancouver, BC, Canada, July, 2019), pp. 1649–1656
5. F. Hutter, L. Kotthoff, J. Vanschoren (eds.), *Automated Machine Learning: Methods, Systems, Challenges* (Springer, 2019)
6. A. Lissovoi, P.S. Oliveto, J.A. Warwicker, Simple hyper-heuristics can control the neighbourhood size of randomized local search optimally for leading ones. Evolutionary Computation **28**(3), 437–461 (2020 September)
7. Z. Liu, I. Guyon, J. Jacques Junior, M. Madadi, S. Escalera, A. Pavao, H.J. Escalante, W.-W. Tu, Z. Xu, S. Treguer, Autocv challenge design and baseline results, in *In CAp 2019 - Conference sur lÁpprentissage Automatique* (July, 2019)
8. Y. Mei, M.A. Ardeh, M. Zhang, Knowledge transfer in genetic programming hyper-heuristics, in *Automated Design of Machine Learning and Search Algorithms*, ed. by N. Pillay, R. Qu (Springer, 2020)
9. W. Meng, R. Qu, A survey of learning in automated design of search algorithms, in *IEEE Computational Intelligence Magazine*, under review
10. M. Misir, Hyper-heuristics: autonomous problem solvers, in *Automated Design of Machine Learning and Search Algorithms*, ed. by N. Pillay, R. Qu (Springer, 2020)
11. G. Ochoa, M. Hyde, T. Curtois, J.A. Vazquez-Rodriguez, J. Walker, M. Gendreau, G. Kendall, B. McCollum, A.J. Parkes, S. Petrovi, E.K. Burke, HyFlex: a benchmark framework for cross-domain heuristic search, in *Proceedings of Evolutionary Computational Combinatorial Optimization* (Málaga, April 11–13, 2012), pp. 136–147
12. P.S. Oliveto, Rigorous performance analysis of hyper-heuristics, in *Automated Design of Machine Learning and Search Algorithms*, ed. by N. Pillay, R. Qu (Springer, 2020)
13. N. Pillay, D. Beckedahl, EvoHyp - a Java toolkit for evolutionary algorithm hyper-heuristics, in *Proceedings of IEEE Congress on Evolutionary Computation* (San Sebastian, June 5-8, 2017), pp. 2707–2713
14. N. Pillay, T. Nyathi, Automated design of classification algorithms, in *Automated Design of Machine Learning and Search Algorithms*, ed. by N. Pillay, R. Qu (Springer, 2020)
15. N. Pillay, R. Qu, *Hyper-heuristics: Theory and Applications* (Springer Nature, 2018)
16. N. Pillay, R. Qu, Assessing hyper-heuristic performance. J. Oper. Res. Soc. accepted (2020)

17. R. Poli, M. Graff, There is a free lunch for hyper-heuristics, genetic programming and computer scientists, in *European Conference on Genetic Programming* (Tubingen, April 15–17, 2009), pp. 195–207
18. R. Qu, A general model for automated algorithm design, in Automated Design of Machine Learning and Search Algorithms, ed. by N. Pillay, R. Qu (Springer 2021)
19. R. Qu, G. Kendall, N. Pillay, The general combinatorial optimisation problem - towards automated algorithm design. IEEE Comput. Intell. Mag. **15**, 14–23 (2020). May
20. C. Stone, E. Hart, B. Paechter, A cross-domain method for generation of constructive and perturbative heuristics, in *Automated Design of Machine Learning and Search Algorithms*, ed. by N. Pillay, R. Qu (Springer, 2021)
21. T. Stützle, Automated algorithm configuration: advances and prospects, in *Intelligent Distributed Computing VIII. Studies in Computational Intelligence*, vol 570, ed. by D. Camacho, L. Braubach, S. Venticinque, C. Badica (Springer, Cham, 2015)
22. D.H. Wolpert, W.G. McReady, No free lunch theorems for optimisation. IEEE Trans. Evol. Comput. **1**(1), 67–82 (1997). April
23. H. Zhu, Y. Jin. Towards real-time federated evolutionary neural architecture search, in *Automated Design of Machine Learning and Search Algorithms*, ed. by N. Pillay, R. Qu (Springer, 2021)

Chapter 2
Automated Machine Learning—A Brief Review at the End of the Early Years

Hugo Jair Escalante

Abstract Automated machine learning (AutoML) is the sub-field of machine learning that aims at automating, to some extend, all stages of the design of a machine learning system. In the context of supervised learning, AutoML is concerned with feature extraction, preprocessing, model design, and post processing. Major contributions and achievements in AutoML have been taking place during the recent decade. We are, therefore, in perfect timing to look back and realize what we have learned. This chapter aims to summarize the main findings in the early years of AutoML. More specifically, in this chapter an introduction to AutoML for supervised learning is provided and a historical review of progress in this field is presented. Likewise, the main paradigms of AutoML are described and research opportunities are outlined.

2.1 Introduction

Automated Machine Learning or AutoML is a term coined by the machine learning community to refer to methods that aim at automating the design and development of machine learning systems and applications [33]. In the context of supervised learning, AutoML aims at relaxing the need of the user in the loop from all stages in the design of supervised learning systems (i.e., any system relying on models for classification, recognition, regression, forecasting, etc.). This is a tangible need at present, as data are being generated vastly and in practically any context and scenario, however, the number of machine learning experts available to analyze such data is overseeded.

H. J. Escalante (✉)
Computer Science Departments, Centro de Investigación y de Estudios Avanzados del IPN, Zacatenco, Mexico city 07360, Mexico
e-mail: hugo.jair@gmail.com

Instituto Nacional de Astrofísica, Óptica y Electrónica, Tonanzintla, Puebla, Puebla 72840, Mexico

N. Pillay and R. Qu (eds.), *Automated Design of Machine Learning and Search Algorithms*, Natural Computing Series,
https://doi.org/10.1007/978-3-030-72069-8_2

AutoML for supervised learning has been the focus of research for more than ten years now,[1] and great progress has been achieved so far, consider for instance the useful AutoML methods in the most popular machine learning toolkits [17, 62], and the AutoML mechanisms in large scale platforms (e.g., Azure[2] or H2O.ai[3] [36]). In fact, AutoML is nowadays a *hot topic* within machine learning that is receiving much attention from industry, academy, and even the general public.

With such progress and interest from the community, it is necessary to go through the fundamentals and main findings achieved in the last decade. This is the aim of the present chapter, which aims at reviewing the most notable developments in the last few years, explaining the fundamentals of AutoML, and highlighting open issues and research opportunities in the subject.

This chapter is complimentary to excellent surveys and reviews in the field that can be found in [9, 30, 33, 51, 63, 69, 71]. Compared with these references, this chapter offers an introduction to AutoML, and a brief review of progress in the field, all of this at a superficial but broad-reaching focus.

The remainder of the chapter is organized as follows. In Sect. 2.2, the fundamentals of AutoML are introduced, including definitions, notions, and components of AutoML systems. Then, in Sect. 2.3, a brief review on the most representative AutoML methodologies is presented. Next, in Sect. 2.4, a brief review on AutoML challenges and their role in the development of the field are presented. Then in Sect. 2.5, open issues and research opportunities are highlighted. Finally, in Sect. 2.6, a summary of the chapter and take-home messages are presented.

2.2 Fundamentals of AutoML

Autonomous[4] Machine Learning (AutoML) is the field of study dealing with methods that aim at reducing the need for user interaction in the design of machine learning systems and applications. The topic has been mostly studied in the context of supervised learning, although unsupervised [1] and semi supervised learning [39] efforts are emerging as well. This chapter deals with AutoML in the supervised learning context.

[1] Please note that although model selection and other efforts for hyperparameter optimization have been out there for decades, see e.g., [24]; this chapter focuses on full model or pipeline selection and design [11, 33].

[2] https://docs.microsoft.com/en-us/azure/machine-learning/service/concept-automated-ml.

[3] http://docs.h2o.ai/h2o/latest-stable/h2o-docs/automl.html.

[4] Often referred to as Automatic Machine Learning.

2.2.1 Supervised Learning

Supervised learning is perhaps the most studied topic within machine learning, as it has wide applicability. Spam filtering methods, face recognition systems, handwritten character recognition techniques, and text classification methodologies are only a few of the *classical* applications relying in supervised learning. The distinctive feature of supervised learning methods is that they must *learn* to map objects to labels, based on a sample of labeled data (i.e., the supervision).

More formally, under the supervised learning setting, we have available a data set $\mathcal{D}$ formed by N pairs of d-dimensional samples, $\mathbf{x}_i \in \mathbb{R}^d$, and labels[5] $y_i \in \{-1, 1\}$, that is: $\mathcal{D} = \{(\mathbf{x}_i, y_i)\}_{i \in 1,\ldots,N}$. The samples $\mathbf{x}_i$ codify objects of interest (e.g., documents, images or videos) with a set of numerical descriptors, while the labels y_i determine the *class* of objects (e.g., spam vs. no-spam). The overall goal of supervised learning is to find a function $f : \mathbb{R}^d \rightarrow \{-1, 1\}$ mapping inputs to outputs, i.e., $y_j = f(\mathbf{x}_j)$, that can generalize beyond $\mathcal{D}$. Where options for the form of f include linear models, decision trees, instance based classifiers among others. Regardless of the form of f, the learning process reduces to find the f that *best* fits dataset $\mathcal{D}$.

Usually, $\mathcal{D}$ is split into training and validation partitions, hence the goal is learning f from $\mathcal{D}$ such that label predictions can be made for any other instance sampled from the same underlying distribution as $\mathcal{D}$. If we denote $\mathcal{T}$ to the *test* set, formed by instances coming from the same distribution as $\mathcal{D}$ but that do not appear in such set. $\mathcal{T}$ can be used to evaluate the generalization capabilities of f. The reader is referred to [2, 4, 29] for definitions and in-depth treatments of supervised machine learning.

2.2.2 Notions of AutoML

Having described the supervised learning setting, we can intuitively describe AutoML as the ***task of finding the*** f ***5that better generalizes in any possible*** $\mathcal{T}$ ***with the less possible human intervention***. Where f can be the composition of multiple functions that may transform the input space, subsampling data, combining multiple predictors, etc. For example, f could be of the form: $f(\mathbf{x}) = \nu_{\theta_\nu}(\Phi_{\theta_\Phi}(\mathbf{x})$, here ν is a classification model (e.g., a random forest classifier [6]) and Φ is a feature transformation methodology (e.g., feature standardization and principal component analysis [23]) with hyperparameters θ_ν and θ_Φ, respectively, and where each of these models could be formed in turn by several other functions/models.

Functions of the form $f(\mathbf{x}) = \nu_{\theta_\nu}(\Phi_{\theta_\Phi}(\mathbf{x})$ are called *full models* [11, 12] or *pipelines* [17], as they comprise all of the processes that have to be applied to the data in order to obtain a supervised learning model. AutoML can be seen as the search of functions ν and Φ, with their corresponding hyperparameters θ_ν and θ_Φ using $\mathcal{D}$. In the following, we present conventional definitions of AutoML, however, the intuitive

[5] Please note that labels could be also real values (for regression tasks) or categorical, for clarity, we instead describe a binary classification problem.

notion is general enough to be inclusive of all existing definitions, and it should be clearer for newcomers to the field.

2.2.2.1 Levels of Automation in AutoML

There are several notions of AutoML for supervised learning dating back to 2006 (see the *Full model selection* definition[6] in [12]), where one of the mostly adopted is that from Feurer et al. [17]. Such definition, however, refers solely to the automatic pipeline generation problem, whereas different related tasks within supervised learning have been considered as AutoML at different times. Actually, any task trying to automate part of the machine learning design process can be considered AutoML. For instance, algorithm selection [55], hyperparameter optimization [20], meta-learning [58, 64], full model selection [12], Combined Algorithm Selection and Hyperparameter optimization (CASH) [62], neural architecture search [9], etc. Because all of these tasks are closely related to each other, we refer to the unifying view proposed by Liu et al. [43] instead.

Liu et al. distinguish at least three levels of automation in which AutoML systems can be categorized, these are summarized as follows:

- α-**level.** *Search of estimators/predictors*. This level refers to the task of defining/determining a function mapping inputs to outputs, for example, manually setting the weights of a linear regressor for approaching a particular task (here $y_i \in \mathbb{R}$), or generating hard-coded classifiers (e.g., based on if-then rules).
- β-**level.** *Search of learning algorithms*. Refers to the task of determining the best learning algorithm for a given task. Including methods that:
  - Explore the space of all estimators of a given class, e.g., hyperparameter optimization of a support vector machine (SVM) classifier [5, 57]. In this case, the form of f is defined as: $f(\mathbf{x}) = sign(\sum_{j=1}^{N} \delta_j y_j k(\mathbf{x}_j, \mathbf{x}) + b)$, with δ denoting the variables associated to the Lagrange multipliers and k an appropriate kernel function. β-level methods in this setting could search for adequate kernel functions k and additional hyperparameters for f (e.g., regularizer term); likewise, these methods should still find the parameters of the model, e.g., δ, $\mathbf{w}$ and b values.
  - Explore the space of all estimators that can be built from a set of learning algorithms and/or related processes like feature selection, normalization of variables, etc. These type of β-level techniques include methods that automatically generate classification pipelines like: PSMS [12] and Auto-WEKA [62]. These methods are capable of determining the type of function f (e.g., choosing an SVM or a decision tree classifier), but also they can specify additional procedures to be applied to the training data and/or the model, before, during or after f is learned. For instance, typical processes could be: feature selec-

[6] Although this article was published in 2009, the main concepts and ideas were presented in a NIPS workshop in 2006 [11, 25].

tion/extraction, building ensembles with partial solutions, and adjusting the outputs of models (e.g., according to class imbalance rations). β-level techniques are also in charge of determining the hyperparameters associated with any component of the *full model*.

- γ-**level.** *Search for meta-learning algorithms*. This level refers to methods that aim at exploiting a knowledge base of tasks-solutions to learn to recommend/select β-level methods given a new task. This level includes techniques from the early meta-learning approaches for *recommending* an algorithm from a number of options [58, 65], to portfolio optimization methods [37], to surrogate models used in modern AutoML solutions [17, 18], to cutting edge few-shot meta-learning methodologies [66]. Examples of γ-level AutoML techniques include AutoSklearn that incorporates meta-learning as warm start for the optimization process [17], and early AutoML solutions incorporating surrogates [18, 19]. The distinctive feature of γ-level approaches is that they take advantage of task-level information and use it for any aspect of the AutoML process.

Under Liu et al.'s notion, most methodologies aiming to automate the design of machine learning systems can be covered [43]. From the (manual) optimization of parameters for a fixed model, to the automation of any aspect of the design process. A remarkable feature of the above notion is that authors consider budgets (in time and space) for the different levels. Also, one should note that this notion is transverse to the categorization[7] of *model selection* techniques into filters, wrappers, and embedded methods by Guyon et al. [24, 27]. Please refer to [43] for details and examples of tasks/methods falling under each of these categories.

2.2.3 Disentangling AutoML Methods

The field of AutoML has grown rapidly in the last few years and because of that, a vast number of solutions are out there. In order to make it easier for the reader to distinguish across different AutoML techniques, in this section, we describe the key components of any AutoML method.

In the author's opinion, one can distinguish three main components, namely: *Optimizer, Meta-learner*, and *data-model processing methods*. This categorization is graphically depicted in Fig. 2.1.

The **optimizer** is the core of the AutoML method and it comprises the optimization algorithm itself, together with the objective function (usually a loss function for supervised learning). Resource controlling mechanisms are often associated to the optimizer, and the goal is to deal with the optimization problem while meeting time and memory budget constraints. Whereas generic optimization methods (e.g.,

[7] Guyon et al. distinguish methods performing a search intensive procedure, called wrappers, (mostly associated to β-level techniques), those that are not data-driven, called filters, (where γ-level methods can be framed) and embedded techniques (related to β and α level methodologies).

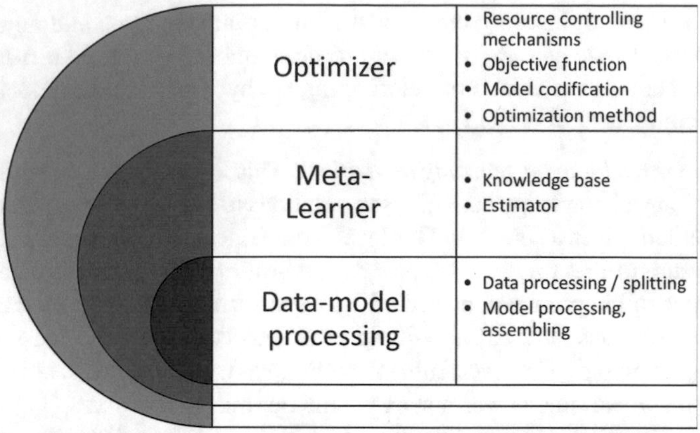

Fig. 2.1 Graphical diagram of the main components of an (γ-level) AutoML method

evolutionary [18, 60] and bio-inspired algorithms [12], pattern search [48], etc.) have been traditionally used for this core component of AutoML, *ad-hoc* optimization techniques tailored to the AutoML scenario are preferred. This include on a budget, anytime, and derivative free based methodologies. Likewise, multi objective techniques and methods that can operate over complex structures can have a positive impact in the overall performance of AutoML methodologies. Some of this methods are covered in other chapters of this book.

A **meta-learner** refers to any estimator that is used during the AutoML optimization process, this could be a meta-learning technique for making recommendations on potentially useful models, or any other estimator (e.g., of expected performance or running time) used by the optimizer. Meta-learners are part of any γ-level approach. The meta-learner is often coupled with the optimizer (e.g., in Auto-WEKA [62] and AutoSklearn [17])). One should note that meta-learning by itself can be seen as an AutoML methodology: early approaches were used to make *coarse* model suggestions to solve supervised learning problems [65]. This form of algorithm recommendation/selection has been out there before the first AutoML formulations appeared. However, most of the early meta-learning efforts focused on recommending a classification model, rarely they also suggested hyperparameters. Therefore, full pipelines were not considered initially in meta-learning. Nowadays meta-learning is a hot topic by itself, see [64, 66], and it has been *synergistically* used in AutoML systems [17]. We refer the reader to [64, 66] for a complete review on meta-learning.

Data processing mechanisms are those that modify, organize data according to the need of AutoML methods. These include data sampling and splitting for the assessment of solutions (e.g., successive halving methods [38]). Finally, **model processing** techniques are those that enhance the model with *ad hoc* mechanisms for improving AutoML solutions. For instance, building ensembles with partial solutions like in [14, 17, 18].

Although this is not a strict categorization, most γ-level AutoML solutions adhere to it. Also, the interaction among these components is very flexible, for instance, there are AutoML methods that use the meta-learner before the optimization process while others use it during the search. This will be clearer in the next section where the most popular AutoML methodologies are described.

2.3 AutoML Methodologies

As previously mentioned, progress in AutoML has resulted in several methodologies that automate the design and development of supervised learning systems at different levels. It is out of the scope of this chapter to provide a complete review of existing methodologies, instead, in this section, the most representative AutoML methodologies out there are described. The reader is referred to recent surveys in AutoML for complete description of the available methodologies [9, 30, 33, 63, 69, 71].

Table 2.1 summarizes the most representative methodologies of the early years of AutoML. These are shown in chronological order and the most important innovation or contribution from each methodology is briefly mentioned in the table. The goal of this table is just to provide a glimpse of the chronological development of AutoML. In the following, we briefly describe some of these methodologies for further discussion below. We have divided this into waves that encompass methods that dealt with the problem similarly and that are chronologically close to each other.

2.3.1 First Wave: 2006–2010

Particle Swarm Model Selection (PSMS) is among the first existing AutoML methods dealing with the full pipeline generation problem [11, 12]. Authors formulated the so-called *full model selection* problem, that consists of finding the best combination of data preprocessing, feature selection/extraction, and classification models, together with the optimization of all of the associated hyperparameters. A heterogenous vector-based representation was proposed to codify models into vectors and Particle Swarm Optimization (PSO) was used to solve the problem. A number of data sampling procedures were adopted to make the method tractable. In the same line, Gorissen et al. proposed a similar evolutionary algorithm to search for surrogates, where a wide variety of data preprocessing, feature selection/extraction, and model postprocessing techniques could be considered to build the model [19]. To the best of the author's knowledge, this was the first work that proposed building ensembles as part of the AutoML process. This notion inspired other methodologies like Ensemble PSMS [14], in which ensemble models of partial solutions found during the PSMS search process were returned as solutions. Building ensembles is nowadays part of most successful AutoML solutions like AutoSkLearn [17]. The last AutoML method from the early years of AutoML that we would like to mention

Table 2.1 Overview of main AutoML methodologies shown in chronological order. Please note that α-level methods are not included in this table as they refer to any methodology for fitting a model to a dataset (e.g., least-squares for linear regression)

Year	Ref.	Method	Type	Description	Innovative aspects
2006	[11, 12]	PSMS	β	Vectorial representation of solutions, PSO used as optimizer, subsampling, CV	Formulation of the full model selection task
2007	[18, 19]	Hetero-geneous surrogate evolution	β	Parallel co evolution of models, ensemble generation	Returned ensemble of solutions, large and heterogenous space of models
2010	[14]	Ensemble PSMS	β	Enhanced PSMS with ensemble of solutions	Returned an ensemble of solutions as output
2012	[60]	GPS: GA-PSO-FMS	β	GAs were used to search for a model template, PSO was used for hyperparameter optimization	Separation of template search and hyperparameter optimization
2013	[62]	Auto-WEKA	γ	SMBO with SMAC, approached the CASH problem	Definition of the combined algorithm selection and hyperparameter optimization problem
2014	[56]	Multi-objective surrogate-based FMS	γ	Multi objective (complexity/performance) evolutionary method, surrogates were used to approximate the fitness function	Among the first methods using a meta-learner for AutoML, multi-objective formulation
2015	[17]	AutoSk-Learn	γ	SMBO, warm starting with a classifier, ensemble generation	AutoML definition, warm-starting with meta-learner, winner of AutoML challenge
2016	[49, 50]	TPOT	β	Genetic programming/NSGA-II selection, cross validation, data sampling	Models naturally codified as GP trees
2017–2020	[9, 10, 35, 52, 70]	Neural Architecture search	γ	Reinforcement Learning, Evolutionary Algorithms, SMBO for Neural Architecture search	Novel codifications for architectures, comparison of architectures, *ad-hoc* NAS surrogates

is GPS [60], Quan et al. approached the full model selection problem with a quite novel formulation: in a first step, authors looked for a promising template for a classification pipeline and in a second stage author optimized hyperparameters for the selected template. In the author's view, this was a form of warm-starting the AutoML process, something that is common in contemporaneous AutoML solutions.

From the above discussion, it is interesting that several core contributions widely used in current state of the art AutoML solutions were proposed during the first wave. Namely, a first formulation of the AutoML problem [12, 18], the idea of building ensembles with information derived form the AutoML process [14, 18], and initial ideas on warm-starting the search process [60].

2.3.2 Second Wave: 2011–2016

A second wave of AutoML started in the early 2010s with the introduction of models based on Bayesian Optimization/Sequential Model-Based Optimization (SMBO) for hyperparameter optimization and algorithm selection [32, 59]. The intuitive idea of these methods is to use a sort of surrogate model to estimate the relations between performance and hyperparameters, and using this estimate to guide the optimization process via an acquisition function. In 2013, Thornton et al. introduced Auto-WEKA, an AutoML method based on SMBO capable of building classification pipelines in the popular WEKA platform [28]. The authors formulated the CASH problem, which resembles similarities with the full model selection task. Auto-WEKA relied on a SMBO method called SMAC [32] with a random forest estimator. This method boosted research in SMBO for AutoML that nowadays is the dominant optimization approach in this field.

Interestingly, alternative methodologies not adhering to a probabilistic formulation were proposed as well. For example, Rosales et al. developed an AutoML methodology based on multi-objective optimization and surrogate models [56]. A regressor (and later a classifier) was used to estimate the performance of solutions such that only the promising ones were evaluated with the costly objective function. This solution shares the spirit of SMBO but approaches the task in a different way.

In the following years, solutions based on SMBO have been proposed, most notably AutoSklearn [17]. This method arose in the context of an academic challenge (see Sect. 2.4). AutoSklearn is based on SMBO with the distinctive feature that the search process is first initialized with a meta-learner that aims at reducing the search space and directing it towards promising models. Also, this method generates an ensemble of solutions explored during the search process. AutoSklearn won a series of AutoML challenges with large margin at some stages [27], and even outperformed humans that aimed to fine-tune a model.[8] AutoSklearn was made publicly available and it is very popular nowadays.

Among the novel AutoML methodologies released after AutoSklearn is TPOT (Tree-based Pipeline Optimization Tool), a method based on evolutionary computation with a particular twist [50]. The distinctive feature of TPOT, when compared to early efforts based on evolutionary computation, is that TPOT uses genetic programming as an optimizer and models are coded as syntactic trees formed by primitives

[8] During a live competition on manual model tuning that lasted a couple of days and was organized with WCCI2016 [27].

that correspond to models. Each tree represents a full classification pipeline and these are evolved to optimize performance while reducing the complexity (number of primitives used) of the pipeline. Codifying pipelines as trees is a natural solution that has not been explored elsewhere.

To summarize, the second wave can be credited by the emergence of Bayesian Optimization as the *de facto* optimizer for AutoML, most AutoML solutions nowadays implement such modeling framework and differ in the way the estimators are defined or how they are used and coupled with other processes. This wave also witnessed the resurgence of meta-learning as a critical step towards automating the selection of classification models. Likewise, progress in hyperparameter optimization resulted in techniques (e.g., multi-fidelity approaches [8, 34, 38]) that have boosted research on AutoML, see [16] for an up-to-date review on progress in this area.

2.3.3 *Third Wave: 2017 and On*

The current[9] trend in AutoML is that of techniques for Neural Architecture Search (NAS) [9, 10, 53, 61, 71]. The outstanding achievements of deep learning across many fields, together with the enormous complexity that takes to manually tune a model to obtain the desired performance in a particular dataset has moved AutoML into the deep learning arena (in fact, several authors use as synonym AutoML with NAS). NAS deals with the problem of searching for the best architecture and hyperparameters of deep learning models. Being this a very complex problem because of the number of associated parameters (of the order of billions) and the size of datasets that are required by these models to perform decently. Also, a specific difficulty that must be addressed by NAS methodologies is the need for comparing heterogeneous structures (i.e., deep learning architectures). NAS is out of the scope of this chapter, however, the reader is referred to [9, 10, 53, 61] for up-to-date surveys on this dynamic and fast evolving field. NAS together with few shot learning, and the use of reinforcement learning for AutoML processes comprise the third wave, great progress is expected in these fields as these topics are in the spotlight of the machine learning community.

This section has provided a broad review on the evolution of AutoML during the last decade. Although the review is not exhaustive, it gives the reader a clear idea on how the field has progressed, and most importantly, introduces the fundamentals of AutoML. In the remainder of this chapter, we describe the role that challenges have had in the development of AutoML and we highlight open issues and research opportunities in the area.

---

[9] One should note that efforts to automatically design neural networks arose in the early 90's, see, e.g., [3, 47].

2.4 AutoML Challenges

It is well known that competitions have helped to advance the state of the art and to solve extremely complex problems that otherwise would have took much time, even centuries, see e.g., the *Longitude Act*.[10] In the case of AutoML, they have played a major role, and although it is arguable, in the authors' opinion, AutoML was born in the core of academic challenges. The *2006 Prediction challenge* [20] and the *2007 agnostic learning vs. prior knowledge competition* [25, 26] challenged participants to develop methodologies that, with the less possible domain knowledge, could solve generic classification tasks. This competition gave rise to a number of early AutoML solutions, see e.g. [7, 13, 45, 54, 67]. Although most of them dealt with the hyperparameter optimization problem, for the first time were assessed the advantages of including domain knowledge vs. developing completely agnostic methods when building generic classifiers. The outcomes of the challenge brought light in that building an autonomous black box able to solve many classification problems was actually feasible. Please refer to [25, 26] for detailed analyses on the outcomes of the challenges and the developed solutions.

The initial efforts of the previous competitions were consolidated years later throughout a series of challenges that were critical to boost the interest of the community in the AutoML field: *the ChaLearn AutoML series* [21, 22, 27]. ChaLearn[11] lead the organization of a series of competitions that aimed at developing the *dreamed AutoML black box* in a 5-stage evaluation protocol. Initially, participants dealt with binary classification problems, then supervised learning problems of greater difficulty (regression, multiclass and multi-label classification) were incorporated in subsequent stages. In each stage, five new datasets were released, where participants did not know anything about the data, in fact, data was private, remained in the cloud until evaluation, so no code had access to the data beforehand. This was among the most novel feature of the AutoML challenge when compared to competitions at that time: solutions from participants of the AutoML challenge were evaluated autonomously in the cloud without any user intervention. Every AutoML solution was evaluated under the same conditions and using the same resources, it was during this challenge that budget restrictions were explicitly considered. The competition also allowed the comparison of pure AutoML solutions with standard offline manually-tuned solutions. It was found that there was still a gap between fully autonomous vs. *tweaked* approaches, motivating further research for the forthcoming editions. It is important to emphasize that it was in the context of this challenge that a popular and very effective AutoML method arose: AutoSklearn [17].

The first edition of the AutoML challenge series focused on midsize tabular data associated with supervised learning tasks. The complexity of the approached tasks was increased in the subsequent editions that focused on more realistic settings and more challenging scenarios. For instance, the Life Long AutoML challenge asked participants to develop solutions that could learn continuously in large-scale

[10] https://worddisk.com/wiki/Longitude_Act/.

[11] http://chalearn.org/.

datasets coming from real applications [15] and using non-standard data formats (e.g., temporal and relational data[12]). Because of the large scale of these datasets, solutions of the challenge focused on efficiency, hence the other aspects of AutoML were not targeted by participants (e.g., extensive search or overfitting avoidance mechanisms) Also, the *life long* setting motivated participants to develop incremental solutions, in fact, top ranked participants relied in boosting ensembles of trees, see e.g., [68]. One of the most important outcomes of the challenge was that efficiency in AutoML has not received enough attention from the community. Also, it was evidenced the lack of capabilities of state-of-the-art methods to handle non-tabular data. For a detailed description of the challenge please refer to [15].

The latest edition of the AutoML challenge series features the AutoDL[13] competition [41]. In this challenge, participants are required to build AutoML methodologies able to work directly with raw data, where data can be heterogeneous (e.g., text, images, time series, videos, speech signals, etc.). Although the competition focus is on deep learning methodologies, any kind of method can be submitted. As in previous editions, solutions are evaluated in the CodaLab[14] platform without any user intervention, methods do not have access to data until evaluation takes place, and there are budget restrictions. In preliminary evaluation phases of AutoDL that have focused on a single modality of data (e.g., images), very effective and efficient deep learning architectures have been already proposed [42]. Top ranked participants of these evaluation phases have developed efficient auto augmentation techniques [40] and have relied on *light* architectures that are used as warmstart for the AutoML process (e.g., on mobile net [31]). See [41, 42, 44] for details on the already existing methodologies that solve recognition tasks from raw data without user intervention and by consuming reasonable resources.

This section has provided an overview of academic competitions dealing with the AutoML problem under very different and challenging conditions. By providing data, resources, and accurate evaluation protocols, AutoML challenges have boosted research in different fronts of machine learning. From the *2006 prediction challenge* to the 2020 AutoDL competition, the AutoML field has seen its rise within the machine learning community. Several effective methods for approaching the problem have been proposed so far, some of them being widely used nowadays. AutoML is a clear example of what challenges can do, the field is growing with a large portion of the machine learning community actively working on it. AutoML challenges have also made a contribution to setting the basis for fair and standardized evaluations. Such evaluations are highly needed in AutoML, being a data-driven and resource-consuming process, ensuring autonomy, and delivering solutions within a reasonable time is critical.

[12] https://www.4paradigm.com/competition/kddcup2019.

[13] https://autodl.chalearn.org/.

[14] https://codalab.lri.fr/.

2.5 Open Issues and Research Opportunities

In the last decade, AutoML has achieved a tremendous progress in trying to automate model design and development, mainly in the context of supervised learning. From initial efforts in trying to approach the problem with straightforward black box optimizers based on vector representations, to the most recent studies aiming to compare graphs, and adopting meta-learning schemes. With such progress, the reader may be deceived that the AutoML task is solved (at least for tasks like classification), this, however, is still a faraway goal. As there are several challenges that deserve attention from the community. In the following, some of the most promising problems for which research could make a tremendous impact are listed.

- **Explainable AutoML models**. AutoML solutions are, in general, black boxes that aim at exploring the space of models that can be built with a set of primitives. Effective AutoML solutions are out there that can be used by any user without any formation in machine learning. Despite the progress, a direction that has not been explored by the community is that of developing *transparent* AutoML methodologies. In the author's view, AutoML models should be equipped with explainability and interpretability mechanisms. This enhancement could bring important benefits for making AutoML accessible to everyone. Although this venue has not been explored yet, we are not faraway from having transparent AutoML techniques, as AutoML is, in general, a search intensive procedure that generates vast amounts of information that can be exploited to generate explainable and interpretable AutoML solutions.
- **AutoML in feature engineering**. Although data processing, including feature selection and extraction, have been considered as components of pipelines generated by AutoML techniques, the feature engineering process by itself has received little attention from the community. It is only recently that efforts aiming to process raw data directly are emerging, see [41, 42, 46]. We believe this research venue will be decisive for the full automation of the AutoML process.
- **AutoML for non tabular data**. Related to the previous point, AutoML methods for dealing with non tabular data, including raw data (e.g., text, images, etc.) and structured data (e.g., graphs, networks, etc.) are becoming more and more necessary, hence this area could also be a fruitful venue for research.
- **Large scale AutoML**. Large scale problems are still an open problem for state-of-the-art AutoML solutions. This was evidenced in the recent AutoML challenges, where only a few solutions could perform search intensive AutoML procedures [15]. This represents an open problem that deserves further attention from the community. Likewise, in deep learning models, AutoML has to be efficient and there are already several *efficient* implementations of NAS models.
- **Transfer learning in AutoML**. As previously mentioned, current AutoML solutions generate vast and rich information that can be useful for a number of purposes. A promising purpose for taking advantage of such information is to perform transfer learning to enhance the performance of AutoML models. Meta-learning procedures already perform a sort of transfer learning, however, a promising research

venue is to transfer knowledge on information on the optimization process (e.g., transferring information on the dynamics of the optimization process from task to task).

- **Benchmarking and reproducibility in AutoML**. Since AutoML is an optimization process that involves data, efforts on developing platforms and frameworks for the evaluation and fair comparison among AutoML methodologies is an open issue. Whereas challenges offer such platforms, they may become obsolete rapidly given the speed at which AutoML is growing. Likewise, code sharing and the mechanisms that encourage the reproducibility of results in AutoML could have a huge positive impact on the maturity of the field.
- **Interactive AutoML methods.** While the main goal of AutoML is to *automate* processes and remove as much as possible to the user from design loop, interactive AutoML methodologies could take the performance of AutoML models far away from its current status. Mechanisms for including prior knowledge into the AutoML process could have a positive impact.

2.6 Conclusions

Automated machine learning aims at helping users with the design of machine learning systems. From the optimization of hyperparameters of fixed models to model type selection and full model/pipeline generation to the automatic design of deep learning architectures, AutoML is now an established field with wide applicability in the *data science era*. Great progress has been achieved in the early years, with very effective methodologies readily to use for users with limited knowledge in machine learning. Likewise, solutions making *easier* the design task even for machine learning experts.

This chapter has provided an overview of the major achievements during this first decade, the most representative methodologies were presented and the fundamentals of the AutoML task were provided. Perhaps the most important conclusion one can draw from these early years of progress is that nowadays we have evidence that AutoML is a feasible task, this is a very important result as in the early years the machine learning community was very skeptical about the future of the field. Hence, even when the black box all-problem solution is far from being reached, today we can leverage AutoML techniques to approach problems that traditionally required considerable effort. Also, it is clear the importance that AutoML challenges have had in the establishment of the field. With the progress seen in this first decade, much is expected from AutoML in the next few years. In particular, it will be exciting to know the methodologies that can approach the open problems highlighted in the previous section. Also, it is intriguing to what extent will it be possible to take automation in deep learning.

Acknowledgements The author is grateful to the editors for their support in the preparation of this manuscript. The ChaLearn collaboration (http://www.chalearn.org/) is acknowledged for the organization of the ChaLearn AutoML challenges series. This research was partially supported by CONACyT under the project CB-26314: *Integración de Visión y Lenguaje mediante Representaciones Multimodales Aprendidas para Clasificación y Recuperación de Imágenes y Videos.*

References

1. J. U. Allingham, Unsupervised automatic dataset repair. Master's thesis, Computer Laboratory, University of Cambridge (2018)
2. E. Alpaydin, *Introduction to Machine Learning*, 3rd edn. Adaptive computation and machine learning (MIT Press, 2014)
3. P.J. Angeline, G.M. Saunders, J.B. Pollack, An evolutionary algorithm that constructs recurrent neural networks. Trans. Neur. Netw. **5**(1), 54–65 (1994). January
4. C. Bishop, *Pattern Recognition and Machine Learning*, 1st edn. (Springer, 2006)
5. B.E. Boser, I.M. Guyon, V.N. Vapnik, A training algorithm for optimal margin classifiers, in *Proceedings of the Fifth Annual Workshop on Computational Learning Theory*, COLT '92 (Association for Computing Machinery, New York, NY, USA, 1992), pp. 144–152
6. L. Breiman, Random forests. Mach. Learn. **45**, 5–32 (2001)
7. G.C. Cawley, N.L.C. Talbot, Agnostic learning versus prior knowledge in the design of kernel machines, in *Proceedings of the International Joint Conference on Neural Networks, IJCNN 2007, Celebrating 20 years of neural networks, Orlando, Florida, USA, August 12–17, 2007* (2007), pp. 1732–1737
8. T. Domhan, J.T. Springenberg, F. Hutter, Speeding up automatic hyperparameter optimization of deep neural networks by extrapolation of learning curves, in *Proceedings of the 24th International Conference on Artificial Intelligence*, IJCAI'15 (AAAI Press, 2015), pp. 3460–3468
9. T. Elsken, J. Hendrik Metzen, F. Hutter, A survey, Neural architecture search (2018)
10. T. Elsken, J.H. Metzen, F. Hutter, *Neural Architecture Search* (Springer International Publishing, Cham, 2019), pp. 63–77
11. H.J. Escalante, Results on the model selection game: towards a particle swarm model selection algorithm. NIPS2016 Multi-level Inference Workshop and Model Selecion Game (2006)
12. H.J. Escalante, M. Montes, L.E. Sucar, Particle swarm model selection. J. Mach. Learn. Res. **10**, 405–440 (2009)
13. H.J. Escalante, M. Montes-y-Gómez, L.E. Sucar, PSMS for neural networks on the IJCNN 2007 agnostic vs prior knowledge challenge, in *Proceedings of the International Joint Conference on Neural Networks, IJCNN 2007, Celebrating 20 years of neural networks, Orlando, Florida, USA, August 12-17, 2007* (2007), pp. 678–683
14. H.J. Escalante, M. Montes-y-Gómez, L.E. Sucar, Ensemble particle swarm model selection, in *International Joint Conference on Neural Networks, IJCNN 2010, Barcelona, Spain, 18-23 July, 2010* (2010), pp. 1–8
15. H.J. Escalante, W.-W. Tu, I. Guyon, D.L. Silver, E. Viegas, Y. Chen, W. Dai, Q. Yang, Automl @ neurips 2018 challenge: design and results, in *The NeurIPS '18 Competition*, ed. by S. Escalera, R. Herbrich, (Springer International Publishing, Cham, 2020), pp. 209–229
16. M. Feurer, F. Hutter, *Hyperparameter Optimization* (Springer International Publishing, Cham, 2019), pp. 3–33
17. M. Feurer, A. Klein, K. Eggensperger, J.T. Springenberg, M. Blum, F. Hutter, *Auto-sklearn: Efficient and Robust Automated Machine Learning* (Springer International Publishing, Cham, 2019), pp. 113–134
18. D. Gorissen, T. Dhaene, F. De Turck, Evolutionary model type selection for global surrogate modeling. J. Mach. Learn. Res. **10**, 2039–2078 (2009)

19. D. Gorissen, L.D Tommasi, J. Croon, T. Dhaene, Automatic model type selection with heterogeneous evolution: an application to RF circuit block modeling, in *Proceedings of the IEEE Congress on Evolutionary Computation, CEC 2008, June 1-6, 2008, Hong Kong, China* (2008), pp. 989–996
20. I. Guyon, A. Reza Saffari Azar Alamdari, G. Dror, J.M. Buhmann, Performanceprediction challenge, in *Proceedings of the International Joint Conference on Neural Networks, IJCNN 2006, part of the IEEE World Congress on Computational Intelligence, WCCI 2006, Vancouver, BC, Canada, 16-21 July 2006* (2006), pp. 1649–1656
21. I. Guyon, K.P. Bennett, G.C. Cawley, H.J. Escalante, S. Escalera, T.K. Ho, N. Macià, B. Ray, M. Saeed, A.R. Statnikov, E. Viegas, Design of the 2015 chalearn automl challenge, in *2015 International Joint Conference on Neural Networks, IJCNN 2015, Killarney, Ireland, July 12-17, 2015* (2015), pp. 1–8
22. I. Guyon, I. Chaabane, H.J. Escalante, S. Escalera, D. Jajetic, J.R. Lloyd, N. Macià, B. Ray, L. Romaszko, M. Sebag, A.R. Statnikov, S. Treguer, E. Viegas, A brief review of the chalearn automl challenge: any-time any-dataset learning without human intervention, in *Proceedings of the 2016 Workshop on Automatic Machine Learning, AutoML 2016, co-located with 33rd International Conference on Machine Learning (ICML 2016), New York City, NY, USA, June 24, 2016* (2016), pp. 21–30
23. I. Guyon, A. Elisseeff, An introduction to variable and feature selection. J. Mach. Learn. Res. **3**(null), 1157–1182 (2003)
24. I. Guyon, A. Saffari, G. Dror, G. Cawley, Model selection: beyond the bayesian/frequentist divide. J. Mach. Learn. Res. **11**, 61–87 (2010). March
25. I. Guyon, A. Saffari, G. Dror, G.C. Cawley, Agnostic learning vs. prior knowledge challenge, in *Proceedings of the International Joint Conference on Neural Networks, IJCNN 2007, Celebrating 20 years of neural networks, Orlando, Florida, USA, August 12-17, 2007* (2007), pp. 829–834
26. I. Guyon, A. Saffari, G. Dror, G.C. Cawley, Analysis of the IJCNN 2007 agnostic learning vs. prior knowledge challenge. Neural Netw. **21**(2-3), 544–550 (2008)
27. I. Guyon, L. Sun-Hosoya, M. Boullé, H.J. Escalante, S. Escalera, Z. Liu, D. Jajetic, B. Ray, M. Saeed, M. Sebag, A.R. Statnikov, W.-W. Tu, E. Viegas, Analysis of the automl challenge series 2015-2018, in *Automated Machine Learning - Methods, Systems, Challenges* (2019), pp. 177–219
28. M. Hall, E. Frank, G. Holmes, B. Pfahringer, P. Reutemann, I.H. Witten, The weka data mining software: an update. SIGKDD Explor. Newsl. **11**(1), 10–18 (2009). November
29. T. Hastie, R. Tibshirani, J. Friedman, *The Elements of Statistical Learning*, 2nd edn. (Springer, 2009)
30. X. He, K. Zhao, X. Chu, Automl: a survey of the state-of-the-art (2019)
31. A.G. Howard, M. Zhu, B. Chen, D. Kalenichenko, W. Wang, T. Weyand, M. Andreetto, H. Adam, Mobilenets: Efficient convolutional neural networks for mobile vision applications, in *CoRR*, abs/1704.04861 (2017)
32. F. Hutter, H.H. Hoos, K. Leyton-Brown, Sequential model-based optimization for general algorithm configuration, in *Learning and Intelligent Optimization*, ed. by C.A. Coello Coello (Springer Berlin Heidelberg, Berlin, Heidelberg, 2011), pp. 507–523
33. F. Hutter, L. Kotthoff, J. Vanschoren, eds, in *Automated Machine Learning - Methods, Systems, Challenges*. The Springer Series on Challenges in Machine Learning (Springer, 2019)
34. K.G. Jamieson, A. Talwalkar, Non-stochastic best arm identification and hyperparameter optimization, in *Proceedings of the 19th International Conference on Artificial Intelligence and Statistics, AISTATS 2016, Cadiz, Spain, May 9-11, 2016*, vol. 51. JMLR Workshop and Conference Proceedings, ed. by A. Gretton, C.C. Robert (JMLR.org, 2016), pp. 240–248
35. H. Jin, Q. ong, X. Hu, Auto-keras: an efficient neural architecture search system, in *Proceedings of the 25th ACM SIGKDD International Conference on Knowledge Discovery & Data Mining*, KDD '19(Association for Computing Machinery, New York, NY, USA, 2019), pp. 1946–1956
36. E. LeDell, H2o automl: scalable automatic machine learning, in *Proceedings of the AutoML Workshop at ICML 2020* (2020)

37. B. Li, S.C.H. Hoi, Online portfolio selection: a survey. ACM Comput. Surv. **46**(3) (2014)
38. L. Li, K. Jamieson, G. DeSalvo, A. Rostamizadeh, A. Talwalkar, Hyperband: a novel bandit-based approach to hyperparameter optimization. J. Mach. Learn. Res. **18**(1), 6765–6816 (2017)
39. Y.-F. Li, H. Wang, T. Wei, W.-W. Tu, Towards automated semi-supervised learning, in *The Thirty-Third AAAI Conference on Artificial Intelligence, AAAI 2019, The Thirty-First Innovative Applications of Artificial Intelligence Conference, IAAI 2019, The Ninth AAAI Symposium on Educational Advances in Artificial Intelligence, EAAI 2019, Honolulu, Hawaii, USA, January 27 - February 1, 2019* (AAAI Press, 2019), pp. 4237–4244
40. S. Lim, I. Kim, T. Kim, C. Kim, S. Kim, Fast autoaugment, in *CoRR*, abs/1905.00397 (2019)
41. Z. Liu, I. Guyon, J. Jacques Junior, M. Madadi, S. Escalera, A. Pavao, H. Jair Escalante, T. Wei-Wei, X. Zhen, S. Treguer, AutoCV challenge design, baseline results, in *CAp 2019 - Conférence sur l'Apprentissage Automatique, Toulouse, France* (2019)
42. Z. Liu, Z. Xu, S. Escalera, I. Guyon, J.C.S. Jacques Junior, M. Madadi, A. Pavao, S. Treguer, W.-W. Tu, Towards Automated Computer Vision: Analysis of the AutoCV Challenges 2019. working paper or preprint, November (2019)
43. Z. Liu, Z. Xu, M. Madadi, J. Jacques Junior, S. Escalera, S. Rajaa, I. Guyon, Overview and unifying conceptualization of automated machine learning, in *Proceedings of Automating Data Science Workshop @ECML-PKDD* (2019)
44. Z. Liu, Z. Xu, S. Rajaa, M. Madadi, J.C.S. Jacques Junior, S. Escalera, A. Pavao, S. Treguer, W.-W. Tu, I. Guyon, Towards automated deep learning: analysis of the autodl challenge series 2019 zhengying liu, in *Proceedings of Machine Learning Research*, vol. 123 (2020), pp. 242–252
45. R.W. Lutz, Logitboost with trees applied to the WCCI 2006 performance prediction challenge datasets, in *Proceedings of the International Joint Conference on Neural Networks, IJCNN 2006, part of the IEEE World Congress on Computational Intelligence, WCCI 2006, Vancouver, BC, Canada, 16-21 July 2006* (2006), pp. 1657–1660
46. J.G. Madrid, H. Jair Escalante, Meta-learning of text classification tasks, in *Progress in Pattern Recognition, Image Analysis, Computer Vision, and Applications - 24th Iberoamerican Congress, CIARP 2019, Havana, Cuba, October 28-31, 2019, Proceedings*, vol. 11896, ed. by I. Nyström, Y.H. Heredia, V.M. Núñez. Lecture Notes in Computer Science (Springer, 2019), pp. 107–119
47. G.F. Miller, P.M. Todd, S.U. Hegde, Designing neural networks using genetic algorithms, in *Proceedings of the Third International Conference on Genetic Algorithms* (Morgan Kaufmann Publishers Inc, San Francisco, CA, USA, 1989), pp. 379–384
48. M. Momma, K.P. Bennett, *A Pattern Search Method for Model Selection of Support Vector Regression* (SIAM, 2002), pp. 261–274
49. R.S. Olson, J.H. Moore, TPOT: a tree-based pipeline optimization tool for automating machine learning, in *Proceedings of the 2016 Workshop on Automatic Machine Learning, AutoML 2016, co-located with 33rd International Conference on Machine Learning (ICML 2016), New York City, NY, USA, June 24, 2016* (2016), pp. 66–74
50. R.S. Olson, J.H. Moore, *TPOT: A Tree-Based Pipeline Optimization Tool for Automating Machine Learning* (Springer International Publishing, Cham, 2019), pp. 151–160
51. N. Pillay, Q. Rong, D. Srinivasan, B. Hammer, K. Sorensen, Automated design of machine learning and search algorithms [guest editorial]. Comp. Intell. Mag. **13**(2), 16–17 (2018). May
52. E. Real, S. Moore, A. Selle, S. Saxena, Y.L. Suematsu, J. Tan, Q.V. Le, A. Kurakin, Large-scale evolution of image classifiers, in *Proceedings of the 34th International Conference on Machine Learning - Volume 70*, ICML'17 (JMLR.org, 2017), pp. 2902–2911
53. P. Ren, Y. Xiao, X. Chang, P.-Y. Huang, Z. Li, X. Chen, X. Wang, Challenges and solutions: a comprehensive survey of neural architecture search (2020)
54. J. Reunanen, Model selection and assessment using cross-indexing, in *Proceedings of the International Joint Conference on Neural Networks, IJCNN 2007, Celebrating 20 years of neural networks, Orlando, Florida, USA, August 12-17, 2007* (2007), pp. 2581–2585
55. J.R. Rice, The algorithm selection problem, in *Advances in Computers*, vol. 15, ed. by M. Rubinoff, M.C. Yovits (Elsevier, 1976), pp. 65–118

56. A. Rosales-Pérez, J.A. Gonzalez, C.A. Coello Coello, H.J. Escalante, C.A. Reyes García, Multi-objective model type selection. Neurocomputing **146**, 83–94 (2014)
57. B. Scholkopf, A.J. Smola, *Learning with Kernels: Support Vector Machines, Regularization, Optimization, and Beyond* (MIT Press, Cambridge, MA, USA, 2001)
58. K.A. Smith-Miles, Cross-disciplinary perspectives on meta-learning for algorithm selection. ACM Comput. Surv. **41**(1) (2009)
59. J. Snoek, H. Larochelle, R.P. Adams, Practical bayesian optimization of machine learning algorithms (2012)
60. Q. Sun, B. Pfahringer, M. Mayo, Full model selection in the space of data mining operators, in *Proceedings of the 14th Annual Conference Companion on Genetic and Evolutionary Computation*, GECCO '12 (Association for Computing Machinery, New York, NY, USA, 2012), pp. 1503–1504
61. E.-G. Talbi, Optimization of deep neural networks: a survey and unified taxonomy. working paper or preprint, June (2020)
62. C. Thornton, F. Hutter, H.H. Hoos, K. Leyton-Brown, Auto-WEKA: combined selection and hyperparameter optimization of classification algorithms, in *Proceedings of KDD-2013* (2013), pp. 847–855
63. L. Tuggener, M. Amirian, K. Rombach, S. Lörwald, A. Varlet, C. Westermann, T. Stadelmann, Automated machine learning in practice: state of the art and recent results, in *CoRR*, abs/1907.08392 (2019)
64. J. Vanschoren, Meta-learning: a survey, in *CoRR*, abs/1810.03548 (2018)
65. R. Vilalta, Y. Drissi, A perspective view and survey of meta-learning. Artif. Intell. Rev. **18**(2), 77–95 (2002)
66. Y. Wang, Q. Yao, Few-shot learning: a survey, in *CoRR*, abs/1904.05046 (2019)
67. J.D. Wichard, Agnostic learning with ensembles of classifiers, in *Proceedings of the International Joint Conference on Neural Networks, IJCNN 2007, Celebrating 20 years of neural networks, Orlando, Florida, USA, August 12-17, 2007* (IEEE, 2007), pp. 2887–2891
68. J. Wilson, A.K. Meher, B.V. Bindu, S. Chaudhury, B. Lall, M. Sharma, V. Pareek, Automatically optimized gradient boosting trees for classifying large volume high cardinality data streams under concept drift, in *The NeurIPS '18 Competition*, ed. by S. Escalera, R. Herbrich (Springer International Publishing, Cham, 2020), pp. 317–335
69. Q. Yao, M. Wang, Y. Chen, W. Dai, Y.-F. Li, T. Wei-Wei, Q. Yang, Y. Yu, A survey on automated machine learning, Taking human out of learning applications (2018)
70. B. Zoph, Q.V. Le, Neural architecture search with reinforcement learning, in *CoRR*, abs/1611.01578 (2016)
71. M.-A. Zöller, M.F. Huber, Survey on automated machine learning (2019)

Chapter 3
A General Model for Automated Algorithm Design

Rong Qu

Abstract This chapter presents a newly defined novel combinatorial optimisation problem, namely, the General Combinatorial Optimisation Problem (GCOP), whose decision variables are a set of elementary algorithm components. The combinations of these algorithm components, i.e. solutions of GCOP, thus represent different search algorithms. The objective of GCOP is to find the optimal combinations of algorithm components for solving optimisation problems. Solving the GCOP is thus equivalent to automatically designing the best search algorithms for optimisation problems. The definition of the GCOP is presented with a new taxonomy which categorises relevant literature on automated algorithm design into three lines of research, namely, automated algorithm configuration, selection and composition. Based on the decision space under consideration, the algorithm design itself is defined as an optimisation problem. Relevant literature is briefly reviewed, motivating a new line of exciting and challenging directions on the emerging research of automated algorithm design.

3.1 Introduction

Combinatorial Optimisation Problems (COPs) represent an important topic in operational research [42]. Subject to given constraints, a COP consists of assigning discrete domain values to a finite set of decision variables. The aim is to optimise an objective function which evaluates the solutions, i.e. different assignments of domain values to decision variables. In the literature, the mostly studied COPs include travelling salesman problem, knapsack problem, job shop scheduling, personnel scheduling and timetabling. Well-established benchmark COPs (e.g. the OR Library [8]) have motivated advanced research on designing effective search algorithms.

---

[1] http://people.brunel.ac.uk/~mastjjb/jeb/info.html.

R. Qu (✉)
University of Nottingham, Nottingham, United Kingdom
e-mail: rong.qu@nottingham.ac.uk

N. Pillay and R. Qu (eds.), *Automated Design of Machine Learning and Search Algorithms*, Natural Computing Series,
https://doi.org/10.1007/978-3-030-72069-8_3

Effectively addressing the extensions of the benchmark COPs with different constraints and features has a direct impact on improving the efficiency of operations across business and industry sectors in real world. Due to their complex constraints and non-convex problem structure, most of the COPs are NP-hard [21]. Exhaustive search in mathematical optimisation is often not applicable due to the exponential search spaces of COPs. In the last few decades, evolutionary computation and meta-heuristic search algorithms have been extensively investigated and successfully applied to real-world COP applications.

The increasing demand of real-world optimisation requires fast developments of search algorithms with less involvement of human expertise. This leads to one of the fast emerging recent advances on automated algorithm design in optimisation research and evolutionary computation. That is, without the extensive knowledge from human experts, to automatically design search algorithms or solvers for unseen problem instances. This echoes the recent fast developments of AI which automatically models extensive human intelligence to address problems in various domains.

In [51], a new taxonomy of automated algorithm design has categorised the latest research into automated algorithm configuration, automated algorithm selection and automated algorithm composition. Based on this taxonomy, this chapter further defines automated algorithm design as a COP with decision variables of parameters, algorithms and components for automated algorithm configuration, selection and composition, respectively. Solving a classic COP usually concerns a search space of problem solutions. Automated algorithm design can be seen as a COP concerning a search space of decisions in designing algorithms.

In [51], a new model, the General Combinatorial Optimisation Problem (GCOP), is defined with the new taxonomy to formally model automated algorithm composition as a COP. Algorithm design decisions have been defined as elementary algorithm components and modelled as decision variables in the search space, optimisation of which automatically composes and designs new generic search algorithms. The GCOP thus also presents a general model capable of defining a wide range of selection hyper-heuristics as shown in [51].

In this chapter, a brief overview of the three lines of research in automated algorithm design is presented with the new taxonomy in Sect. 3.2. With this context the fundamentals of the GCOP model are discussed in Sect. 3.3. Section 3.4 presents some examples of search algorithms defined with the GCOP model, followed by discussions on research issues and future directions in Sect. 3.5. Section 3.6 concludes the chapter.

3.2 Automated Algorithm Design

To design evolutionary algorithms or meta-heuristics for solving optimisation problems, different decisions need to be made. These include, at a lower level for the chosen target algorithms, how to fine-tune their parameters (e.g. temperatures in simulated annealing, tabu tenure in tabu search, population size in genetic algorithms), how to design operators (e.g. neighbourhood operators in local search algorithms, genetic operators in evolutionary algorithms); and at a higher level, which are the most appropriate algorithms, and how to integrate or hybridise different heuristics for solving the problems/instances at hand.

In the existing scientific literature, the majority of search algorithms have been designed manually. Some of the decisions designing effective algorithms have been made online while solving the problems by adaptively adjusting parameter settings, choosing appropriate operators using some learning mechanisms. Many other decisions have been made offline with domain knowledge, human expertise or based on experimental results on testing instances. Nevertheless, making these different decisions is highly dependent on human expertise, and presents a challenge for researchers of different skills.

Automated algorithm design aims to make these above-mentioned decisions with less or no human involvement. In [51], recent research advances in automated algorithm design have been categorised with the following different focuses and objectives:

- Automated algorithm configuration: given some pre-defined target algorithm(s), to automatically configure their parameters on a given set of training problem instances offline so as to solve unseen instances.
- Automated algorithm selection: from a portfolio of chosen algorithms with their associated parameters, to select the most appropriate one(s) based on a set of training instances for solving unseen instances.
- Automated algorithm composition: given heuristics or components of some algorithms, to automatically compose or combine them into new general algorithms while solving the problem instances online.

Although not specifically defined in the literature, these above three lines of research on automated algorithm design mostly concern discrete decisions in a *search space* of possible *algorithms*, i.e. solutions for the problem of algorithm design. Automated algorithm design itself thus can be transferred to an optimisation problem, with different decision variables as follows:

- Automated algorithm configuration: explores a search space of different parameter settings of some target algorithm(s), i.e. decision variables are parameters of certain domain within a template of the target algorithm(s). The target algorithm(s) with the best parameter configurations are applied to solve unseen problem instances offline.
- Automated algorithm selection: explores a search space of a family or portfolio of target algorithms, i.e. decision variables are different algorithms or solvers themselves; in some cases, associated with their parameters. These algorithms are usually selected against a set of features identified to categorise typical training problem instances into clusters, thus to solve unseen similar instances offline.
- Automated algorithm composition: explores a search space of different heuristics or components, i.e. decision variables are heuristics or algorithm components of some chosen target algorithm(s) or general algorithms. The best composition(s) of these heuristics or components are explored to solve the problem instances online.

With these fundamental differences on the decision/search spaces, the above-defined taxonomy aims to categorise the existing research on automated algorithm design, where terminologies have been used interchangeably at places. The first two lines of research take a top-down approach, with pre-defined target algorithm(s) or pool of algorithms. The resulting configured or selected algorithms are likely to be new variants of the same target algorithm(s) or of the same family of algorithms. The third line of research on automated algorithm composition takes a bottom-up approach, with the given heuristics or components, to freely compose usually new general algorithms.

The following sections briefly review some selected literature on automated design of meta-heuristics for COPs with the above taxonomy. As an emerging topic potentially across different disciplines, it is challenging to review exclusively all relevant literature in automated algorithm design. For example, in automated algorithm configuration, tree search solvers [26] have been extensively investigated, resulting in highly strong solvers winning SAT competitions. Heuristic search in constraint programming [38] represents another interesting topic. In genetic programming [35], operations upon problem attributes are considered as decisions designing new heuristics. One stream of research focuses on solving SAT [59], where stochastic local search and tree search in a large number of solvers have been investigated across the three lines of research in automated configuration, selection and composition. This broad literature is not the focus in this chapter; however, some of the techniques reviewed could be adopted or transferred to design exact search techniques addressing other optimisation problems.

3.2.1 Automated Algorithm Configuration

Among the three lines of research on automated algorithm design, automated algorithm configuration has been the mostly studied in the last two decades, aiming to reduce the human efforts on this important and time-consuming task in algorithm design. The target meta-heuristic search algorithms cover mainly heuristics, local search, evolutionary algorithms and swarm intelligence algorithms.

Compared to evolutionary algorithms, heuristics and local search algorithms attracted relatively less attention in automated algorithm configuration. Algorithms considered include Tabu Search [3], Simulated Annealing [43] and Variable Neighbourhood Descent [2]. Early research focused on tuning numerical values [3, 7, 11, 18, 43]. Neighbourhood operators have also been automatically configured in recent research [1, 19]. COPs considered include flowshop scheduling [3, 43], VRP [1, 18, 19] and TSP [1].

In evolutionary algorithms, different types of parameters have been automatically configured. Most research concern configuring numerical parameters [22, 49, 52], including mutation/crossover rate, population size, chromosome length, number of iterations/evaluations, etc. Other types include categorical [56], symbolic [54], conditional [12] and mixed of these parameters [12, 30, 31, 41, 53, 54]. Types of algorithms cover genetic algorithms [53], evolutionary algorithms [20, 41, 49, 54], memetic algorithms [22, 31] as well as continuous evolutionary algorithms [30]. The problem domains concern a wide range of applications, from function optimisation [20, 30, 54], NK landscape [31, 53], CSP [56], TSP [33, 41] to multiple COPs [22].

Automated configuration has also addressed swarm intelligence, including (multi-objective) ant colony optimisation mainly for TSP [7, 12, 33] and particle swarm optimisation for scheduling and function optimisation [4, 57]. Within the template of ant colony optimisation, automated configurations have been made upon numerical, categorical and conditional parameters. Compared to other meta-heuristic algorithms, the search space of parameters is usually much larger, requiring efficient automated configuration methods.

Different platforms, frameworks and methods have been developed to automatically configure the large number of parameters in the target algorithms using statistical techniques [3, 18, 20, 22, 49, 52], sequential model-based optimisation [19] and evolutionary computation methods [41, 54, 56, 57]. The mostly adopted platforms include ISAC [27], F-Race [12], ParamILS [26] and their extensions I/F-race [12] and irace [33]. In F-Race, the automated parameter tuning is defined as a machine learning problem [10], for which the racing technique is used to statistically eliminate poor configurations of ant colony optimisation [12] and evolutionary algorithms [30] upon training instances offline. In ParamILS [26], iterative local search is employed to effectively explore the configuration space of search algorithms. Although it is mainly used to configure local search algorithms in tree search and SAT solvers [26], it can also be used to configure any parameterised algorithms including heuristics or meta-heuristics [53]. Based on GGA [6] and stochastic offline programming, ISAC [27], which configures mainly SAT solvers, can also be used to configure meta-heuristics.

The majority of automated configuration is conducted offline, usually upon a set of training instances, aiming to solve unseen similar testing instances. This opens a new line of research, with regard to algorithm performance, on the choice of the instance features [4], landscape [25, 31] and the choice of the benchmark instances themselves [30]. It has been shown that some of the existing ant colony optimisation algorithms could be replicated by automated configuration of parameters in the defined framework [34]. The new algorithms automatically generated, even of the same family of the target algorithms, are superior to those manually designed, producing highly promising results [3, 54] especially for SAT [59]. Note that manually designed algorithms often require and highly depend on extensive and different human expertise in algorithm design.

3.2.2 Automated Algorithm Selection

Research on automated algorithm selection started about a decade ago [29], and received relatively less research attention compared to automated algorithm configuration. The portfolios of algorithms cover a diverse range of approaches and techniques, from different parametric SAT solvers [32, 59], specific heuristics [13, 45], meta-heuristics [16, 24, 37], evolutionary algorithms [5, 55] and swarm intelligence [44].

One main research topic in automated algorithm selection focuses on the analysis and clustering of training instances according to their features, thus to select the best algorithms or solvers accordingly for unseen test instances of the same cluster [32]. This follows the same idea as that of automated algorithm configurations in Sect. 3.2.1 for unseen instances of similar features. Techniques analysing and clustering problem instances include mainly machine learning [16, 45] and statistical analysis [13, 23, 24, 44].

Several frameworks have been built in automated algorithm selection. Population-based algorithm portfolios (PAP) [55] and Hydra [59] have been developed for optimisation functions [55], Boolean satisfiability problem and travelling salesman problem [32]. During the algorithm selection from the portfolios, configuration of the target algorithms has been considered at the same time, using existing platforms as discussed in Sect. 3.2.1. In Hydra [59], a large number of parameters are configured using stochastic local search in ParamILS, and configurations are iteratively combined into a portfolio, from which the best solvers based on training instances are selected for solving new SAT instances. In [36], algorithm configuration using GGA [6] integrated with algorithm selection using SATzilla [60] obtains highly promising results solving SAT instances.

3.2.3 Automated Algorithm Composition

In automated algorithm composition, a set of components or heuristics are automatically combined online to produce new generic algorithms. A main line of research is on hyper-heuristics [15, 47], which aim to decide 'at a higher abstraction level which low-level heuristics to apply' [17]. Constructive or perturbative low-level heuristics are selected or generated to solve optimisation problems. By searching the given low-level heuristics, high-level methods can thus solve multiple COPs with the same or adaptive algorithms online. With the taxonomy defined above, this can be seen as to automatically design new algorithms by composing the low-level heuristics as the algorithm components.

Besides hyper-heuristics, research in automated algorithm composition is underdeveloped. Some research in the literature concerns components (also called building blocks) for a type of target algorithms, e.g. evolutionary algorithms [9, 41]. Compositions of these building blocks thus can be seen as designing new variants of evolutionary algorithms in a more flexible way. In [51], elementary components of general search algorithms rather than building blocks in evolutionary algorithms have been defined within a new GCOP model. As a result, new generic algorithms rather than specific type of algorithms can be automatically designed. Details of the GCOP model are discussed in Sect. 3.3 in this chapter.

Frameworks have been developed in hyper-heuristics, including HyFlex [14] and EvoHyp [46], supporting automatic composition of low-level heuristics across multiple COPs [47] including those in Cross-Domain Heuristic Search Challenge [14].

3.3 The General Combinatorial Optimisation Problem

In [51], a new problem model, namely, General Combinatorial Optimisation Problem (GCOP), is formally defined to model the problem of algorithm design as a COP. In the new GCOP model, the most *elementary algorithm components* associated with different heuristics and parameters are defined as decision variables. Different techniques applied to explore the search space of these decisions in algorithm design can thus be seen as to automatically design new generic algorithms for solving the problems under consideration online. The resulting optimised compositions of basic algorithm components thus represent new generic search algorithms automatically designed.

Definition of the GCOP[51]

The **General Combinatorial Optimisation Problem** (GCOP) is a combinatorial optimisation problem. The decision variables of GCOP take domain values a from A, a finite set of algorithm components, $a \in A$. The solution space C of GCOP consists of algorithm compositions c upon the decision variables a. The objective function of GCOP, $F(c) \rightarrow R, c \in C$, evaluates the performance of c for solving the optimisation problem(s) p.

The decision variables of p take values from a finite set of problem-specific values. The solution space S for p consists of the direct solutions s explored and obtained by the corresponding algorithm compositions c, i.e. $c \rightarrow s$. The objective function $f(s) \rightarrow R$ evaluates $s \in S$ for p. The problem p could be extended to other optimisation problems including continuous optimisation, multi-objective optimisation problems, etc.

Objective Functions of the GCOP

Let M be a mapping function M: $f(s) \rightarrow F(c)$, i.e. each algorithm composition c for the GCOP maps to solutions s for p, i.e. $c \rightarrow s$, thus the generated s reflects the performance of c. The objective of the GCOP is to search for the optimal $c^* \in C$ which produces the optimal $s^* \in S$ for p, so that $F(c^*)$ is optimised, as defined in $Objective$ (3.1).

$$F(c^*|c^* \rightarrow s^*) \leftarrow f(s^*) = \mathbf{min}(f(s)) \quad (3.1)$$

$Objective$ (3.1) can be extended to measure various aspects of c, e.g. the performance of c for solving multiple p and computational time of c, etc. to inform the search for solving the GCOP.

Domains of Decision Variables in the GCOP

In [51], a domain $A_{1.0}$ has been established with a set of most basic algorithm components a of two categories, namely, operators $A_{1.0\_o}$ and acceptance criteria $A_{1.0\_a}$, each with their associated heuristics and parameters. This provides a general algorithm design model for automatically designing a large number of existing meta-heuristics in the literature, i.e. local search algorithms and selection hyper-heuristics. The GCOP can be extended in different ways to sustain advanced research in automated algorithm design. For experienced users, the domain A can be extended with user-defined components for different problems under consideration as shown in [51]. Research is ongoing to extend the elementary components to define and automatically design other main types of meta-heuristics, i.e. population-based algorithms.

The basic idea of the GCOP is to breakdown search algorithms into a set of elementary components, which are modularised into general search operators associated with different heuristics, as the decision variables. In the existing literature, these elementary components are quite often 'hard-wired' manually into integrated or compound operators or heuristics using human expertise. The idea with the GCOP is that the most basic elementary components can thus be freely optimised to automatically generate new generic algorithms which significantly expand the scope which human experts may not be able to explore. In [51], it has been demonstrated that many of the selection hyper-heuristics can be defined using the unified GCOP model. Section 3.4 presents more examples of existing search algorithms in the literature defined using $A_{1.0}$ in the GCOP model.

Search Spaces in the GCOP

The search space C for GCOP consists of all possible compositions $c \in C$. It is fundamentally different from that of S for p, which consists of all possible problem solutions $s \in S$. The encodings of c and s are different, upon which different techniques or methods could be applied to analyse and explore the search spaces of different characteristics. The search space of c is usually of a much lower dimension compared to s which depends on the specific p, and has a different upper bound. Furthermore, the objective function of the GCOP, i.e. performance of c, can be more than just the direct evaluation of s for p.

The concept of two search spaces has been firstly analysed in [50] in the context of hyper-heuristics [47], where high-level methods explore the search space of general or problem-specific low-level heuristics, which are then applied to solve the problems online. This concept is generalised in the GCOP to model algorithm design. The search space on decisions of algorithm design is explored at a higher level, leading to the best compositions of algorithm components addressing the problems at hand. In other words, the GCOP can be seen as modelling the problem of algorithm design as a COP at a higher level.

The underlying theory of the GCOP model is fundamentally different from that of hyper-heuristics, where the low-level heuristics are designed and selected manually by human experts. In another word, many of the low-level heuristics can be seen as specific or compound heuristics integrating subsets of the elementary components as modelled in the GCOP. The idea of hyper-heuristics which search upon these specific pre-defined low-level heuristics to solve COPs is fundamentally different from that of GCOP, which is upon general elementary algorithm components to support evolving new generic algorithms modelled in a search space.

Along with the advances in evolutionary computation, different frameworks, platforms and toolkits have been established, supporting fast developments of algorithms with certain consistency. However, there is a lack of common or general standard of search algorithms in the optimisation research community [28]. The GCOP provides a new standard which formulates various search algorithms in a unified model with the most basic elementary algorithm components. Such a standard can thus support systematic investigations within coherent frameworks to gain insights in automated algorithm design upon the most elementary general components. To sustain such research advances, the latest developments and resources have been made available at a dedicated GCOP website.[2]

3.4 Search Algorithms Defined with the GCOP Model

In [51], with the basic elementary operators $A_{1.0}\_o$ and general acceptance criteria $A_{1.0}\_a$ in $A_{1.0}$, various selection hyper-heuristics for solving vehicle routing problems (VRP) and nurse rostering problems (NRP) have been defined with the GCOP model. The unified GCOP model supports insightful analysis across different search algorithms for the two COPs.

With the GCOP model, analysis on $a \in A_{1.0}$ adopted in selection hyper-heuristics for NRP and VRP leads to interesting findings [51]. For solving VRP variants of different constraints, it was observed that a subset of the basic $a \in A_{1.0}$ is enough to design a large number of selection hyper-heuristics. Among them the mostly used operators include *swap*, *interchange* or *k-opt*. Some of the operators used can be seen as compound operators, combining more than one $a \in A_{1.0}$. For NRP, on the one hand, various acceptance criteria $a \in A_{1.0}\_a$ have been studied, which is not the case for VRP. This may be due to the highly constrained nature of NRP, requiring complicated constraint-handling techniques. On the other hand, most of the NRP algorithms can be formulated using operators $a \in A_{1.0}\_o$, while for VRP problem-specific operators often needed to extend $A_{1.0}\_o$. This may be due to the fixed solution structure in NRP, where shifts can be easily exchanged on the same days, while the variable solution structure in VRP, i.e. different lengths of the routes for each vehicle, calls for effective problem-specific operators addressing different problem features in the wide range of variants.

In this chapter, Table 3.1 presents more selected examples of various local search algorithms defined using subsets of $A_{1.0}$ in the GCOP. In the literature, a large amount of advanced algorithms have been developed with different mechanisms, enhancing the basic variants as shown in Table 3.1. For example, learning has been recently

---

[2] https://sites.google.com/view/general-cop.

Table 3.1 Examples of local search algorithms modelled in GCOP

Algorithm *c*	$o \in A_{1.0}$ and $a \in A_{1.0}$ used to define algorithm *c*
Greedy local search (GLS)	Different operators with $a_{oi}(n)$: only the best out of *n* neighbours are accepted. *n* can be set as a fixed or variable value
GLS variant 1	With $a_{oi}(n)$, $o_{xchg}(k,m,h1_w)$, where values of *k* and *m* decision variables selected by heuristic $h1_w$ in two parts of a solution *s* are swapped
GLS variant 2	With $a_{oi}(n)$, $o_{chg}(k,h1_w,h1_b)$, *k* decision variables selected by $h1_w$ are changed using heuristic $h1_b$
Tabu Search (TS)	Different operators with $a_{tabu}(n,l)$: the best out of *n* neighbours and not in the tabu list is accepted,. *l* (tabu length) and *n* are set as a fixed or variable value
TS variant 1	With $a_{tabu}(n,l)$, $o_{xchg}(k,m,h1_w)$ or $o_{chg}(k,h1_w,h1_b)$ as defined above
TS variant 2	With $a_{tabu}(n,l)$, $o_{ins}(k,h1_w,h1_b)$, where *k* decision variables selected by $h1_w$ are inserted to another position selected by $h1_b$
Simulated Annealing (SA)	Different operators with $a_{gd}(n,t,r)$: worse solutions sampled from *n* neighbours are accepted by a probability subject to a temperature *t* decreased at rate *r*. Better solutions are always accepted
SA variant 1	With $a_{gd}(n,t,r)$, $o_{xchg}(k,m,h1_w)$ or $o_{chg}(k,h1_w,h1_b)$ as defined above
SA variant 2	With $a_{gd}(n,t,r)$, $o_{rr}(k,h1_w,h1_b)$, where values of a section of *k* decision variables in solution *s* selected by $h1_w$ are removed, and then reassigned using $h1_b$
Variable Neighbourhood Search	$a_{oi}(n)$ with more than one operator as above

integrated in evolutionary computation and meta-heuristics, greatly improving algorithm performance. Of course, domain knowledge usually significantly improves the efficiency of search algorithms, however, usually at the cost of computational expenses and/or human expertise, and thus reduces the generality of the algorithms in real-world applications.

In the literature, it is not always clear how some decisions in algorithm design have been made. For example, the acceptance criteria $A_{1.0\_a}$ or the number of *n* neighbours explored in local search algorithms are not always clearly specified. This led to some ambiguity in reproducing the published algorithms. With the consistent modular components with parametric and heuristic settings in the GCOP model, these details can be clearly defined with $a \in A$, sustaining consistent research findings reported in the literature.

3.5 Challenges in Automated Algorithm Design with the GCOP

The search space of the GCOP as a COP increases exponentially with A. Identifying a single best $a \in A_{1.0}$, i.e. using a single algorithm component with the best parametric settings, to design algorithms as shown in Table 3.1 might be manageable using advanced computational techniques. However, exploring or exploiting the exponential search space of algorithm compositions freely composed upon different $a \in A$ is a challenging research issue, similar to that for COPs in optimisation research. This presents a new challenge to evolutionary computation and computational intelligence.

With the advances in automated algorithm design, new algorithms generated are likely to be highly different from those manually designed. Those manually designed algorithms in Table 3.1, i.e. search algorithms using the fixed components, represent only a small subset of C, which are combinations of different components used in search algorithms. These newly identified algorithms provide an interesting subject of research across different disciplines including artificial intelligence, evolutionary computation and machine learning.

The GCOP model provides a new standard to formulate various search algorithms, and also serves a consistent data structure to collect, store and process data of algorithm design for potential knowledge discovery using machine learning. Statistical methods have been used to identify a compact subset of low-level heuristics in hyper-heuristics towards building general effective methods [39]. Further systematic analysis using machine learning with standards like the GCOP may reveal new knowledge such as behaviours and speed of algorithm components, synergy between the basic components, etc. The new standard bridging search algorithms in optimisation and machine learning in artificial intelligence potentially contributes to a significantly improved understanding on effective search algorithms.

Heuristic search algorithms have been criticised with lacking theoretical fundamentals, replying highly on experience to solve problems where exhaustive search is not realistic. Most established heuristic search algorithms and frameworks in the literature are defined descriptively, lacking a fundamentally consistent structure and standard. As a result, although numerous algorithms have been manually designed in optimisation research, the rich but scattered experience is difficult to model and reuse. The novel GCOP model supports the establishment of a new standard to retain such knowledge into structured and optimised general components, which may serve as the training data for machine learning to sustain data-driven automated design of new algorithms.

Recent research advances in automated algorithm design made some progress on the generality [12, 15] and reusability of algorithms; however, much more needs to be done to significantly reduce human expertise and development barriers. In automated algorithm configuration and selection, existing research has aimed to reuse the configured or selected algorithms upon training instances for solving unseen problems or instances categorised by similar problem features identified [32, 55]. In automated algorithm composition, hyper-heuristics have been developed to address cross-domain COPs [40]. An assessment method [48] has also been proposed to evaluate the generality, rather than the optimality, of search algorithms. The scope of generality and reusability, subject to the No Free Lunch Theorems [58], presents a challenging and interesting theoretical issue to the optimisation research community. Collaborative research across disciplines is needed, especially with recent advances in machine learning, to reveal new knowledge transferable to solve different optimisation algorithms, thus to enhance the reusability and generality of search algorithms.

3.6 Conclusions

With the advanced research in evolutionary computation and optimisation research, a large number of meta-heuristics and evolutionary algorithms have been designed in scientific literature for solving benchmark and real-world combinatorial optimisation problems (COPs). The extensive knowledge on algorithm design led to the emerging new research challenges on automated algorithm design.

A recently defined new model, the General Combinatorial Optimisation Problem (GCOP), is discussed in this chapter, where the design of search algorithms itself is transferred and defined as a COP. In solving the GCOP, automated compositions of elementary algorithm components evolve new generic algorithms which may be difficult to design manually. The novel GCOP opens a new line of interesting research directions in optimisation research. In addition to extending the GCOP domain with more algorithm components to define population-based algorithms, the objective function can be also extended to measure the generality, reusability and computational time of the newly evolved algorithms. The new algorithms automatically designed may also introduce new knowledge on algorithm design in the literature for solving other optimisation problems, including continuous optimisation problems and multi-objective optimisation problems.

This chapter also discusses a recently proposed new taxonomy on automated algorithm design, which categorises relevant literature into automated algorithm configuration, selection and composition, concerning a search space of algorithm parameters, a portfolio of algorithms and algorithm components or heuristics, respectively. It is shown in the literature that automatically designed algorithms can outperform those designed manually. Research along the three streams of work may lead to further findings specifically on algorithm parameters, algorithm components and algorithm portfolios, respectively, to explore the scope of improved performance automated algorithm design involving less human involvement. Further investigations along the coherent streams of research hopefully will lead to increased knowledge and stimulate more advances in evolutionary computation and optimisation research, impacting on real-world complex optimisation problems.

References

1. T. Adamo, G. Ghiani, A. Grieco, E. Guerriero, E. Manni, MIP neighborhood synthesis through semantic feature extraction and automatic algorithm configuration. Comput. Oper. Res. **83**, 106–119 (2017)
2. T. Adamo, G. Ghiani, E. Guerriero, E. Manni, Automatic instantiation of a variable neighborhood descent from a mixed integer programming model. Oper. Res. Perspect. **4**, 123–135 (2017)
3. B. Adenso-Díaz, M. Laguna, Fine-tuning of algorithms using fractional experimental designs and local search. Oper. Res. **54**(1), 99–114 (2006)
4. T. Agasiev, A. Karpenko, The program system for automated parameter tuning of optimization algorithms. Procedia Comput. Sci. **103**, 347–354 (2017)
5. R. Akay, A. Basturk, A. Kalinli, X. Yao, Parallel population-based algorithm portfolios: an empirical study. Neurocomputing **247**, 115–125 (2017)
6. C. Ansótegui, M. Sellmann, K. Tierney, Gga: a gender-based genetic algorithm for the automatic configuration of algorithms, in *Proceedings of 2009 15th International Conference on Principles and Practice of Constraint Programming* (Lisbon, Portugal, 2009), pp. 142–157
7. P. Balaprakash, M. Birattari, T. Stützle, Improvement strategies for the f-race algorithm: sampling design and iterative refinement, in *HM 2007: Hybrid Metaheuristics* (Dortmund, Germany, October 8-9, 2007), pp. 108–122
8. J. Beasley, OR-library: distributing test problems by electronic mail. J. Oper. Res. Soc. **41**(11), 1069–1072 (1990)
9. L. Bezerra, M. Lòpez-Ibáñez, T. Stützle, Automatic design of evolutionary algorithms for multi-objective combinatorial optimization, in *Proceedings of Parallel Problem Solving from Nature* (Ljubljana, September 13–17, 2014), pp. 508–517
10. M. Birattari, *The Problem of Tuning Metaheuristics As Seen From a Machine Learning Perspective* (IOS Press, US, 2005)
11. M. Birattari, T. Stützle, L. Paquete, K. Varrentrapp, A racing algorithm for configuring metaheuristics, in *Proceedings of the 4th Annual Conference on Genetic and Evolutionary Computation (GECCO'02)* (2002), pp. 11–18
12. M. Birattari, Z. Yuan, P. Balaprakash, T. Stützle, F-race and iterated F-race: an overview, in *Experimental Methods for the Analysis of Optimization Algorithms* (2010), pp. 311–336
13. B. Bischl, O. Mersmann, H. Trautmann, M. Preuss, M. Preuß, Algorithm selection based on exploratory landscape analysis and cost-sensitive learning, in *GECCO '12: Proceedings of the 14th Annual Conference on Genetic and Evolutionary Computation* (Philly, 2012), pp. 313–320
14. E.K. Burke, M. Gendreau, M. Hyde, G. Kendall, B. McCollum, G. Ochoa, A.J. Parkes, S. Petrovic, The cross-domain heuristic search challenge - an international research competition, in *Proceedings of Intelligent Conference Learning and Intelligent Optimization* (Rome, January 17-21, 2011), pp. 631–634
15. E.K. Burke, M. Gendreau, M. Hyde, G. Kendall, G. Ochoa, E. Özcan, Hyper-heuristics: a survey of the state of the art. J. Oper. Res. Soc. **64**(12), 1695–1724 (2013)
16. T. Carchrae, J.C. Beck, Applying machine learning to low-knowledge ccontrol of optimisztion algorithms. Comput. Intell. **4**(21), 372–387 (2005)
17. P. Cowling, G. Kendall, E. Soubeiga, A hyperheuristic approach to scheduling a sales summit, in *Proceedings of Practice and Theory of Automated Timetabling* (Konstanz, August 16–18, 2000), pp. 176–190
18. S.P. Coy, B.L. Golden, G.C. Runger, E.A. Wasil, Using experimental design to find effective parameter settings for heuristics. J. Heuristics **1**(7), 77–97 (2001)
19. N.T.T. Dang, P. De Causmaecker, Characterization of neighborhood behaviours in a multi-neighborhood local search algorithm, in *LION 2016: Learning and Intelligent Optimization*. Lecture Notes in Computer Science 10079 (2016), pp. 234–239
20. O. François, C. Lavergne, Design of evolutionary algorithms - a statistical perspective. IEEE Trans. Evol. Comput. **5**(2), 129–148 (2001)

21. M.R. Garey, D.S. Johnson, *Computers and Intractability: A Guide to the Theory of NP-Completeness* (W.H. Freeman, New York, 1979)
22. D.B. Gümüs, E. Özcan, J. Atkin, An analysis of the taguchi method for tuning a memetic algorithm with reduced computational time budget, in *ISCIS 2016: Computer and Information Sciences* (Poland, 2016), pp. 12–20
23. Y. He, S.Y. Yuen, Y. Lou, X. Zhang, A sequential algorithm portfolio approach for black box optimization. Swarm Evol. Comput. **44**, 559–570 (2019)
24. B.A. Huberman, R.M. Lukose, T. Hogg, An economics approach to hard computational problems. Science **275**(5296), 51–54 (1997)
25. F. Hutter, H.H. Hoos, K. Leyton-Brown, Sequential model-based optimization for general algorithm configuration, in *LION 2011: Learning and Intelligent Optimization* (Rome, Italy, 2011), pp. 507–523
26. F. Hutter, H.H. Hoos, K. Leyton-Brown, T. Stützle, ParamILS: An automatic algorithm configuration framework. Journal of Artificial Intelligence Research **36**, 267–306 (2009)
27. S. Kadioglu, Y. Malitsky, M. Sellmann, K. Tierney, and K. Tierney. Isac - instance-specific algorithm configuration. In *Proceedings of the 2010 conference on ECAI 2010: 19th European Conference on Artificial Intelligence*, pages 751–756, Lisbon, Portugal, Aug, 2010
28. G. Kendall, R. Bai, J. Blazewicz, P. De Causmaecker, M. Gendreau, R. John, J. Li, B. McCollum, E. Pesch, R. Qu, N. Sabar, G. Vanden Berghe, and A. Yee. Good laboratory practice for optimization research. *Journal of Operational Research Society*, 67(4):676–689, Apr. 2016
29. P. Kerschke, H.H. Hoos, F. Neumann, H. Trautmann, Is evolutionary computation evolving fast enough? Evolutionary Computation **27**(1), 3–45 (2019)
30. T. Liao, D. Molina, T. Stützle, Performance evaluation of automatically tuned continuous optimizers on different benchmark sets. Applied Soft Computing **27**, 490–503 (2015)
31. A. Liefooghe, B. Derbel, S. Verel, H. Aguirre, K. Tanaka, Towards landscape-aware automatic algorithm configuration: preliminary experiments on neutral and rugged landscapes, in *Evo-COP 2017: Evolutionary Computation in Combinatorial Optimization* (2017), pp. 215–232
32. S. Liu, K. Tang, X. Yao, Automatic construction of parallel portfolios via explicit instance grouping, in *Proceedings of AAAI Conference on Artificial Intelligence* (New Orleans, 2018), pp. 2–7
33. M. López-Ibáñez, J. Dubois-Lacoste, L. P. Cáceres, T. Stützle, M. Birattari, The irace package: Iterated racing for automatic algorithm configuration. Oper. Res. Perspect. **3**, 43–58 (2016)
34. M. López-Ibáñez, T. Stützle, The automatic design of multi-objective ant colony optimization algorithms. IEEE Trans. Evol. Comput. **16**(6), 861–875 (2012)
35. J. MacLachlan, Y. Mei, J. Branke, M. Zhang, Genetic programming hyper-heuristics with vehicle collaboration for uncertain capacitated arc routing problems, in *Evolutionary Computation* **28**(4), 563–593 (2020)
36. Y. Malitsky, M. Sellmann, Instance-specific algorithm configuration as a method for non-model-based portfolio generation (2012), pp. 244–259
37. T. Messelis, P. De Causmaecker, An automatic algorithm selection approach for the multi-mode resource-constrained project scheduling problem. Eur. J. Oper. Res. **233**(3), 511–528 (2014)
38. S. Minton, Automatically configuring constraint satisfaction programs: a case study. Constraints **1–2**(1), 7–43 (1996)
39. M. Misir, K. Verbeeck, P. De Causmaecker, G.V. Berghe, An investigation on the generality level of selection hyper-heuristics under different empirical conditions. Appl. Soft Comput. **13**(7), 3335–3353 (2013)
40. G. Kendall, R. Qu, N.R. Sabar, M. Ayob, A dynamic multiarmed bandit-gene expression programming hyper-heuristic for combinatorial optimization problems. IEEE Trans. Cybern. **45**(2), 217–228 (2015)
41. M. Oltean, Evolving evolutionary algorithms using linear genetic programming. Evol. Comput. **13**(3), 387–410 (2005)
42. C. Papadimitriou, K. Steiglitz, *Combinatorial Optimization: Algorithms and Complexity* (Dover Publications Inc., 1982)

43. M.-W. Park, Y.-D. Kim, A systematic procedure for setting parameters in simulated annealing algorithms. Comput. Oper. Res. **25**(3), 207–217 (1998)
44. J. Pérez, R.A. Pazos, J. Frausto, G. Rodríguez, D. Romero, L. Cruz, A statistical approach for algorithm selection, in *WEA 2004: Experimental and Efficient Algorithms* (Angra dos Reis, Brazil, May, 2004), pp. 417–431
45. J. Pihera, N. Musliu, Application of machine learning to algorithm selection for tsp, in *2014 IEEE 26th International Conference on Tools with Artificial Intelligence* (Limassol, Cyprus, 2014), pp. 47–54
46. N. Pillay, D. Beckedahl, EvoHyp - a Java toolkit for evolutionary algorithm hyper-heuristics, in *Proceedings of IEEE Congress on Evolutionary Computation* (San Sebastian, June 5-8, 2017), pp. 2707–2713
47. N. Pillay, R. Qu, *Hyper-Heuristics: Theory and Applications* (Springer Nature, 2019)
48. N. Pillay, R. Qu, Assessing hyper-heuristic performance. J. Oper. Res. Soc. accepted (2020)
49. M. Preuss, T. Bartz-Beielstein, Sequential parameter optimization applied to self-adaptation for binary-coded evolutionary algorithms, in *Parameter Setting in Evolutionary Algorithms* (2007), pp. 91–120
50. R. Qu, E.K. Burke, Hybridisations withing a graph based hyper-heuristic framework for university timetabling problems. J. Oper. Res. Soc. **60**, 1273–1285 (2009)
51. R. Qu, G. Kendall, N. Pillay, The general combinatorial optimisation problem - towards automated algorithm design. IEEE Comput. Intell. Mag. **15**(2), 14–23 (2020)
52. I.C.O. Ramos, M.C. Goldbarg, E.G. Goldbarg, A.D.D. Neto, Logistic regression for parameter tuning on an evolutionary algorithm, in *2005 IEEE Congress on Evolutionary Computation* (Edinburgh, Scotland, 2-5 Sept. 2005)
53. M.-C. Riff, E. Montero, A new algorithm for reducing metaheuristic design effort, in *2013 IEEE Congress on Evolutionary Computation* (Mexico, 2013)
54. S.K. Smit, A.E. Eiben, Comparing parameter tuning methods for evolutionary algorithms, in *2009 IEEE Congress on Evolutionary Computation* (Trondheim, Norway, 2009)
55. K. Tang, F. Peng, G. Chen, X. Yao, Population-based algorithm portfolios with automated constituent algorithms selection. Inf. Sci. **279**, 94–104 (2014)
56. H. Terashima-Marín, P. Ross, M. Valenzuela-Rendón, Evolution of constraint satisfaction strategies in examination timetabling, in *GECCO'99: Proceedings of the 1st Annual Conference on Genetic and Evolutionary Computation* (1999), pp. 635–642
57. A.A. Visheratin, M. Melnik, D. Nasonov, Automatic workflow scheduling tuning for distributed processing systems. Procedia Comput. Sci. **101**, 388–397 (2016)
58. D.H. Wolpert, W.G. McReady, No free lunch theorems for optimisation. IEEE Trans. Evol. Comput. **1**(1), 67–82 (1997)
59. L. Xu, H. Hoos, K. Leyton-Brown, Hydra: automatically configuring algorithms for portfolio-based selection, in *Proceedings of AAAI Conference on Artificial Intelligence* (Atlanta, July 11–15, 2010)
60. L. Xu, F. Hutter, H.H. Hoos, K. Leyton-Brown, Satzilla: portfolio-based algorithm selection for sat. J. Artif. Intell. Res. **32**, 565–606 (2008)

Chapter 4
Rigorous Performance Analysis of Hyper-heuristics

Pietro S. Oliveto

Abstract We provide an overview of the state-of-the-art in the time complexity analysis of selection hyper-heuristics for combinatorial optimisation. These algorithms aim at automating the optimisation process by using a set of low-level heuristics and a machine learning mechanism to decide online which heuristic is the most appropriate one at the current stage. We mainly focus on work that establishes the performance gains that simple and sophisticated hyper-heuristics can achieve compared to the low-level heuristics applied in isolation, and that compares the expected runtime of the hyper-heuristics against the best possible one achievable with the given set of low-level heuristics. We cover examples where mixing heuristics is necessary, as well as others where learning from the past performance of the applied heuristics is crucial for the algorithms to be efficient. We emphasise that simple and sophisticated hyper-heuristics from the literature can achieve *optimal* performance for some standard unimodal and multimodal benchmark functions. Problem characteristics are highlighted for which more or less machine learning sophistication is required, and insights are provided of how a rigorous theory can guide the design of more efficient hyper-heuristics.

4.1 Introduction

Rather than manually trying to identify which heuristic and related parameter settings perform well for a given class of computational problems, several approaches have been proposed in recent years that attempt to automate the design of the (meta) heuristic for the class of problems at hand. Differently from the more traditional optimisation heuristics, these methodologies operate on a search space of heuristics rather than directly on the search space of the solutions of the optimisation problem to be solved. For this reason, they are often referred to as hyper-heuristics.

P. S. Oliveto (✉)
Department of Computer Science, University of Sheffield, Sheffield, UK
e-mail: p.oliveto@sheffield.ac.uk

N. Pillay and R. Qu (eds.), *Automated Design of Machine Learning and Search Algorithms*, Natural Computing Series,
https://doi.org/10.1007/978-3-030-72069-8_4

Many different classes of automated algorithm design methodologies have been proposed. Algorithm configurators, also commonly referred to as automated parameter tuners, aim to identify optimal parameter settings for the application of an algorithm to a problem class [31, 41]. Algorithm generation methodologies aim to identify a well performing heuristic combining elements of a set of given algorithmic components [3, 5, 50]. Both algorithm configurators and algorithm generators typically work *offline* on a training set of instances of the problem class, and the goal is that the resulting heuristic will perform well on unseen instances of the problem and also on other (related) problem classes. A considerably different class of automated algorithm design systems are those that select which heuristic to use during the actual optimisation process (i.e., *online*) from a portfolio of heuristics, often referred to as the set of low-level heuristics [25]. Selection hyper-heuristics belong to this class. We refer the reader to [4, 25, 34, 51, 54] for surveys regarding the state-of-the-art.

Despite the numerous successful applications of automated algorithm design systems that have been reported, there is a very limited rigorous foundational understanding of their behaviour and performance. In particular, it is unclear how good the resulting algorithms actually are both in terms of what solution quality they can efficiently guarantee and how much time they require to achieve a given solution quality. A natural question is to quantify the gains of using automated methods over the traditional manual algorithm selection and parameter tuning. One may wonder whether the gains due to the automation are mainly in the time saved by humans not having to manually design algorithms of comparable quality, or whether the evolved algorithms may be actually better than those designed by humans. Rigorous statements that quantify the performance of these systems allow a more informed appreciation of their benefits and, together with their proofs, provide insights that can allow the development of better performing automated algorithm design methodologies.

In this chapter, we provide an overview of what has been rigorously proven regarding the behaviour and performance of the methodologies that have been considered experimentally in the literature. To the best of our knowledge all the available time complexity analyses are related to *selection hyper-heuristics*, i.e., that use some machine learning mechanism to choose online from a set of low-level heuristics which one to apply at different stages of the optimisation process. Particular focus will be placed on evaluating to what extent the sophistication of the machine learning mechanism impacts the performance of the hyper-heuristics. A different, but related (and somewhat overlapping) field, is that of parameter control which aims at dynamically changing the parameter values during the optimisation process of a *fixed* algorithm (i.e., the algorithm does not change, only the values of its parameters). We refer to a recent excellent book chapter for an overview of the theory of this field [19].

Algorithm 1 Single Trajectory Selection Hyper-Heuristic [1, 13, 14]

```
1: Choose s ∈ S uniformly at random
2: while stopping conditions not satisfied do
3:     Choose h ∈ H according to the heuristic selection methodology
4:     s' ← h(s)
5:     s ← MoveAcceptance(s', s)
```

4.2 Selection Hyper-heuristics

In this section, we introduce the main hyper-heuristic framework that will be considered in this chapter. It is depicted in Algorithm 1. Although there is a growing number of studies regarding multi-point (i.e., population-based) hyper-heuristics, the majority of perturbative selection hyper-heuristics in the literature conduct a single point search (i.e., the algorithm aims to iteratively improve one candidate solution) [4].

Essentially, a single trajectory selection hyper-heuristic consists of two separate components:

1. a heuristic selection methodology, often referred to as the *learning mechanism*, and,
2. a move acceptance methodology.

A set of low-level heuristics H is provided that contains the different heuristics that may be applied to the current candidate solution in each stage of the optimisation process. The learning mechanism is used to decide which low-level heuristic should be applied. The move acceptance operator is used to decide whether to accept the outcome of the application of the low-level heuristic or whether to keep the previous search point. This general description presents high modularity. Single trajectory hyper-heuristics differ from each other according to which methodologies are used for heuristic selection and move acceptance.

While the initial search point may be chosen in several ways, Algorithm 1 just selects it uniformly at random. Unless stated otherwise, this will be the case for all the presented results. The performance of the hyper-heuristics will be measured using the expected number of fitness function evaluations performed until the optimum is found for the first time, i.e., *expected runtime*, the traditional measure used in the randomised search heuristics community. An asymptotic notation will be used for the purpose: see [7] for the precise meaning of the Ω, O, Θ, o, and ω symbols. We will say that a hyper-heuristic is *efficient* for a problem if its expected runtime grows at most as a polynomial function of the problem size n (i.e., the length of the bit-string representing candidate solutions). Otherwise, we will say that it is *inefficient*. We will say that a hyper-heuristic has *optimal* performance, if no better (asymptotic) expected runtime can be achieved with the available low-level heuristics applied in any combination.

4.2.1 Heuristic Selection Methods

The majority of heuristic selection methodologies in the literature use some reinforcement learning mechanism that generates online scores for each low-level heuristic based on past applications [4]. These scores are usually generated by rewarding successful heuristics and penalising unsuccessful ones. Furthermore, the importance given to the performance in older iterations usually decreases as time goes by (i.e., *memory length*). With these scores, different strategies may be used to choose which low-level heuristic to apply next. The heuristic with the best score (i.e., *max strategy*, e.g., [14]) may be selected, or each heuristic is selected with some probability according to how the heuristic scores or ranks compared to the others (e.g., *roulette wheel strategy* [44]).

When the concept of a hyper-heuristic was first formally introduced, also simpler heuristic selection methods were considered. The main motivation for these is that *"hyper-heuristics should be cheap and fast to implement, yet robust enough to handle a wide range of problems and problem instances from a variety of domains"* [13]. Hence, important research questions are how sophisticated a hyper-heuristic should be to achieve some desired performance quality, and what performance gains may be achieved with greater sophistication. A natural way to assess the performance quality of a complex hyper-heuristic is to compare it with that of more basic ones (and with its low-level heuristics applied on their own). Since these simple hyper-heuristics naturally constitute the basis for a rigorous foundational study, we introduce them precisely [4, 13]:

- SIMPLERANDOM: At each iteration, a randomly chosen heuristic is applied. This choice may be made uniformly at random (i.e., for all heuristics i, $p_i = 1/|H|$) or according to some probability distribution over the set of low-level heuristics.
- RANDOMGRADIENT: (also known as Random Descent): A low-level heuristic is chosen at random and is applied repeatedly as long as it improves in each application.
- RANDOMPERMUTATION: Generates a random ordering of the low-level heuristics and at each step applies them in that predefined order.
- PERMUTATIONGRADIENT: Follows the permutation order but continues applying the chosen heuristic as long as it improves in each application.
- GREEDY: Applies all the low-level heuristics and returns the best found solution.
- GREEDYGRADIENT: Applies all the low-level heuristics once and then applies the one that has generated the best improved solution as long as it continues to improve.

The definitions provided above are the most commonly used in the literature and the ones that will be used in this chapter. However, in the literature, the same names may be used for variations of these selection mechanisms. For example, in [13] GREEDYGRADIENT is used but it is simply called "Greedy" (omitting the "gradient" - while GREEDY as defined above is not applied at all). An important remark is that the RANDOMGRADIENT hyper-heuristic considered in [13] has a considerably different behaviour to the one presented here. In [13] the randomly chosen low-level heuristic

Algorithm 2 SIMPLERANDOM Selection Hyper-heuristic with OI Move Acceptance

```
Choose s ∈ S uniformly at random
while stopping conditions not satisfied do
    Choose h_i ∈ H with probability p_i (SIMPLERANDOM heuristic selection)
    s' ← h(s)
    if f(s') > f(s) then
        s ← s' (ONLYIMPROVEMENTS acceptance operator)
```

is applied until a local optimum is identified. On problems defined over bit-strings as the ones presented in this chapter, this makes the difference between using the heuristic until no improvements are possible with it anymore (e.g., no single bit flip may improve the current solution, i.e., local optimum), and stopping to use it the first time the heuristic does not find an improvement (e.g., a bit is flipped and it does not provide an improvement but there may still exist single bit flips that improve the current solution, i.e., it is not necessarily on a local optimum). We consider the latter formulation in this chapter because it adapts better to randomised local search heuristics since they typically do not check for local optimality (versus deterministic local search) and because, to the best of our knowledge, all existing time complexity analyses of random gradient hyper-heuristics have used this formulation.

4.2.2 *Move Acceptance Operators*

The most common move acceptance operators used in the literature are [4]:

- ONLYIMPROVEMENTS (OI): which accepts new solutions only if they are better than the current one.
- IMPROVEMENTSANDEQUAL (IE): which accepts new solutions if they are not worse than the current one.
- ALLMOVES (AM): which accepts all new solutions independent of their quality.

More sophisticated move acceptance operators that accept worsenings according to some probability distribution have also been used in the literature. Such probability distributions may be static (i.e., they do not change during the run) or dynamic (e.g., by applying cooling schedules similarly to simulated annealing).

Except for Sect. 4.7 on move acceptance operators, the hyper-heuristics considered in this chapter will use the ONLYIMPROVEMENTS acceptance operator (and therefore, OI is simply assumed in the theorem statements). The results also hold for the IE operator. On the other hand, using AM for the considered hyper-heuristic framework would degenerate into random searches, hence poor performance (if, for example, the low-level heuristics were to inherently apply some selection mechanism, then the AM operator may be safely used). As an example, Algorithm 2 provides the pseudo-code of the SIMPLERANDOM hyper-heuristic using the OI operator.

4.3 Hyper-heuristics Are Necessary

The first-time complexity analyses of hyper-heuristics concentrated on providing example problem classes where using different heuristics at different stages of the optimisation process is essential for the optimal solution to be identified. Lehre and Özcan constructed a benchmark function called GAPPATH. The function contains points in the search space where a heuristic that always flips one bit (i.e., RLS_1 - Randomised Local Search with neighbourhood size 1) cannot improve and others where the same occurs for a heuristic that always flips two distinct bits (i.e., RLS_2 - neighbourhood size 2) [35]. The function is defined as follows, where x is the bit-string of length n representing a candidate solution, and x_i is the value of the i_{th} bit in x:

$$\text{GapPath}(x) := \begin{cases} \text{ZeroMax}(x) & \text{if Ridge}(x) \equiv (\text{mod } 3) \\ \text{ZeroMax}(x) + 2n\text{Ridge}(x) & \text{otherwise.} \end{cases} \tag{4.1}$$

Here ZeroMax $:= \sum_{i=1}^{n}(1 - x_i)$ and

$$\text{Ridge}(x) := \begin{cases} i & \text{if } x = 1^i 0^{n-i} \text{ for } i \in [0..n] \\ 0 & \text{otherwise.} \end{cases} \tag{4.2}$$

are respectively the standard benchmark functions that return the number of 0-bits in a bit-string, and a path of consecutive 1-bits followed by consecutive 0-bits with fitness increasing with the number of ones. The GAPPATH function differs from RIDGE in the path part due to some gaps, placed at regular intervals (i.e., points of the form $1^i 0^{n-i}$ where $i \equiv 1(\text{mod}3)$), of inferior fitness compared to the rest of the path. Hence, while it is sufficient to use 1-bit flips to optimise the ZEROMAX part and most of the ridge, it is often necessary to flip two bits to jump over the gaps on the ridge. On the other hand, when the current solution is a path point, but two bits away from a gap, then 2-bit flips will not be able to improve. These arguments are formalised in the following theorem. A similar example in the context of multiobjective optimisation was also recently provided [52].

Theorem 4.1 (Theorems 4 and 5 in [35]) *If $p_1 = 0$ or $p_1 = 1$ then the expected time of the* SIMPLERANDOM *hyper-heuristic with $H=\{RLS_1, RLS_2\}$ to optimise* GAPPATH *is infinite. The expected runtime of the algorithm initialised in the search point 0^n with $p_1 \in [0, 1]$ is $\left(\frac{n^3-3n^2}{6(1-p_1)} + \frac{n^2}{3(1-p_1)p_1}\right)$.*

While the former result was the first one to prove the necessity of using more than one heuristic in the context of hyper-heuristics, previous work had already implicitly shown such a necessity (although hyper-heuristics were not the focus of the studies). For identifying minimum spanning trees in graphs, Neumann and Wegener [45] considered an algorithm which flips one bit and two bits, respectively, with probability 1/2 - essentially the SIMPLERANDOM hyper-heuristic with $p_i = 1/2$

and H=$\{RLS_1,RLS_2\}$. Solutions were represented as bit-strings of length m, i.e., the number of edges in the graph, and the fitness function returned the sum of the weights of the edges in the current solution but gave a very large penalty to the number of connected components and a smaller penalty to the total number of selected edges. In this setting using RLS_1 is necessary to identify the first spanning tree with positive probability, while RLS_2 is necessary to find better ones once the current solution is a spanning tree, although not one of minimal weight (i.e., to find a new spanning tree it is necessary to remove one edge and insert a different one - a 2-bit flip).

Theorem 4.2 (Adapted from Theorem 6.8.2 in [19]) *The* SIMPLERANDOM *hyper-heuristic with H=$\{RLS_1,RLS_2\}$ solves the minimum spanning tree problem in connected undirected graphs with n vertices, m edges and integral edge weights in $[1,..w_{\max}]$ in polynomial expected time if and only if $p_1 \notin \{0,1\}$. If $p_1 = \Omega(1)$, then the expected optimisation time is $O(m^2 \log(nw_{\max}))$.*

Similar results, in the sense that both 1-bit and 2-bit flips are necessary, have also been implicitly shown for identifying maximum matchings in undirected graphs [27].

4.4 Learning is Necessary

In the previous section, evidence was provided that it may be necessary to use different heuristics (or different variation operators) during the optimisation process for effective search to occur. To provide such examples it was sufficient to consider a simple random gradient hyper-heuristic that chooses which low-level heuristic to apply at each step according to some fixed probability distribution. In particular, the hyper-heuristic makes no effort to try and identify which low-level heuristic is more promising in the optimisation phase at hand as more generally applied hyper-heuristics strive to do. In this section, we present the theoretical results from the literature that have provided evidence that deciding which low-level heuristics to select based on the information gained from past choices may be necessary for efficient optimisation.

The first theoretical comparative analysis of different heuristic selection methodologies was performed by Alanazi and Lehre [1]. They analysed the performance of four simple selection mechanisms from the literature for the standard LEADINGONES$(x) := \sum_{i=1}^{n} \prod_{j=1}^{i} x_j$ benchmark function. The function returns the number of consecutive 1-bits in the bit-string before the first 0-bit. The considered heuristic selection mechanisms were: SIMPLERANDOM, RANDOMPERMUTATION, GREEDY and RANDOMGRADIENT. The first three do not use any feedback from past applications of low-level heuristics to inform future choices. On the other hand, RANDOMGRADIENT does, as its main idea is to continue to use the randomly selected heuristic so long as it continues to provide improvements. Alanazi and Lehre provided a lower bound of

$\frac{n^2}{9}(3\ln(\frac{10}{3}) + o(n^2))$[1] and an upper bound of $2n^2(\ln(5/2) + o(1))$ on the expected runtime of RANDOMGRADIENT. On the other hand, they provided a lower bound of $\frac{n^2}{6}\ln(3)$ and an upper bound of approximately $n^2\ln(3)$ for the other three mechanisms. Hence, the analysis did not allow to appreciate whether RANDOMGRADIENT outperforms the other three, or not, for the LEADINGONES function. Lissovoi, Oliveto and Warwicker later showed that it does not. In particular, they proved that the four hyper-heuristics have all identical performance for the problem up to lower order terms [37, 40]. In the following theorem SIMPLERANDOM chooses each low-level heuristic uniformly at random, i.e., $p_i = 1/2$.

Theorem 4.3 (Theorem 5, Corollary 6, Theorem 12, Corollary 13 and Lemma 18, in [40]) *The expected runtime of the* SIMPLERANDOM, RANDOMPERMUTATION, GREEDY *and* RANDOMGRADIENT *hyper-heuristics using H={RLS_1,RLS_2} or H={1-BitFlip, 2-BitFlip}*[2] *for* LEADINGONES *is* $\frac{1}{2}\ln(3)n^2 + o(n^2) \approx 0.549n^2$. *Furthermore, if* $k = \Theta(1)$ *low-level heuristics are used H={$RLS_1, \ldots, RLS_k$} or H={1-BitFlip,... k-BitFlip}, then for each k the above mentioned hyper-heuristics all have identical leading constants in their expected runtimes which increase with k.*

The theorem provides several insights on the working principles of these hyper-heuristics. Firstly, the expected runtimes of the four hyper-heuristics for LEADINGONES are greater than the expected runtime of one of its constituent heuristics, RLS_1, which has an expected runtime of exactly $0.5n^2$ for the problem [6]. Secondly, the performance of the hyper-heuristics deteriorates with the size of the set of low-level heuristics they are allowed to select from. Thirdly, the RANDOMGRADIENT hyper-heuristic does not display any significant advantage in terms of performance for the standard LEADINGONES benchmark function. The former two insights may be considered as an inevitable consequence of the greater generality of hyper-heuristics compared to simple heuristics (i.e., some loss over optimal performance for given problems might have to be accepted for the sake of being efficient for larger classes of problems). However, the third insight is more worrying as the idea behind the design of the RANDOMGRADIENT hyper-heuristic is to select better performing low-level heuristics more often than worse performing ones. As a result, better performance over random selection *should* be expected, at least for LEADINGONES where there is a clear phase distinction in the performance of the different heuristics during the optimisation process. While at the beginning flipping many bits is advantageous, once half of the leading ones have been identified it is always preferable to flip only one bit [2]. In particular, the analysis reveals that RANDOMGRADIENT is not capable of appreciating whether a selected low-level heuristic is effective or not because it does not run it long enough to determine whether it is beneficial or detrimental in the current region of the search space (i.e., it is unlikely that a beneficial random local search operator improves in two consecutive applications).

---

[1] In [1] the reported lower bound is larger, i.e., $\frac{n^2}{9}(4 + 3\ln(\frac{10}{3}) + o(n^2))$ due to a small mistake in the proof [40].

[2] The difference between RLS_k and k-BitFlip is that the former flips k bits without replacement while the latter does so with replacement (i.e., the same bit may flip more than once).

Building upon this result, Lissovoi, Oliveto and Warwicker provided a simple framework to study the learning capabilities of heuristic selection methodologies [37]. For this purpose, they modified the GAPPATH function introduced by Lehre and Ozcan [35] such that only hyper-heuristics that can appreciate whether the currently chosen low-level heuristic is effective can optimise the function efficiently. The modified function is called GENERALISEDGAPPATHWITHTRAPS. Essentially, after a successful 1-bit flip several 2-bit flips are necessary to make progress. Hence, hyper-heuristics that learn to use 2-bit flips more often will be quicker. Furthermore, they introduce trap points at the end of each 2-bit flip improving stage reachable by flipping one bit. As a result, hyper-heuristics that have not learnt to prefer the best operator during the 2-bit-flip stages have a good probability of falling into the trap by flipping one bit and getting stuck forever. By reiterating several such stages, hyper-heuristics that fail to learn which operator is preferable will get stuck with overwhelming probability. We refer the reader to [37] for a formal definition of the GENERALISEDGAPPATHWITHTRAPS$_k$ benchmark function.

Theorem 4.4 (Theorem 3.3 in [37][3]) *The* SIMPLERANDOM *($p_i = 1/2$),* RANDOMPERMUTATION*,* GREEDY *and* RANDOMGRADIENT *hyper-heuristics using H={RLS$_1$,RLS$_2$} or H={1-BitFlip, 2-BitFlip} fail to find the global optimum of* GENERALISEDGAPPATHWITHTRAPS$_k$ *in finite time with overwhelming probability* $1 - n^{-\Omega(n)}$.

They then proceed to show that if the RANDOMGRADIENT hyper-heuristic is allowed to run the randomly selected low-level heuristic for sufficient time to detect whether it is effective or not, then it can optimise the function efficiently.[4] The pseudo-code of such hyper-heuristic is given in Algorithm 3. The hyper-heuristic applies the randomly chosen low-level heuristic for τ steps (i.e., the learning period). If an improvement is found, then the learning period time counter is immediately re-initialised.

Theorem 4.5 (Theorem 3.4 in [37]) *The* RANDOMGRADIENT *hyper-heuristic with a learning period $\tau = \Omega(n^3)$ will find the global optimum of the* GENERALISEDGAPPATHWITHTRAPS$_k$ *within at most $\frac{4\tau n}{2k+1} + \frac{kn^3}{2(2k+1)} + O(n^2)$ steps with overwhelming probability $1 - 2^{-\Omega(n)}$. However, for $\tau = O(n^2)$ the* RANDOMGRADIENT *hyper-heuristic will fail to reach the optimum in finite time with probability at least* $1 - 2^{-\Omega(n)}$.

Hence, if given appropriate time to evaluate the performance of its selected low-level heuristics, RANDOMGRADIENT can learn to appreciate their effectiveness or

[3] While theorems 4 and 5 in [37] are only proven for H={1-BitFlip, 2-BitFlip} they also naturally hold for H={RLS$_1$,RLS$_2$}.

[4] They also show that a similar modification applied to a GREEDYGRADIENT hyper-heuristic may make it 'intelligent': once the greedy selection has returned the first found improvement, then the operator that made the improvement should be exploited by applying it for some time before another greedy selection step is made. Such a modification to the GREEDYGRADIENT hyper-heuristic makes it also efficient for the function.

Algorithm 3 RANDOMGRADIENT Hyper-Heuristic with Learning Period τ

```
Choose x ∈ S uniformly at random
while stopping conditions not satisfied do
    Choose h ∈ H uniformly at random
    c_t ← 0 (learning period time counter)
    while c_t < τ do
        c_t ← c_t + 1; x' ← h(x)
        if f(x') > f(x) then
            c_t ← 0; x ← x'
```

their ineffectiveness. In the following section, it will be shown how an appropriate use of such a learning period may make the difference between applying low-level heuristics essentially at random or in an optimal manner.

4.5 Hyper-heuristics Can Achieve Optimal Performance

In the previous two sections, example problem classes were provided (i.e., GAPPATH and GENERALISEDGAPPATHWITHTRAPS$_k$) where the use of more than one low-level heuristic was necessary to optimise instances of those problems. Hence, the considered hyper-heuristics are efficient for those problems while their constituent heuristics cannot solve them if applied in isolation. In this section, we address the question of what performance may be expected from a hyper-heuristic when heuristics in the low-level set are efficient by themselves for the problem. Given that the hyper-heuristic has to learn which heuristic to apply at different stages, it is not obvious how fast a hyper-heuristic will be compared to its low-level heuristics applied on their own. For instance, one may wonder whether it is faster than the average of the expected runtimes of its low-level heuristics (or of a subset), or if it may learn to apply them in a clever order such that it optimises the problem faster than all of its constituent heuristics if applied on their own. In this section, we will show example problems where the latter is true for two different hyper-heuristics from the literature. In particular, we will argue that for the considered problems, the hyper-heuristics run in *optimal* expected time (i.e., the best expected time achievable with any combination of their low-level heuristics) up to lower order terms.

4.5.1 *The* RANDOMGRADIENT *Hyper-heuristic has Optimal Performance for* LEADINGONES

Theorem 4.3 shows for the standard LEADINGONES benchmark function, that four simple hyper-heuristics from the literature essentially perform equally to a hyper-heuristic that naively selects low-level heuristics uniformly at random in each step.

We also argued that the RANDOMGRADIENT hyper-heuristic should have superior performance if it is allowed to run its low-level heuristics long enough to evaluate whether they are effective or not at different stages of the optimisation process. Lissovoi, Oliveto and Warwicker proved that if the learning period τ is set appropriately, then RANDOMGRADIENT has the best possible performance achievable with the available ingredients up to lower order terms.

Theorem 4.6 (Adapted from Theorem 9 and Lemma 18 in [40]) *Let the low-level heuristic set be H={1-BitFlip, 2-BitFlip, ..., k-BitFlip} or H={RLS_1,RLS_2, ..., RLS_k} and let the learning period satisfy both $\tau = \omega(n)$ and $\tau \leq \left(\frac{1}{k} - \epsilon\right) n \ln n$ for some constant $0 < \epsilon < \frac{1}{k}$. The expected runtime of the* RANDOMGRADIENT *hyper-heuristic for* LEADINGONES *is the best possible for any unbiased (1 + 1) black box algorithm using {1-BitFlip, ... k-BitFlip} or {RLS_1,RLS_2, ..., RLS_k} and is smaller than the best possible expected runtime achievable by using any strict subset of the low-level heuristics.*

The theorem highlights the power that hyper-heuristics may have as general problem-solvers. Theorem 4.3 indicates that the performance of the simple hyper-heuristics *deteriorates* with the increase of the size of the low-level heuristic set if they do not evaluate the effectiveness of chosen heuristics during the run. In sharp contrast, Theorem 4.6 highlights how the inclusion of more low-level heuristics to the set is preferable and leads to better performance. Figure 4.1 provides the expected runtime of the RANDOMGRADIENT hyper-heuristic using respectively two, three, four and five RLS heuristics with different neighbourhood size, for different values of the learning period. The figure clearly shows that the hyper-heuristic using three heuristics has better performance than any possible one using only two. The same holds for five operators versus only four of them.

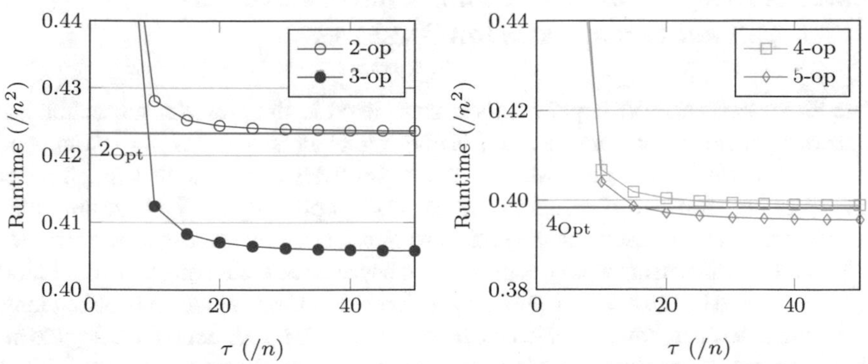

Fig. 4.1 A comparison of the expected runtimes, for different values of the learning period τ, of the RANDOMGRADIENT hyper-heuristic with k RLS heuristics $H = \{RLS_1, RLS_2, \ldots, RLS_k\}$ against the leading constant in the theoretical upper bound of the expected runtime of the RANDOMGRADIENT hyper-heuristic using $k+1$; for $k = 2$ and $k = 4$. 2_{Opt} ($\approx 0.42329n^2$) and 4_{Opt} ($\approx 0.39830n^2$) are the best possible expected runtimes achievable with access to 2 and 4 low-level RLS heuristics respectively [40]

Table 4.1 The upper bounds in the leading constants found from various parameter combinations of the number of heuristics k and the learning period τ. The values reported in the fourth column are the best possible for each k. As the number of operators increases, larger values of τ are required for good performance ($\tau = \omega(n)$ is necessary to achieve optimal performance). Note that the upper bounds provided for large values of k and small values of τ are far from tight due to the generality of the results in [40]

k	$\tau = 5n$	$\tau = 50n$	$\tau = 100n$	$\tau = \frac{1}{10}n\ln(n)$
2	0.46493	0.42363	0.42329	0.42329
3	0.46802	0.40579	0.40525	0.40525
4	0.48102	0.39897	0.39830	0.39830
5	0.49630	0.39568	0.39492	0.39492
11	3.090×10^{23}	8785.8	0.38987	0.38987
18	1.886×10^{44}	5.363×10^{24}	1034.8	0.38899

The technical results presented in [40] allow the derivation of upper bounds on the expected runtime of the hyper-heuristic for any constant number of low-level heuristics k and any learning period $\tau \leq \left(\frac{1}{k} - \epsilon\right) n \ln n$ for some constant ϵ. Some of the most interesting combinations of k and τ are reported in Table 4.1. Doerr and Wagner [24] calculated that the best possible performance achievable by any (1 + 1) black box algorithm (i.e., single trajectory) for LEADINGONES is approximately $0.388n^2$. The table shows that this is reached by the RANDOMGRADIENT hyper-heuristic up to one decimal place using 4 heuristics, up to two decimal places using at least $k = 11$ heuristics and up to three decimal places using at least $k = 18$ heuristics.

4.5.2 A Reinforcement Learning Hyper-heuristic has Optimal Performance for ONEMAX

The RANDOMGRADIENT hyper-heuristic considered in the previous subsection has a learning memory of size one, i.e., it only remembers whether the last applied low-level heuristic was successful or not. Nevertheless, we saw that it can adapt the neighbourhood size of randomised local search optimally for the LEADINGONES benchmark function. Only one theoretical work exists that analyses the performance of hyper-heuristics using a more sophisticated heuristic selection mechanism, similar to those applied by the more advanced hyper-heuristics used in practical applications.

Doerr, Doerr and Yang analysed the performance of a hyper-heuristic using essentially an ϵ-greedy reinforcement learning scheme to adapt the neighbourhood size of randomised local search[5] [20]. The hyper-heuristic uses the low-level heuristic set H= $\{RLS_1, \ldots, RLS_k\}$. The low-level heuristics are chosen uniformly at random

[5] The authors do not explicitly refer to the term 'hyper-heuristic' in their work and simply call their proposed algorithm 'RLS with self-adjusting mutation strength'.

at each step with probability $\epsilon > 0$ (i.e., *learning iterations*) and the progress made in these iterations by the chosen heuristic is stored in an efficient manner. With the remaining probability a greedy choice (i.e., max strategy) of the most promising low-level heuristic is made (i.e., *regular iterations*). An estimate of the future progress (called *velocity*) of each low-level heuristic $\text{RLS}_r \in [RLS_1, \ldots, RLS_k]$ is made via a time-discounted average of the progresses observed during the past learning iterations:

$$v_t[RLS_r] := \frac{\sum_{s=1}^{t} \mathbf{1}_{RLS_s=RLS_r}(1-\delta)^{t-s}(f(x_s) - f(x_{s-1}))}{\sum_{s=1}^{t} \mathbf{1}_{RLS_s=RLS_r}(1-\delta)^{t-s}}$$

where RLS_s is the low-level heuristic used in the s-th learning iteration and the parameter δ, called the *forgetting rate*, determines the decrease of the importance of the performance in older iterations of the heuristic. We refer the readers to [20] for a precise pseudo-code of the algorithm.

The authors prove that for suitably selected parameters ϵ and δ the hyper-heuristic when applied to ONEMAX essentially chooses, for all but a lower order fraction of the iterations, a low-level heuristic that gives an expected progress equal to the best possible progress (again, apart from lower order terms). As a result, the algorithm has the best possible optimisation time achievable by any unary (i.e., mutation-based) unbiased black box algorithm (i.e., $n \ln n - cn \pm o(n)$ for a constant c between 0.2539 and 0.2665 [21]). Consequently the hyper-heuristic is optimal and the best performing unary unbiased black box algorithm known for ONEMAX.[6]

Theorem 4.7 (Adapted from Theorem 6.6.1 in [19]) *Let $T(Best_{RLS_{1..k}})$ be the minimum expected runtime achievable using any combination of $\{RLS_1, \ldots, RLS_k\}$ for* ONEMAX. *Then the expected runtime of the ϵ-greedy reinforcement learning hyper heuristic with parameters $\epsilon = n^{-0.01}$ and $\delta = n^{-0.99}$ using $H = \{RLS_1, \ldots, RLS_k\}$ for* ONEMAX *is $T(Best_{RLS_{1..k}}) + o(n)$.*

Apart from this remarkable result (i.e., the hyper-heuristic has optimal performance up to the first *two* leading constants), the authors have reported excellent experimental performance of the hyper-heuristic also for LEADINGONES and the minimum spanning tree problem. However, rigorously proven statements regarding the actual performance as a function of the problem size are not available for these problems.

4.6 Automatically Adapting the Learning Period is Necessary

Previous sections have provided example problems where appropriately chosen learning periods allow the RANDOMGRADIENT hyper-heuristic to perform effectively. For LEADINGONES optimal performance is even achieved. However, the question

[6] Binary algorithms using crossover such as genetic algorithms may be faster [8, 9, 18].

remains regarding how to set the learning period parameter appropriately for problems that are not well-understood. Indeed, different learning period lengths may considerably affect the performance of the hyper-heuristic. In Sect. 4.4 we saw that a cubic learning period allows RANDOMGRADIENT with $H = \{RLS_1, RLS_2\}$ to optimise GENERALISEDGAPPATHWITHTRAPS$_k$ efficiently, while a quadratic one (or smaller) leads to infinite runtime with overwhelmingly high probability. On the other hand, for optimal performance to be achieved for LEADINGONES the parameter should be asymptotically smaller than quadratic.

While it may not be surprising that widely different problems may require considerably different learning periods, one may wonder how sensitive the learning period is to problem characteristics. It turns out that already for the class of *unimodal functions* considerably different learning periods are required for optimal performance.

Theorem 4.8 (Adapted from Theorems 3, 4, 5 and 6 in [39]) *Starting at* 0^n*, the* RANDOMGRADIENT *hyper-heuristic with* $H=\{RLS_1, RLS_3\}$ *and* $\tau \geq n$ *for* ONEMAX *has expected runtime* $\Omega(n\sqrt{n}/(\sqrt{\log n})) = \omega(n \log n)$*. For positive learning periods of* $\tau = o(n)$ *the expected runtime is at most* $(1 + o(1)) \cdot (6\tau n + 2 \ln n)$*.*

Starting at 0^n*, the* RANDOMGRADIENT *hyper-heuristic with* $H=\{RLS_1, RLS_k\}$*, any* $k = O(1)$ *and* $\tau = o(n)$ *for* RIDGE *has expected runtime* $(1 + o(1)) \cdot 2n^2$*. For positive learning periods of* $\tau \geq (5/2) \cdot n \log n$ *and* $\tau = O(n^2/logn)$ *the expected runtime is* $(1 + o(1)) \cdot n^2$*.*

Hence, for LEADINGONES and RIDGE super quasi-linear static learning periods are required for optimal performance, while for ONEMAX linear periods or higher lead to suboptimal asymptotic performance.[7]

Apart from different static learning periods being required for different problems, the optimal value for the learning period may change at different stages of the optimisation process for a single function. In particular, the ideal learning period should be large enough for the best low-level heuristic to find improvements within the period but, at the same time, low enough such that all the other heuristics fail. To this end, Doerr, Lissovoi, Oliveto and Warwicker, introduced a self-adaptive mechanism for the RANDOMGRADIENT hyper-heuristic to automatically adapt the learning period during the run. The aim of such a mechanism is twofold. On one hand, the user should not need to specify the length of the learning period in advance. On the other hand, the hyper-heuristic should be able to automatically, and appropriately, change the duration of the learning period at different stages of the optimisation process. The ADAPTIVERANDOMGRADIENT hyper-heuristic (ARG) is described in Algorithm 4.

ARG uses an update scheme inspired by the 1/5 rule traditionally used in continuous optimisation to adapt the mutation strength. A low-level heuristic is considered *successful* if it obtains σ improvements in a learning period τ (rather than just one improvement). The algorithm essentially decreases the value of the learning period τ by a multiplicative factor if the currently selected low-level heuristic is successful within a period of τ steps while it increases it by a multiplicative factor if it is

[7] For ONEMAX the set $H = \{RLS_1, RLS_3\}$ was chosen because these are the two fastest RLS algorithms for the problem.

Algorithm 4 ADAPTIVERANDOMGRADIENT Hyper-Heuristic

$\tau \leftarrow \tau_0$
Choose $x \in S$ uniformly at random
while optimum not found **do**
    Choose $h \in H$ uniformly at random
    $c_t \leftarrow 0$; $c_s \leftarrow 0$ (successes counter)
    while $c_t < \tau$ **do**
        $c_t \leftarrow c_t + 1$; $x' \leftarrow h(x)$
        if $f(x') > f(x)$ **then**
            $c_s \leftarrow c_s + 1$; $x \leftarrow x'$
        if $c_s \geq \sigma$ **then**
            $c_s \leftarrow 0$; $c_t \leftarrow 0$
            $\tau \leftarrow \tau \cdot F^{-1/\sigma^2}$
    $\tau \leftarrow \tau \cdot F^{1/\sigma}$

unsuccessful. The multiplicative factors are chosen such that σ decreases counteract exactly one increase, i.e., essentially a $1 - 1/\sigma$ rule.

Hence, ARG is in principle more "powerful" than the static RANDOMGRADIENT hyper-heuristic because it may use different learning period lengths at different times if necessary. Indeed, it has been proven to optimise the LEADINGONES, RIDGE and ONEMAX functions in optimal asymptotic time by tracking the learning period during the run and allowing it to identify the optimal operator with high probability in each iteration of the optimisation process.

Theorem 4.9 (Adapted from Th. 3.1 in [22] and from Th. 7 and Th. 8 in [39]) *Let $\sigma = \Omega(\log^4 n) \cap o(\sqrt{n/\log n})$, $\tau_0 = 1$ and $H = \{RLS_1, RLS_2\}$.*[8] *Then the* ADAPTIVERANDOMGRADIENT *hyper-heuristic optimises* LEADINGONES *in at most $((1 + \ln 2)/4)n^2 + o(n^2)$ expected steps with $F > 1$ a constant, and* RIDGE *starting at 0^n in at most $(1 + o(1))n^2$ expected steps with $F = 1.5$.*

Let $\sigma = \Omega((\log n)^{3/4}) \cap o(\log n)$, $\tau_0 = 1$, $F = 1 + \frac{1}{\sqrt{\log n}}$ and $H = \{RLS_1, RLS_3\}$. Then the ADAPTIVERANDOMGRADIENT *hyper-heuristic optimises* ONEMAX *starting at 0^n in at most $O(n \log n)$ steps.*

It should be noticed that the expected runtimes for LEADINGONES and RIDGE are optimal up to lower order terms (i.e., they have the same leading constant of the best possible expected runtime achievable using the given low-level heuristic sets). At the same time, the expected runtime for ONEMAX is asymptotically optimal, a result which Theorem 4.8 shows is not possible with the same fixed static learning periods (i.e., static periods that allow optimal performance for LEADINGONES and RIDGE lead to suboptimal asymptotic performance for ONEMAX).

Figure 4.2 shows how the learning period is adapted in five experimental runs (and an average over 100 runs) of the algorithm for LEADINGONES. It can be seen that τ quickly increases into the range that allows the operators to produce sigma

[8] The result for LEADINGONES in [22] is proven for 2-bit flips (i.e., with replacement) but there is no reason to believe that it does not hold also for RLS_2.

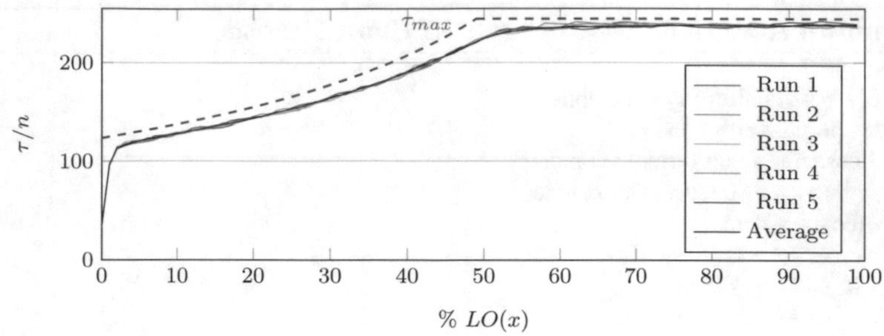

Fig. 4.2 Adapted value of τ over time in five typical runs for $\sigma = \sqrt{n}/\ln n$, $n = 10^7$, and an average of over 100 runs for LEADINGONES. $\tau_{\max}$ is a threshold value for the learning period that is proven in the proof of Theorem 3.1 in [22] to be unlikely to be reached by the learning period throughout the run [22]

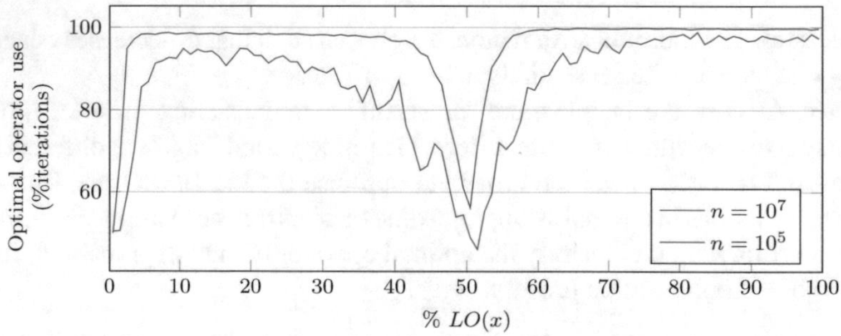

Fig. 4.3 Percentage of the iterations ARG applies the optimal mutation operator for $\sigma = \sqrt{n}/\ln n$, average of over 100 runs. The dip around the middle of the graph corresponds to the middle region of the optimisation process, where both operators perform similarly well [22]

improvements within a learning period. Furthermore, the algorithm tracks the length of the learning period appropriately: at the beginning of the runs, it is smaller since improvements are found more easily by RLS_2, while it becomes larger towards the end of the run when improvements become harder and RLS_1 is preferable. Figure 4.3 shows the effectiveness of the identified learning periods by plotting the percentage of iterations averaged over 100 runs where the optimal low-level heuristic is applied (i.e., RLS_2 for the first $n/2$ leading ones and RLS_1 for the last $n/2$).

An important consideration is that ARG has two parameters, σ and F, which need to be set compared to the single learning period τ of the static RANDOMGRADIENT hyper-heuristic. This comes at the expense of allowing the hyper-heuristic the power of automatically changing the duration of the learning period during the run. In particular, the values for σ and F for which Theorem 4.9 holds are different for ONEMAX compared to those for the other two functions. The values for σ do not even intersect. While these are required for the proofs to hold, Figs. 4.4 and 4.5 show empirically that the hyper-heuristic is robust to a wide range of parameter values. The experiments use $F = 1.5$. For all tested values of σ the experiments suggest that the

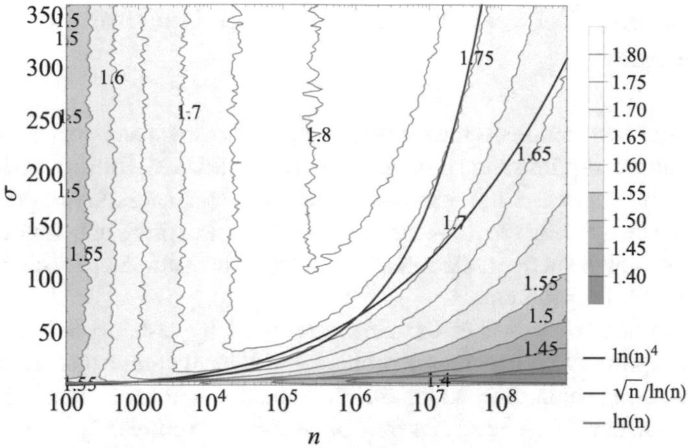

Fig. 4.4 The runtime of ADAPTIVERANDOMGRADIENT with $H = \{RLS_1, RLS_3\}$ for ONEMAX starting at 0^n, for various problem sizes n and parameter values σ, with contour values showing the average observed runtime over 1000 runs divided by $n \ln n$. Several strategies for setting σ depending on n are shown as line plots [39]

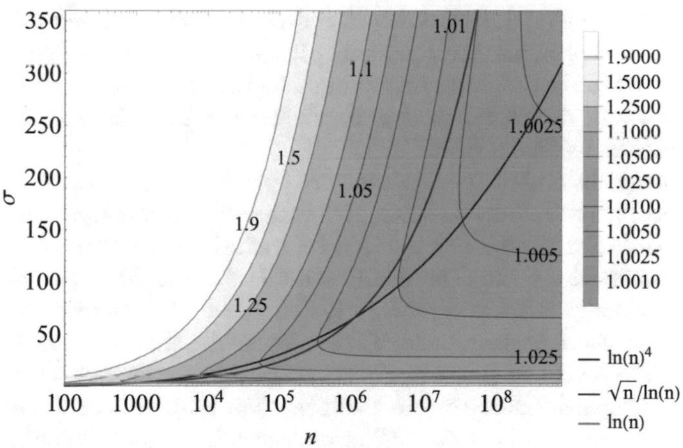

Fig. 4.5 The runtime of ADAPTIVERANDOMGRADIENT starting at 0^n with $H = \{RLS_1, RLS_2\}$ for RIDGE, for various problem sizes n and parameter values σ, with contour values showing the average observed runtime over 1000 runs divided by n^2. Several strategies for setting σ depending on n are shown as line plots [39]

algorithm has asymptotically optimal performance for ONEMAX (i.e., $O(n \log n)$) and is very close to the optimal expected runtime up to the leading constant, i.e., 1, for RIDGE (the performance for LEADINGONES is expected to be similar to the latter).

4.7 Switching Between Move Acceptance Operators is Necessary

In the previous two sections, optimal performance was shown for two hyperheuristics for some unimodal optimisation problems (i.e. LEADINGONES, RIDGE and ONEMAX). For such problems, non-elitist selection operators are not necessary as progress can always be made by using the low-level heuristics and accepting only improvements. Hence, smart low-level heuristic selection mechanisms sufficed to achieve optimal performance for the problems.

In this section, we consider the performance of hyper-heuristics for standard multimodal optimisation benchmark problems with local optima that are difficult to escape from using variation operators such as mutation or recombination. Hence, for such problems, non-elitist heuristics may be necessary to efficiently identify optimal solutions. As a result, also the choices made by the *move acceptance* operators of the hyper-heuristics may become crucial for their effectiveness. The main question that will be addressed is whether, and when, hyper-heuristics may outperform both traditional elitist and non-elitist optimisation heuristics.

The most common acceptance operators used in hyper-heuristics are the elitist ONLYIMPROVING (OI) and IMPROVINGANDEQUAL (IE) operators and the non-elitist ALLMOVES (AM) operator. Their working principles are pretty obvious from their names. The first one only accepts improving solutions, the second accepts solutions that are not worse than the current one, while the last one accepts any solution independent from its fitness value.

Traditionally, the chosen move acceptance operator is fixed throughout the run, with the hyper-heuristic only switching between different low-level heuristics [4]. However, theoretical studies have avoided the exclusive use of the AM acceptance operator throughout the run. The main reason is that the AM operator, used all the time, essentially leads to a random search where all identified solutions are accepted independent of their quality (unless some selection operator is implicitly used by the low-level heuristics: this is never the case for the hyper-heuristics for which time complexity analyses are available). For a hyper-heuristic to excel on sophisticated combinatorial optimisation problems, it is more desirable that they use elitist acceptance operators during the hill climbing phases of the process while switching to non-elitism during the exploration phases, e.g., to escape from local optima. The question is whether and how this may be accomplished automatically and efficiently.

Lehre and Özcan considered a hyper-heuristic which at each step uses the strict selection OI move acceptance operator with some probability and the non-elitist AM operator with the remaining probability. The so-called SIMPLERANDOMMOVEACCEPTANCE hyper-heuristic (SRMA) is depicted in Algorithm 5. It is essentially a random local search algorithm which always flips 1 bit (i.e., RLS_1) and accepts the new solution independent from the quality (i.e., AM) with probability p and with the remaining probability $1 - p$ only accepts it if it is an improvement (i.e., OI). Hence, the algorithm accepts worsening solutions with a fixed probability. Lehre and Özcan

Algorithm 5 SIMPLERANDOMMOVEACCEPTANCE Hyper-Heuristic [35]

1: Choose $x \in \{0, 1\}^n$ uniformly at random
2: **while** termination criteria not satisfied **do**
3: $\quad x' \leftarrow$ FLIPRANDOMBIT(x)
4: $\quad$ ACC $\leftarrow \begin{cases} \text{ALLMOVES} & \text{with probability p} \\ \text{ONLYIMPROVING} & \text{otherwise} \end{cases}$
5: $\quad$ **if** ACC(x, x') **then** $x \leftarrow x'$

performed an analysis of the algorithm for the standard ROYALROAD$_k$ benchmark function with $k > 1$ where it is necessary to set blocks of k bits correctly to observe an improvement. Thus, the only way to escape from local optima using a 1-bit flip mutation operator is to use the non-elitist AM move acceptance operator. They provided an upper bound on the expected runtime for the SRMA hyper-heuristic of $O(n^3 k^{2k-3})$ if the parameter p is chosen appropriately. Hence, it is efficient for any ROYALROAD$_k$ instance with constant k. However, since using the IE operator (or the $(1+1)$ EA with standard bit mutation $1/n$) all the time leads to an upper bound on the expected runtime of $O(n \log n \cdot (2^k/k))$ [23], the advantages of switching between elitism and non-elitism could not be appreciated from this analysis.

A more illustrative analysis of the power of the SRMA hyper-heuristic was performed by Lissovoi, Oliveto and Warwicker [38]. First, they identified values for the parameter p that allow the hyper-heuristic to hill climb the standard unimodal benchmark function ONEMAX. Afterwards they identified what kinds of basins of attraction of local optima SRMA can escape efficiently, and which not, using the identified parameter value p. The first result shows that p should not be too large to efficiently hill climb the ONEMAX benchmark function.

Theorem 4.10 (Adapted from Theorems 4, 5, 6 and Corollary 7 of [38]) *The expected runtime of* SRMA *for* ONEMAX *is* $O(n \log n)$ *if* $p = 1/((1+\epsilon)n)$ *for any constant* $\epsilon > 0$. *On the other hand, the runtime of SRMA for* ONEMAX *is at least* $2^{\Omega(n)}$ *with overwhelming probability at least* $1 - 2^{-\Omega(n)}$ *if* $p = \Theta(1)$, *and at least* $n^{\Omega(\log(n))}$ *with overwhelming probability at least* $1 - n^{-\log(n)}$ *if* $p \geq (\sqrt{n} \log^2 n)/n$.

Hence, setting $p \approx 1/n$ allows the hyper-heuristic to select the non-elitist move acceptance operator AM very often while still allowing it to efficiently hill climb the standard ONEMAX benchmark function.

The effectiveness of the hyper-heuristic at escaping from local optima naturally will depend on its basin of attraction. Lissovoi, Oliveto and Warwicker used the standard CLIFF$_d$ and JUMP$_d$ benchmark functions as two extreme cases. Once on the local optimum of the former function class, if solutions of worse fitness can be accepted, it is relatively easy to identify another slope of increasing fitness that leads away from the local optima and to the global one. In the latter function class all gradients are directed towards the local optimum, hence escaping it is much harder. Advantages of SRMA over standard elitist and/or non-elitist algorithms can be highlighted in both cases.

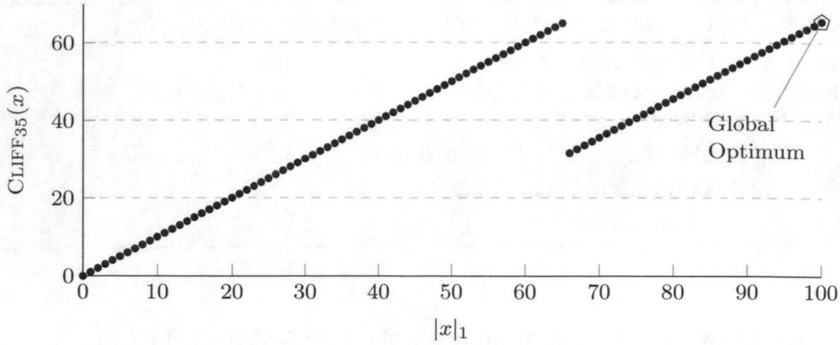

Fig. 4.6 $\text{CLIFF}_d(x)$ with $n = 100$ and $d = 35$

4.7.1 Local Optima with Small Basins of Attraction

The CLIFF_d class of functions (for $1 < d < n/2$) is defined as follows and depicted in Fig. 4.6:

$$\text{CLIFF}_d(x) := \begin{cases} \text{ONEMAX}(x) & \text{if } |x|_1 \leq n - d, \\ \text{ONEMAX}(x) - d + 1/2 & \text{otherwise.} \end{cases}$$

The function class captures real-world problem characteristics when local optima have small basins of attraction. Algorithms which accept worsening moves to the bottom of the cliff may then follow the second slope leading to the global optimum, i.e., the 1^n bit-string. The function class was designed to show the advantages of non-elitist evolutionary algorithms over elitist ones. If the location of the cliff is far away from the local optimum (i.e., large values for parameter d) then elitist algorithms need to perform prohibitively large mutations to identify the global optimum (which is the only better solution). The behaviour of such algorithms is the same as that for the well studied JUMP_d benchmark function. In particular, the expected runtime of traditional elitist evolutionary algorithms increases exponentially with the distance of the cliff to the global optimum (i.e., mutation-based EAs have an expected runtime of $\Theta(n^d)$ [26] while standard steady-state GAs have been proven to be at least a linear factor faster but would still require exponential expected runtimes for large d [16]). On the other hand, traditional non-elitist algorithms may also struggle to optimise instances of the function class. The (1,λ) EA (which generates λ offspring, always discards the current best solution and accepts the best offspring) has to create the whole population on the second slope to escape from the local optima, which makes the problem prohibitive for the algorithm. If the population size is too large, then the algorithm is unlikely to escape the local optimum efficiently, while if it is too small, it is unlikely that it can hill climb efficiently up to the local optima. Jägersküpper and Storch provided an upper bound of approximately $O(n^{25})$ expected fitness evaluations for appropriately chosen neither too small nor too large population sizes (i.e., of logarithmic size) [32].[9] Lissovoi, Oliveto and Warwicker showed that well-established single trajectory non-elitist heuristics such as METROPOLIS [43] fail to optimise the function efficiently. The main reason is that the difference between the fitness of the local optimum and that of search points at the bottom of the cliff is so large that very large temperatures are required for the algorithm to accept such solutions. However, such temperature values would not allow the algorithm to hill climb efficiently up to the local optimum as worsening moves would be accepted too often. On the other hand, they show that SRMA is extremely efficient for the problem, especially when the location of the Cliff is in its hardest position (i.e., at a linear distance from the global optimum).

Theorem 4.11 (Adapted from Theorems 9 and 10 of [38]) *The expected runtime of the* SRMA *hyper-heuristic for* CLIFF_d *with* $p = 1/((1+\epsilon)n)$ *for any constant* $\epsilon > 0$ *is* $O(n \log n + n^3/d^2)$. *The expected runtime of* METROPOLIS *for* CLIFF_d *is at least* $\left\{\frac{1}{2} \cdot \frac{n-d+1}{d-1} \cdot \left(\frac{n}{\log n}\right)^{d-3/2}, n^{\omega(1)}\right\}$.

It can be noticed that when the cliff is at a linear distance from the optimum (hence requiring exponential expected time also for elitist algorithms) the upper bound on the expected runtime of SRMA reduces to $O(n \log n)$. Given the hardness of the instance for traditional algorithms, this performance is impressive because mutation-only unbiased randomised search heuristics cannot solve any problem defined over bit-strings in an expected runtime smaller than $\Theta(n \log n)$ [36]. It has recently been proven that artificial immune systems are also asymptotically as efficient as the SRMA if equipped with ageing operators that allow them to escape from local optima [10–12].

4.7.2 Local Optima with Large Basins of Attraction

The JUMP_d class of functions (for $1 < d < n/2$) is defined as follows with an example instance depicted in Fig. 4.7 [26]:

$$\text{JUMP}_d(x) := \begin{cases} n+d & \text{if } |x|_1 = n, \\ d + \text{ONEMAX}(x) & \text{if } |x|_1 \leq n-d, \\ n - \text{ONEMAX}(x) & \text{otherwise.} \end{cases}$$

The function class captures real-world applications where the local optima have extremely large basins of attraction. The local optima are separated from the global optimum by a slope of decreasing fitness with a gradient that pushes algorithms back to the local optima. The expected runtimes of elitist algorithms are the same as those

[9] With the mathematical tools available today this upper bound may probably be considerably reduced.

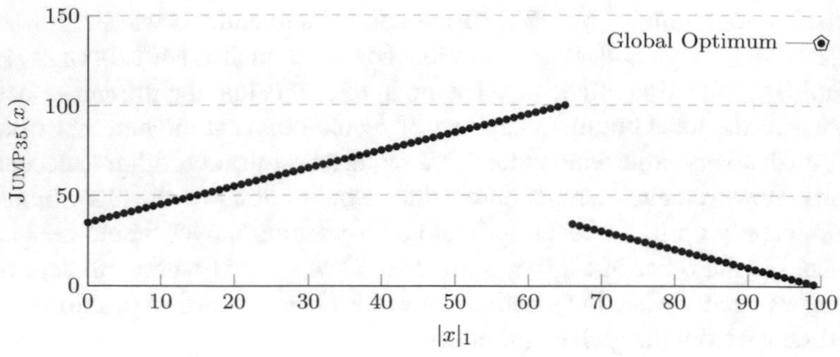

Fig. 4.7 JUMP$_d(x)$ with $n = 100$ and $d = 35$

for CLIFF because the only improving solution from a local optimum is the global one. On the other hand, the function is much more challenging for non-elitist algorithms because no slopes of increasing fitness exist that allow to efficiently escape from the local optima. Nevertheless, Lissovoi, Oliveto and Warwicker show that SRMA is far more efficient than METROPOLIS for the problem class as long as the distance between the global and local optima is not too large.

Theorem 4.12 (Adapted from Theorems 12 and 13 of [38]) *The expected runtime of the* SRMA *hyper-heuristic for* JUMP$_d$ *with* $p = 1/((1+\epsilon)n)$ *for any constant* $\epsilon > 0$ *is* $O(n \log n + (1/d) \cdot n^{2d-1})$*. The runtime of* METROPOLIS *is at least* $2^{\Omega(n)}$ *with probability at least* $1 - 2^{-\Omega(n)}$ *for any* $d > 1$.

Hence, albeit escaping the local optima is as hard as possible for non-elitist algorithms, SRMA can optimise the function class efficiently for any constant jump size, although the provided upper bound on the expected runtime is larger than that of standard elitist evolutionary algorithms (i.e., $\Theta(n^d)$ with standard bit mutation [26] and $O(n^{d-1})$ for crossover-based standard steady-state (μ+1) GAs [16][10]). On the other hand, the established non-elitist METROPOLIS heuristic requires exponential runtime with an overwhelming probability independent of the jump size. Once again the main reason is that the latter algorithm accepts new solutions depending on the difference in quality with the current solution.

[10] Notice that Estimation of Distribution Algorithms (EDAs) can be much faster than all the mentioned algorithms for JUMP$_d$ up to super-constant jump sizes (i.e., $O(n \log n)$ for jump lengths $k < (1/20) \log n$) [17, 55]. If diversity mechanisms are used in the (μ+1) GA, then its expected runtime can be reduced to $O(n \log n + dn + 4^d)$ [15]. It is unclear whether SRMA is really slower since the lower bound provided in [38] is only of order $\Omega(n \log n + 2^{cd})$ for some constant $c > 0$.

4.8 Conclusion

We have provided an overview of the time complexity analyses available in the literature regarding selection hyper-heuristics for combinatorial optimisation. The foundational understanding of these automated algorithm selection methodologies is rapidly growing, yet further work is required for a clear comprehension of their behaviour and performance.

We have motivated the use of hyper-heuristics by providing rigorous evidence of their benefits over using single heuristics in isolation. Results regarding example benchmark functions for which the hyper-heuristics excel have been overviewed, and we have highlighted when more or less sophistication in the hyper-heuristic setup is required. Future work should evaluate the time complexity of simple and complex hyper-heuristics on larger classes of problems to establish how much machine learning sophistication is required to achieve efficient systems of wide and general applicability with performance guarantees. Such an understanding will greatly aid the design of better performing hyper-heuristics.

We have remarked how even extremely simple hyper-heuristics can be very efficient for classical problems such as the minimum spanning tree and the maximum matching problems in graphs. Nevertheless, to the best of our knowledge, no time complexity results are available regarding the performance of the hyper-heuristics used in the literature for classical problems from combinatorial optimisation. While most selection hyper-heuristics from the literature use a single trajectory, some population-based hyper-heuristics have been proposed. No results are available that quantify their expected performance for any problem. The only related analysis that we are aware of is that of Oliveto, Lehre and Neumann where different mutation operators are used by different individuals of the population of a so-called Rank EA [49].

This chapter has overviewed *selection* hyper-heuristics because most of the literature has focused on this class of algorithms. Very little is known about the performance of other classes of automated optimisation algorithms. To the best of our knowledge no time complexity analyses are available regarding *generative* hyper-heuristics that aim to evolve optimisation algorithms offline using training sets of problem instances. There is an urgency for such results. Some time complexity analyses of algorithm configurators for parameter tuning have recently appeared concerning both the worst-case performance [33, 56, 57], and that for standard benchmark functions [28–30].

Apart from quantifying the expected runtime of hyper-heuristics, insights into their behaviour and performance may also be achieved using alternative and complementary perspectives. We encourage experimental analyses of the theory-driven hyper-heuristics overviewed in this chapter for standard combinatorial optimisation problems (e.g., using HyFlex which has become a standard benchmark for comparing hyper-heuristics [46]) and real-world applications to assess the practical usefulness of the theory. Fitness landscape analyses [42, 47, 48, 53] should also focus on expanding the understanding gained from the time complexity and empirical analyses as well as informing them.

Acknowledgements This work was supported by the ESPRC under grant agreement N. EP/M00425 2/1.

References

1. F. Alanazi, P.K. Lehre, Runtime analysis of selection hyper-heuristics with classical learning mechanisms, in *Proceedings of the IEEE Congress on Evolutionary Computation*, CEC '14 (IEEE, 2014), pp. 2515–2523
2. S. Böttcher, B. Doerr, F. Neumann, Optimal fixed and adaptive mutation rates for the leadingones problem, in *Parallel Problem Solving from Nature*, PPSN '10 (Springer, 2010), pp. 1–10
3. J. Branke, S. Pickardt, M. Zhang, Automated design of production scheduling heuristics: a review. IEEE Trans. Evol. Comput. **20**(1), 110–124 (2016)
4. E.K. Burke, M. Gendreau, M. Hyde, G. Kendall, G. Ochoa, E. Özcan, R. Qu, Hyper-heuristics: a survey of the state of the art. J. Oper. Res. Soc. **64**(12), 1695–1724 (2013)
5. E.K. Burke, M.R. Hyde, G. Kendall, J. Woodward, Automating the packing heuristic design process with genetic programming. Evol. Comput. **20**(1), 63–89 (2012)
6. M. Buzdalov, A. Buzdalova, Can OneMax help optimizing LeadingOnes using the EA+RL method? in *IEEE Congress on Evolutionary Computation*, CEC '15 (IEEE, May 2015), pp. 1762–1768
7. T.H. Cormen, C.E. Leiserson, R.L. Rivest, C. Stein, *Introduction to Algorithms* (MIT Press, 2001)
8. D. Corus, P.S. Oliveto, Standard steady state genetic algorithms can hillclimb faster than mutation-only evolutionary algorithms. IEEE Trans. Evol. Comput. **22**(5), 720–732 (2018)
9. D. Corus, P.S. Oliveto, On the benefits of populations on the exploitation speed of standard steady-state genetic algorithms, in *Proceedings of the 2019 Genetic and Evolutionary Computation Conference*, GECCO '19 (ACM Press, 2019), pp. 1452–1460
10. D. Corus, P.S. Oliveto, D. Yazdani, Fast artificial immune systems, in *Proceedings of the international conference on parallel problem solving from nature*, PPSN XV (2018), pp. 67–78
11. D. Corus, P.S. Oliveto, D. Yazdani, Artificial immune systems can find arbitrarily good approximations for the NP-hard number partitioning problem. Artif. Intell. **274**, 180–196 (2019)
12. D. Corus, P.S. Oliveto, D. Yazdani, When hypermutations and ageing enable artificial immune systems to outperform evolutionary algorithms. Theor. Comput. Sci. **832**, 166–185 (2020)
13. P. Cowling, G. Kendall, E. Soubeiga, A hyperheuristic approach to scheduling a sales summit, in *Practice and Theory of Automated Timetabling*, PATAT '01 (Springer, 2001), pp. 176–190
14. P. Cowling, G. Kendall, E. Soubeiga, Hyperheuristics: a tool for rapid prototyping in scheduling and optimisation, in *Applications of Evolutionary Computing*, EvoWorkshops '02 (Springer, 2002), pp. 1–10
15. D.-C. Dang, T. Friedrich, T. Kötzing, M.S. Krejca, P.K. Lehre, P.S. Oliveto, D. Sudholt, A.M. Sutton, Escaping local optima with diversity mechanisms and crossover, in *Proceedings of the Genetic and Evolutionary Computation Conference*, GECCO '16 (2016), pp. 645–652
16. D.-C. Dang, T. Friedrich, T. Kötzing, M.S. Krejca, P.K. Lehre, P.S. Oliveto, D. Sudholt, A.M. Sutton, Escaping local optima using crossover with emergent diversity. IEEE Trans. Evol. Comput. **22**, 484–497 (2017)
17. B. Doerr, A tight runtime analysis for the cGA on jump functions: EDAs can cross fitness valleys at no extra cost, in *Proceedings of the 2019 Genetic and Evolutionary Computation Conference*, GECCO '19 (2019), pp. 1488–1496
18. B. Doerr, C. Doerr, A tight runtime analysis of the $(1+(\lambda, \lambda))$ genetic algorithm on OneMax, in *Proceedings of the 2015 Genetic and Evolutionary Computation Conference*, GECCO '15 (2015), pp. 1423–1430

19. B. Doerr, C. Doerr, Theory of parameter control for discrete black-box optimization: provable performance gains through dynamic parameter choices, in *Theory of Evolutionary Computation - Recent Developments in Discrete Optimization*, ed. by B. Doerr, F. Neumann (Springer, 2020), pp. 271–321
20. B. Doerr, C. Doerr, J. Yang, k-bit mutation with self-adjusting k outperforms standard bit mutation, in *In Proceedings of the international conference on Parallel Problem Solving from Nature*, PPSN '16 (Springer, 2016), pp. 824–834
21. B. Doerr, C. Doerr, J. Yang, Optimal parameter choices via precise black-box analysis, in *Proceedings of the Genetic and Evolutionary Computation Conference*, GECCO '16 (ACM, 2016), pp. 1123–1130
22. B. Doerr, A. Lissovoi, P.S. Oliveto, J.A. Warwicker, On the runtime analysis of selection hyper-heuristics with adaptive learning periods, in *Proceedings of the Genetic and Evolutionary Computation Conference*, GECCO '18 (ACM, 2018), pp. 1015–1022
23. B. Doerr, D. Sudholt, C. Witt, When do evolutionary algorithms optimize separable functions in parallel? in *Proceedings of the workshop on foundations of genetic algorithms*, FOGA '13 (ACM, 2013), pp. 51–64
24. C. Doerr, M. Wagner, Simple on-the-fly parameter selection mechanisms for two classical discrete black-box optimization benchmark problems, in *Proceedings of the Genetic and Evolutionary Computation Conference*, GECCO '18 (ACM, 2018), pp. 943–950
25. J.H. Drake, E. Özcan A. Kheiri, E.K. Burke, Recent advances in selection hyper-heuristics (In press - Online). *European Journal of Operational Research* (2019)
26. S. Droste, T. Jansen, I. Wegener, On the analysis of the (1+1) evolutionary algorithm, in *Theoretical Computer Science* (2002), pp. 51–81
27. O. Giel, Evolutionary algorithms and the maximum matching problem, in *Proceedings of 20th Annual Symposium on Theoretical Aspects of Computer Science*, STACS '03 (2003), pp. 415–426
28. G.T. Hall, P.S. Oliveto, D. Sudholt, On the impact of the cutoff time on the performance of algorithm configurators, in *Proceedings of the Genetic and Evolutionary Computation Conference*, GECCO '19 (ACM, 2019), pp. 907–915
29. G.T. Hall, P.S. Oliveto, D. Sudholt, Analysis of the performance of algorithm configurators for search heuristics with global mutation operators, in *Proceedings of the Genetic and Evolutionary Computation Conference (GECCO '20)* (ACM, 2020), pp. 823–831
30. G.T. Hall, P.S. Oliveto, D. Sudholt, Fast perturbative algorithm configurators, in *Parallel Problem Solving from Nature*, PPSN '20 (2020). arXiv:2007.03336
31. F. Hutter, H.H. Hoos, K. Leyton-Brown, ParamILS: an automatic algorithm configuration framework. J. Artif. Intell. Res. **36**(1), 267–306 (2009)
32. J. Jägersküpper, T. Storch, When the plus strategy outperforms the comma strategy and when not, in *Proceedings of the International Symposium on Foundations of Computational Intelligence*, FOCI '07 (IEEE, 2007), pp. 25–32
33. R. Kleinberg, K. Leyton-Brown, B. Lucier, Efficiency through procrastination: approximately optimal algorithm configuration with runtime guarantees, in *Proceedings of the 26th International Joint Conference on Artificial Intelligence*, IJCAI '17 (AAAI Press, 2017), pp. 2023–2031
34. L. Kotthoff, Algorithm selection for combinatorial search problems: a survey. AI Mag. **35**(3), 48–60 (2014)
35. P.K. Lehre, E. Özcan, A runtime analysis of simple hyper-heuristics: to mix or not to mix operators, in *Proceedings of the Workshop on Foundations of Genetic Algorithms*, FOGA '13 (ACM, 2013), pp. 97–104
36. P.K. Lehre, C. Witt, Black-box search by unbiased variation. Algorithmica **64**(4), 623–642 (2012)
37. A. Lissovoi, P.S. Oliveto, J.A. Warwicker, On the runtime analysis of generalised selection hyper-heuristics for pseudo-boolean optimisation, in *Proceedings of the Genetic and Evolutionary Computation Conference*, GECCO '17 (ACM, 2017), pp. 849–856

38. A. Lissovoi, P.S. Oliveto, J.A. Warwicker, On the time complexity of algorithm selection hyper-heuristics for multimodal optimisation, in *Proceedings of the thirty-third international AAAI conference on artificial Intelligence*, AAAI-19 (AAAI Press, 2019), pp. 2322–2329
39. A. Lissovoi, P.S. Oliveto, J.A. Warwicker, How the duration of the learning period affects the performance of random gradient selection hyper-heuristics, in *Proceedings of the thirty-fourth international AAAI conference on artificial Intelligence*, AAAI-20 (AAAI Press, 2020), pp. 2376–2383
40. A. Lissovoi, P.S. Oliveto, J.A. Warwicker, Simple hyper-heuristics can control the neighbourhood size of randomized local search optimally for leading ones. Evolutionary Computation **28**(3), 437–461 (2020)
41. M. López-Ibáñez, J. Dubois-Lacoste, L. Pérez Cáceres, M. Birattari, T. Stützle, The irace package: iterated racing for automatic algorithm configuration. Oper. Res. Perspect. **3**, 43–58 (2016)
42. I. Maden, S. Uyar, E. Özcan, Landscape analysis of simple perturbative hyper-heuristics, in *Proceedings of the 15th International Conference on Soft Computing*, MENDEL 2009 (2009), pp. 16–22
43. N. Metropolis, A.W. Rosenbluth, M.N. Rosenbluth, A.H. Teller, E. Teller, Equation of state calculations by fast computing machines, in *Journal of Chemical Physics* (1953), pp. 1087–1092
44. A. Nareyek, Choosing search heuristics by non-stationary reinforcement learning, in *Metaheuristics: Computer Decision-Making*, ed. by M.G.C. Resende, J.P. de Sousa (Kluwer, 2003), pp. 523–544
45. F. Neumann, I. Wegener, Randomized local search, evolutionary algorithms and the minimum spanning tree problem. Theor. Comput. Sci. **378**, 32–40 (2007)
46. G. Ochoa, M. Hyde, T. Curtois, J.A. Vazquez-Rodriguez, J. Walker, M. Gendreau, G. Kendall, B. McCollum, A.J. Parkes, S. Petrovic, E.K. Burke, Hyflex: a benchmark framework for cross-domain heuristic search. European conference on evolutionary computation in combinatorial optimization, in *Proceedings of the European Conference on Evolutionary Computation in Combinatorial Optimization*, EvoCOP '12 (2012), pp. 136–147
47. G. Ochoa, R. Qu, E.K. Burke, Analyzing the landscape of a graph based hyper-heuristic for timetabling problems, in *Proceedings of the 2009 Genetic and Evolutionary Computation Conference (GECCO '09)* (2009), pp. 341–348
48. G. Ochoa, J.A. Vazquez-Rodriguez, S. Petrovic, E.K. Burke, Landscape analysis of simple perturbative hyper-heuristics, in *Proceedings of the 2009 IEEE Congress on Evolutionary Computation*, CEC '09 (2009), pp. 1873–1880
49. P.S. Oliveto, P.K. Lehre, F. Neumann, Theoretical analysis of rank-based mutation - combining exploration and exploitation, in *Proceedings of the 2009 IEEE Congress on Evolutionary Computation*, CEC '09 (2009), pp. 1455–1462
50. N. Pillay, Evolving hyper-heuristics for the uncapacitated examination timetabling problem. J. Oper. Res. Soc. **63**(1), 47–58 (2012)
51. N. Pillay, R. Qu, *Hyper-heuristics: theory and applications*, Natural Computing Series (Springer Nature, 2018)
52. C. Qian, K. Tang, Z. Zhou, Selection hyper-heuristics can provably be helpful in evolutionary multi-objective optimization, in *Proceedings of Parallel Problem Solving from Nature*, PPSN '16 (2016), pp. 835–846
53. J.A. Soria-Alcaraz, G. Ochoa, M.A. Sotelo-Figeroa, E.K. Burke, A methodology for determining an effective subset of heuristics in selection hyper-heuristics. Eur. J. Oper. Res. **260**(3), 972–983 (2017)
54. T. Stützle, M. López-Ibáñez, Automated design of metaheuristic algorithms, *Handbook of Metaheuristics*, vol. 272, International Series in Operations Research & Management Science (Springer, 2019), pp. 541–579
55. A.M. Sutton, V. Hasenöhrl. On the runtime dynamics of the compact genetic algorithm on jump functions, in *Proceedings of the 2018 Genetic and Evolutionary Computation Conference*, GECCO '18 (2018), pp. 967–974

56. G. Weisz, A. Gyorgy, C. Szepesvari, LeapsAndBounds: a method for approximately optimal algorithm configuration, in *International Conference on Machine Learning*, ICML '18 (2018), pp. 5254–5262
57. G. Weisz, A. Gyorgy, C. Szepesvári, CapsAndRuns: an improved method for approximately optimal algorithm configuration, in *International Conference on Machine Learning*, ICML '19 (2019), pp. 6707–6715

Chapter 5
AutoMoDe: A Modular Approach to the Automatic Off-Line Design and Fine-Tuning of Control Software for Robot Swarms

Mauro Birattari, Antoine Ligot, and Gianpiero Francesca

Abstract Although swarm robotics is widely recognized as a promising approach to coordinating large groups of robots, a general methodology for designing collective behaviors for robot swarms is still missing. Automatic off-line design is an appealing solution but it is prone to the so-called reality gap, which is the reason for performance drops when control software developed in simulation is deployed on real robots. We present here our research on AutoMoDe, a novel approach to the automatic off-line design of robot swarms, which is based on the principle of modularity. AutoMoDe produces control software for robot swarms by selecting, combining, instantiating, and fine-tuning predefined parametric modules that represent low-level behaviors defined in a mission-agnostic way. By restricting the generation of control software to the instances that can be produced with the given modules, we effectively inject a bias in the design process and consequently reduce its variance. As confirmed by the empirical studies realized so far, this reduces the risk of overfitting simulation models and improves the chances of crossing the reality gap successfully.

The three authors equally contributed to the realization of this chapter and should be considered as co-first authors. The research presented has been conceived and directed by MB; the core experiments were performed by GF; and the manuscript was drafted by AL, revised by MB, and optimized by the three authors. The research has received funding from the European Research Council (ERC) under the European Union's Horizon 2020 research and innovation program (grant agreement No 681872). MB acknowledges support from the Belgian *Fonds de la Recherche Scientifique*–FNRS, of which he is a Research Director.

M. Birattari (✉) · A. Ligot
Université libre de Bruxelles, Brussels, Belgium
e-mail: mbiro@ulb.ac.be

G. Francesca
Toyota Motor Europe, Brussels, Belgium

N. Pillay and R. Qu (eds.), *Automated Design of Machine Learning and Search Algorithms*, Natural Computing Series,
https://doi.org/10.1007/978-3-030-72069-8_5

5.1 An Introduction to Swarm Robotics and Its Design Problem

Swarm robotics [26] is an engineering discipline that found inspiration in swarm intelligence [25] and that is now recognized as a promising approach to design large groups of autonomous robots [87]. Although this discipline has attained a notable position in the scientific literature [36, 53, 69, 74, 83, 86, 88], it has yet to be applied to a real-world scenario. It is the difficulty of reliably generating the desired collective behavior, and more specifically the lack of a general methodology to do so, that hinders the application of the principles of swarm robotics to the real world [16]. In a swarm, robots are completely autonomous and act on the basis of the principle of locality: they take decisions based solely on local information collected through their own sensors or on information communicated by their neighboring peers. Any collective behavior displayed by a swarm is the result of interactions between robots and between robots and the environment. The design problem in swarm robotics is particularly challenging as it is not feasible to directly program the desired collective behavior of a swarm: only the individual robot behaviors can be specified. Obtaining the desired collective behavior requires therefore to master the complex "what, where, when, and how" of the many robot–robot and robot–environment interactions that characterize the operation of a swarm.

Traditional multi-robot systems and software engineering techniques [14, 20, 24, 71], which rely on the formal derivation of the individual behaviors from specifications expressed at the collective level, cannot be applied to swarm robotics, at least in the general case, due to the aforementioned issues. A few principled manual design methods have been proposed [5, 7, 15, 42, 47, 57, 64, 67], but their application is limited to specific classes of missions due to their working hypotheses and constraints. Therefore, experts in swarm robotics usually proceed by trial and error to obtain the desired collective behaviors.

A promising alternative to manually designing the control software exists: the adoption of *optimization-based* design methods. With such methods, the design problem becomes an optimization problem: an optimization algorithm explores the search space composed of all possible individual behaviors, with the objective of finding one that maximizes a performance measure expressed at the collective level. The optimization-based approach regroups different categories of design methods. In the domain literature, the commonly adopted classification distinguishes between online and off-line methods [16, 17, 31]. A second classification, orthogonal to the online/off-line one, distinguishes between semi-automatic and (fully-)automatic design methods [10].

In online methods, the design process is distributed and operates on the physical robots while they perform their mission [18, 41, 48, 52, 73, 82]. Although promising for specific circumstances—for example, to adjust the parameters of control software—online methods do not appear to be the ultimate solution to the design problem in swarm robotics as their application is limited to cases in which the robots are able to evaluate their collective performance [31]. In off-line methods, the design process is performed before the swarm is deployed in the target environment and relies on computer-based simulations. As the assessment of control software is performed in simulation, which allows the computation of any desired performance measure, off-line methods can potentially be applied to any mission. However, they are faced with a problem that does not affect online methods: the so-called *reality gap* [19, 46], which refers to the difference between simulation and reality. Due to the reality gap, one should expect to be deceived by the performance of automatically generated control software when it is deployed on physical robots, as it is likely to drop in comparison with the one obtained in simulation [29].

In semi-automatic design, a human designer utilizes an optimization algorithm as a tool that they operate using their intuition and previous experience. Typically, the designer iterates through a series of steps, which include: the execution of the optimization process, the evaluation and analysis of the behavior produced using simulation and/or physical robot experiments, and the modification of the optimization process. The designer modifies the optimization process so that, on the basis of the evaluation and according to their experience, more performing control software will be produced in the following execution. The elements of the design process that are often modified include the parameters of the optimization algorithm, the characteristics of the control software architecture, or the performance measure to be optimized. This three-step procedure is repeated until the control software produced satisfies the designer and/or they feel that it cannot be improved any further. Many studies have shown that semi-automatic design is an effective way to design robot swarms [4, 22, 27, 28, 39, 45, 59, 66, 76, 78–81, 84]. The drawback of this approach is that it involves an expert designer that must have a good understanding of the optimization process and of the mission at hand. Moreover, because the results obtained are to be partially credited to the expert's ingenuity, they are often hardly reproducible.

In automatic design, one expects from a method to reliably produce control software for a whole class of missions without the need to apply modifications [10]. The optimization process is therefore performed in a fully automatic way, without the need for any per-mission human intervention.

In the rest of this chapter, we take a close look at a novel approach to the off-line automatic design: AutoMoDe, short for *automatic modular design* [34]. The main characteristic of this approach is the modularity of the instances of control software it generates: they are obtained by an optimization algorithm that automatically selects, combines, and fine-tunes predefined modules. These modules include actions to be performed by an individual robot and conditions on the environment perceived or the internal state of the robot that determine whether the robot should transition from one action to another. A number of automatic design methods have been proposed so far that belong in the AutoMoDe approach. In most of them, as we will see in the body of the chapter, the optimization algorithm adopted is either F-race [8, 11] or Iterated F-race [3, 12, 58]. These two algorithms, which were originally developed to automatically design and/or fine-tune metaheuristics, appear to be an ideal choice to handle the high uncertainty that characterizes the operation of a robot swarm. In Sect. 5.2, we elaborate on the reasoning and on the working hypothesis that led to the definition of AutoMoDe; in Sect. 5.3, we describe the different instantiations of AutoMoDe and discuss their achievements; and in Sect. 5.4, we report additional experiments that were conducted to corroborate the working hypothesis discussed in Sect. 5.2. In Sect. 5.5, we summarize the main points made in this chapter and we highlight future research directions.

5.2 From Neuro-Evolutionary Robotics to AutoMoDe

In swarm robotics, the most popular optimization-based approach for designing control software is neuro-evolutionary robotics [29, 56, 76, 77]. In this approach, robots are controlled by a neural network: sensor readings are fed to the neural network as inputs, whereas the robot actuator values are dictated by the network's output. An evolutionary algorithm [2] is used to search for the best possible configuration of the neural network. Thanks to the high flexibility and representational power of neural networks, the neuro-evolutionary approach can produce extremely varied and diverse behaviors [13, 43, 62]. The neuro-evolutionary approach has been successfully used to generate control software for various swarm robotics missions [22, 45, 66, 79]. However, when applied to the off-line case, neuro-evolutionary robotics presents a major limitation: it is unable to cross the reality gap reliably [72], that is, control software developed in simulation does not typically perform satisfactorily when ported to reality.

We conjecture that the inability of evolutionary robotics to cross the reality gap reliably is indeed a side effect of the high representational power of neural networks [34]. Our working hypothesis here is that the reality gap problem faced in the off-line automatic design of robot swarms is somehow reminiscent of the generalization problem faced in machine learning. In supervised learning, a fundamental result is the so-called *bias/variance tradeoff*, which states that the prediction error of an approximator can be decomposed into a bias and a variance component [38, 85]. It is known that these two components are correlated to the representational power of the approximator: a large representational power implies low bias and high variance. It is therefore our contention that, in the context of the automatic off-line design of robot swarms, the high representational power of neural networks can be counterproductive and be the cause of a sort of *overfitting* to the simulation environment, which then hinders performance in the real world.

Based on this reasoning, Francesca et al. introduced a novel approach to the automatic design of robot swarms: *AutoMoDe* [34]. In AutoMoDe, robots are controlled by a modular software architecture (e.g., a finite state machine) automatically generated by assembling predefined modules. Compared to the neural networks used in neuro-evolutionary robotics, the control software generated by AutoMoDe features a lower representational power. In AutoMoDe, the representational power is reduced by injecting bias in the generation of control software: the control software that can be produced is restricted to what can be obtained by assembling some predefined modules. AutoMoDe is a general framework that needs to be *specialized* to a specific robotic platform. To define a specialization of AutoMoDe, an expert needs to: (i) provide a set of modules for the given robotic platform, (ii) select an optimization algorithm, and (iii) define a control software architecture into which the modules must be assembled by the optimization algorithm. The optimization algorithm explores a search space composed of all possible instantiations and combinations of the available modules. It is important to stress that the modules are defined by the expert in a mission-agnostic way. In other terms, the modules are defined on the basis of the capabilities of the robots for then be used to generate control software for any possible mission of interest. The modules are defined once and for all: they are not supposed to be manually modified or tweaked to accommodate the needs of a specific mission for which control software must be designed. The fact that the produced control software is a priori constrained to be a combination of predefined modules introduces a bias and reduces the representational power: it limits the possibility to fine-tune the robot–robot and robot–environment interactions. However, assuming that the expert implements the modules correctly, a specialization of AutoMoDe should be able to generate a sufficient variety of behaviors so as to allow the swarm to perform the possible missions of interest.

The definition and implementation of the modules is critical to the success of specialization of AutoMoDe. To better understand the goals and the implications of the definition of specialization of AutoMoDe, the following conceptual representation of the issue can be helpful. A specialization of AutoMoDe—like any automatic design method—is implemented for a robotic platform on the basis of abstraction of its characteristics and capabilities: what we call a *reference model*. Implicitly, a reference model defines also the class of missions that can be performed by a swarm of robots described by the reference model itself. For example, a mission that requires sorting objects according to their color cannot be performed by robots that are unable to distinguish colors. More formally, consider the class M_I comprising the behaviors that accomplish collective missions that are of interest (within a specific context). Consider also the class B_{RM} comprising all the behaviors that can be produced by a robot swarm whose individuals conform to the given reference model. The intersection between M_I and B_{RM} gives the class M of behaviors that accomplish collective missions that are of interest and that can be produced by robots conforming to the given reference model. A specialization of AutoMoDe and specifically the definition of the modules—like the implementation of any automatic design method—implicitly defines the class B' of the behaviors that can be produced by a swarm of robots whose control software is generated by the specialization of AutoMoDe itself—or by any other automatic design method one might consider. Clearly, B' is a subset of B_{RM}: a specialization of AutoMoDe cannot generate behaviors for a robotic platform that allow it to perform missions requiring capabilities (e.g., sensors and actuators) it does not have—and neither can any other automatic design method. What is important to notice is that the relationship between the classes B_{RM} and B' defines the representational power: the larger B', the higher the representational power. However, what is crucial is M', the intersection between the classes B' and M, which represents the behaviors that can be generated and that solve collective missions of interest. In an ideal case, a specialization of AutoMoDe—or more generally an automatic design

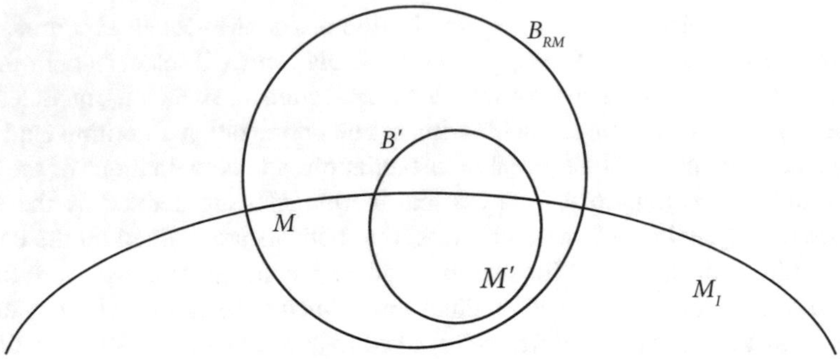

Fig. 5.1 Graphical representation of the sets of behaviors that are relevant when discussing the capabilities of an automatic design method. Note that these sets are purely conceptual and do not need to be explicitly defined in a closed form. M_I is the set of behaviors allowing a swarm to perform collective missions that are of interest (within a specific context). B_{RM} is the set of behaviors that can be achieved by a swarm of robots conforming to the reference model at hand. M is the set of behaviors that can be achieved by a swarm of robots conforming to the reference model and that accomplish collective missions of interest. B' is the set of behaviors that can be produced by a specialization of AutoMoDe—or more generally by a given design method. M' is the set of behaviors that can be produced by the specialization of AutoMoDe—or by a given design method—and that accomplish collective missions of interest. This figure is a modified version of the one previously published in [30]

method—can produce all the behaviors that solve collective missions of interest conforming to the reference model, that is $M \equiv M'$, and no behaviors that are irrelevant, that is $M \equiv M' \equiv B'$. Figure 5.1 gives a graphical representation of the different classes.

5.3 The Specializations of AutoMoDe

Multiple specializations of AutoMoDe have been defined so far, all generating control software for an extended version of the e-puck robot [37, 60]. In the following, we only give a brief overview of these specializations and of the results obtained. We refer the reader to the original publications for the details.

The very first specialization of AutoMoDe was named `Vanilla` [34] and served as a proof-of-concept to assess the core ideas of AutoMoDe. `Vanilla` selects, combines, and fine-tunes predefined modules into control software in the form of a probabilistic finite state machine. In the finite state machine produced by `Vanilla`, the states are associated with low-level behavior modules, whereas the edges or transitions are associated with condition modules. `Vanilla` is based on a set of six low-level behaviors and a set of six conditions. The low-level behaviors are **stop**, which prevents the robot from moving; **exploration**, which makes the robot walk randomly; **attraction** and **repulsion**, which makes the robot move toward or away from its peers, respectively; and **phototaxis** and **anti-phototaxis**, which makes the robot move toward or away from a source of light, respectively. The conditions are **fixed-probability**, which is true with a fixed probability; **white-**, **gray-**, and **black-floor**, which are true when the floor situated below the robot is white, gray, or black, respectively; **neighbor-count**, which is true when a sufficient number of neighboring robots are perceived; and **inverted-neighbor-count**, which is true when sufficiently few neighboring robots are perceived. These modules might have free parameters that are tuned by the optimization algorithm within the optimization process. At every control cycle, the low-level behavior associated with the current state is executed, and the conditions associated to the outgoing edges of the current state are evaluated. The robot executes the same low-level behavior as long as the conditions are evaluated as false. If at least one condition is evaluated as true, one of them is randomly selected, the corresponding transition takes place, and the current state is updated accordingly.

`Vanilla` produces finite state machines with up to four states (or low-level behaviors) to which up to four edges (or conditions) can be connected. To search the space of the possible finite state machine that can be produced by assembling the aforementioned modules and by fine-tuning their parameters, `Vanilla` adopts F-race [8, 11], an optimization algorithm originally developed to configure meta-heuristics. F-race has been designed to handle stochasticity, it is therefore appropriate to use it in the context of swarm robotics as the performance of an instance of control software varies with the operating conditions (e.g., the initial position and orientation of the robots) and with the contingencies encountered by the swarm. An execution of F-race is reminiscent of a race: a number of candidate solutions are incrementally tested and discarded from the race, should they display low performance. The initial set of candidate solutions are generated randomly at the beginning of the optimization process. At each step of the F-race algorithm, using simulation, the surviving candidate solutions (that is, those that have not been discarded in the previous iterations) are evaluated on a test case which is characterized by the initial position and orientation of the robots and (possibly) the configuration of the working environment. Based on the evaluations of all previous steps, the candidate solutions whose expected performance is statistically dominated by at least another one are discarded from the race and are not evaluated any further in the following steps.

`Vanilla` has been studied in two experiments. In the first one, it was compared, on two missions, against an implementation of the neuro-evolutionary approach called `EvoStick` [34]. In the simulation, `EvoStick` was able to find control software that displayed more sophisticated behaviors than those found by `Vanilla`. However, the control software generated by `EvoStick` was unable to reproduce these behaviors once ported on the physical robots and suffered an important performance drop. On the contrary, the control software generated by `Vanilla` transitioned smoothly from simulation to reality and much lesser performance drop was observed. As a result, what we call a *rank inversion* was observed in both missions: `EvoStick` outperformed `Vanilla` in simulation, but `Vanilla` outperformed `EvoStick` in reality.

In the second experiment, the control software produced by `Vanilla` and `EvoStick` was compared against the one produced by five human experts [33]. The experimental protocol devised by Francesca et al. was an original contribution to

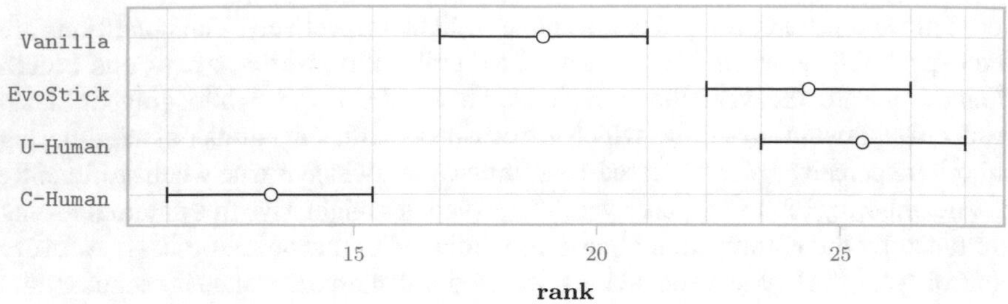

Fig. 5.2 Outcome of the Friedman test performed on the results of the second experiment involving `Vanilla` [34]. For each of the methods, the plot represents the average rank and its 95% confidence interval evaluated on five missions in robot experiments. The lower the rank, the better. `EvoStick` is an implementation of the neuro-evolutionary approach; `U-Human` and `C-Human` are manual methods. The performance of the two methods is to be considered as significantly different if their respective confidence interval do not overlap [23]

swarm robotics on its own: each of the five experts proposed a mission for which control software had to be produced. The five experts did not have any knowledge of the internal functioning of `Vanilla`, therefore, they could not have favored or disfavored `Vanilla` with their choice of a mission. Each expert was then asked to manually produce control software for two missions (other than the one they proposed). For one of them, the expert was left free to design the control software as they deemed appropriate—we call this approach `U-Human`. For the other one, the experts were constrained to use the modules and control architecture of `Vanilla`—we call this approach `C-Human`. In other words, in `C-Human`, the expert plays the role of `Vanilla`'s optimization algorithm. All in all, for each of the five missions, the authors obtained control software produced by `U-Human`, `C-Human` and by `Vanilla` and `EvoStick`.

The results of this second experiment confirm those of the first one: the control software produced by `Vanilla` outperformed the one produced by `EvoStick` when the comparison was performed in reality. Compared to the manual methods, `Vanilla` outperformed `U-Human`, but was outperformed by `C-Human`. The results of this second experiment are reported in Fig. 5.2. Because the only difference between `Vanilla` and `C-Human` lies in the way the space of possible solutions is explored—the former uses the F-race optimization algorithm, the latter relies on an implicit search performed by a human—Francesca et al. argued that `Vanilla` could be improved by adopting a better optimization algorithm [33]. This conclusion gave birth to a second specialization of AutoMoDe: `Chocolate` [32].

`Chocolate` uses an improved version of the optimization algorithm adopted in `Vanilla`: Iterated F-race [3, 12, 58]. Iterated F-race has shown to outperform F-race when used to configure metaheuristics [12]. In Iterated F-race, multiple executions of the F-race algorithm are iteratively conducted. In the first iteration, the initial set of candidates is obtained by uniformly sampling the space of possible solutions. In the following ones, the initial set of candidates are obtained by sampling the space of solutions according to a distribution that gives higher priority to the solutions that

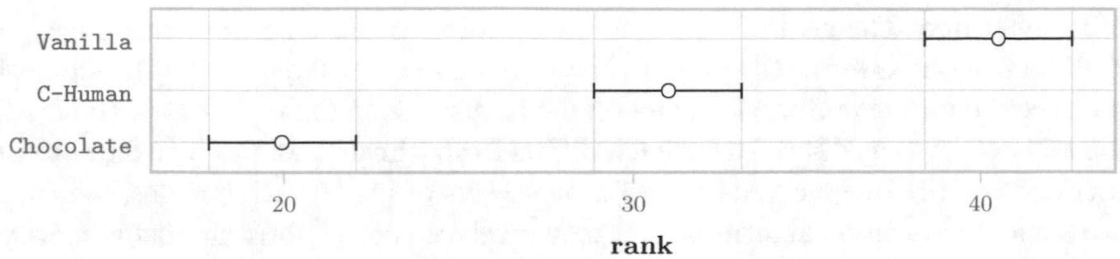

Fig. 5.3 Outcome of the Friedman test performed on the results of the experiment comparing `Vanilla`, `Chocolate`, and `C-Human` [32]. For each of the methods, the plot represents the average rank and its 95% confidence interval, evaluated on the same five missions as in Fig. 5.2. The lower the rank, the better

are close to the surviving solutions of the previous iteration. We refer the reader to [58] for a detailed description of Iterated F-race. `Chocolate` was compared with `Vanilla` and `C-Human` on the basis of the same five missions proposed by the human experts for the previous experiment. The results, depicted in Fig. 5.3, show that `Chocolate` improves over `Vanilla`, and the improvement is such that `Chocolate` also outperforms `C-Human`. The convincing results of `Chocolate` have motivated the creation and study of other further specifications of AutoMoDe: `Gianduja` [44], `Maple` [50], and `Waffle` [70].

With `Gianduja`, Hasselmann et al. [44] studied the emergence of a communication protocol between robots in the automatic design of control software for robot swarms. The authors considered a reference model that comprises an extra capability with respect to the reference model on the basis of which `Chocolate` was developed: the robots are allowed to locally broadcast and receive a message. This message is a priori meaningless, and the authors therefore studied whether an automatic design process is able to assign to the message an appropriate semantics on a per-mission basis. The authors extended the sets of behavioral and conditional modules of `Vanilla` (and `Chocolate`) so as to leverage the enhanced reference model. Two new behavioral modules, **attraction-to-message** and **repulsion-from-message**, were included: the robot moves toward or away from the peers that are broadcasting a message, respectively. Also two new conditional modules, **message-count** and **inverted-message-count**, were included: a transition is enabled if the number of messages received is larger or smaller than a parameter, respectively. Except for the new modules, `Gianduja` is defined as `Chocolate`: like `Chocolate`, it adopts Iterated F-race as an optimization algorithm, and it generates control software in the form of probabilistic finite state machines. The authors tested `Gianduja` on three missions, and for each of them, the design process produced control software that leveraged the communication capability of the robots in a meaningful way.

With `Maple`, Kuckling et al. [50] explored the use of another control architecture for the automatic design of robot swarms: behavior trees. Indeed, instead of combining the predefined modules into a probabilistic finite state machine—as it is done in `Vanilla`, `Chocolate`, and `Gianduja`—`Maple` combines them into a behavior tree. The goal of the authors was not to create a new automatic design method that outperforms Chocolate, but rather to study the impact of the control architecture on the performance and on the robustness to the reality gap. To do so, the authors developed Maple so that it differs from Chocolate only in the control architecture: the two methods share the same sets of predefined modules, they use the same optimization algorithm, and they produce control software that comprise a maximum of four behavioral modules. The authors compared the performance of Chocolate, EvoStick, and Maple on two missions. The results show that Chocolate and Maple performed similarly and that they both displayed a smaller performance drop with respect to EvoStick when the control software produced was ported to the robots. These results confirm the conjecture that the robustness of AutoMoDe to the reality gap originates from its modular nature and indicate that the architecture into which the modules are combined is a secondary issue.

With Waffle, Salman et al. [70] generalized the functionality of AutoMoDe to not only generate control software, but also to concurrently configure the hardware of the swarm itself. Concerning the generation of control software, Waffle is identical to Chocolate. The novelty is the configuration of the robot swarm: Waffle automatically optimizes the hardware configuration of the individual robots and the number of robots comprised in the swarm. In their study, to prove their concept, the authors restricted the hardware configuration of the individual robots to the selection of a local communication module out of a set of hypothetical but realistic candidates. These candidates were defined as variants of an existing infra-red communication module [40]. Some of the candidates are more and some are less capable than the existing module in terms of their transmission range and communication reliability. Those that are more capable are also more expensive and draw more current per unit time and vice versa. The authors studied the performance of Waffle under two types of economic constraints: constraints on the monetary budget available, and/or on the battery capacity of the individual robots. Without these constraints, the design problem is trivial: the design process always selects the largest possible swarm composed of the most capable robots. The constraints make the design problem more interesting and realistic: indeed, every real-world design problem involves trade-offs of an economic nature. Due to the monetary constraint, the automatic design process must choose between: (a) having a swarm composed of many but relatively incapable robots and (b) few capable ones. Due to the power constraint, it must choose between: (a) robots with capable hardware that, due to their high power consumption, can operate for a relatively short time;and (b) robots with less capable hardware that, due to their low power consumption, can operate for a relatively long time. Salman et al. tested Waffle on three missions, and, for each mission performed the design process under nine levels of the aforementioned economic constraint. The results show that the optimal hardware configuration and behavior of the swarm depend on the mission to be accomplished and on the constraint imposed. They also show that the principles of the automatic modular design can be successfully applied to the concurrent design of hardware and control software of robot swarms.

Two other specializations of AutoMoDe were developed: IcePop [51] and Coconut [75]. With IcePop, Kuckling et al. [51] investigated the use of yet another optimization algorithm: simulated annealing [35]. With `Coconut`, Spaey et al. [75] extended the set of behavior modules to include different exploration schemes and investigated their influence on the performance of the swarms that can then be generated.

5.4 Further Corroboration of Our Working Hypothesis

The results of the different specializations of AutoMoDe corroborate our original working hypothesis: the reality gap problem bears similarity with the generalization problem faced in machine learning and reducing the complexity of control architecture by injecting bias produces control software with increased robustness to the reality gap. In this section, we present other studies that further corroborate our insight on the subject.

In supervised machine learning, the phenomenon of overfitting—or alternatively, overtraining—occurs when the learning process is protracted beyond an ideal threshold, which causes the performance on the training set and on the test set to diverge [1, 65]. Indeed, past an optimal level of the training effort, the approximator overspecializes to the examples contained in the training set, which impairs its ability to generalize to a test set. In an experiment, Birattari et al. [9] observed a phenomenon that can be seen as the off-line automatic design counterpart of the overtraining issue faced in supervised machine learning. They called the phenomenon they observed *overdesign*. In this experiment, the authors evaluated both in simulation and in reality the performance of the best instances of control software produced by an neuro-evolutionary design method at different levels of the design effort, that is, after an increasing number of iterations of the evolutionary algorithm. The results reported in Fig. 5.4 show that, past an optimal design effort, the performance that the automatically generated swarm obtains in reality diverges from the one it obtains in simulation.

In addition to corroborating our hypothesis on the similarity between the reality gap problem and the generalization problem in machine learning, these results illustrate the relative nature of the occurrence of the effects of the reality gap. Indeed, not all instances of control software are equally affected by the same reality gap. In this specific case, some instances, notably those produced at the beginning of the design process, display a smaller performance drop than those generated later on in the design process. This can lead to the observation of what the authors call a rank inversion: an instance A of control software outperforms an instance B in simulation, but B outperforms A in reality. In the results of Fig. 5.4, a rank inversion occurred between instances of control software generated by the same design method, but a similar phenomenon has also been observed when comparing different design methods [32, 34].

The phenomena of overdesign and of rank inversion raise two fundamental questions that are core to the off-line automatic design of robot swarms: what design method will produce control software that will yield the best performance once

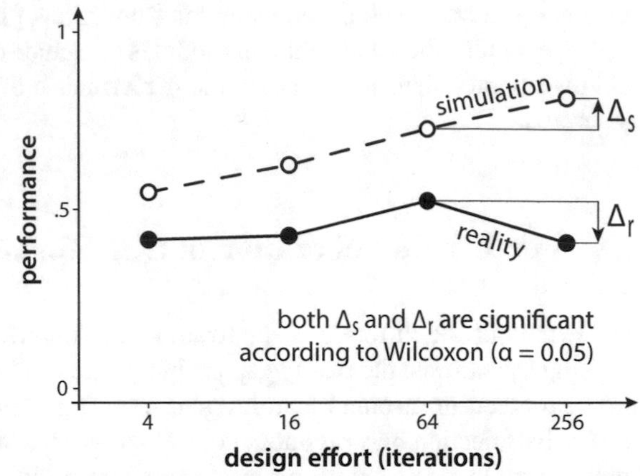

Fig. 5.4 Results of an experiment in which the best artificial neural networks produced after 4, 16, 64, and 256 iterations of an evolutionary algorithm were evaluated in simulation and in reality. We refer the reader to the original publication for the details on experimental protocol and results [9]

uploaded to the robots? When should the design process be stopped? The answers to these questions likely vary from mission to mission and, at the moment, they can be obtained only via robot experiments, which are expensive, time-consuming, and not always feasible [10]. What would be highly desirable to have is a simulation-only procedure that could provide reliable estimations of the real-world performance of control software and of its ability to cross the reality gap. Such a procedure could be used to implement an early stopping mechanism [21, 61, 65] so as to prevent overdesign and also to select among different automatic design methods the one to use.

To the best of our knowledge, Koos et al. [49] were the first to use an artificial, simulation-only reality gap in the context of the automatic design of robot swarms. The authors did so to perform experiments to further assess the performance of a design method they proposed. Ligot and Birattari [54] formally introduced the notion of *pseudo-reality*: a simulation model, different from the one used during the design, used to evaluate the intrinsic robustness of control software to the reality gap. In that paper, a pseudo-reality was generated by hand so as to replicate previously observed performance drop and rank inversion. With the notion of pseudo-reality, the authors investigated the conditions under which the effects of the reality gap manifest. The results show that the effects of the reality gap manifest themselves regardless of whether the evaluation context is more or less complex than the context in which the control software has been designed. These results also substantiate our contention that the effects of the reality gap are due to the fact that control software overfits the context in which it has been designed, and hence those design methods overfit the context in which they operate. In further experiments, Ligot and Birattari [55] obtained similar results with multiple simulation models used as pseudo-reality, all being uniformly sampled around the model used during the design. We foresee that the notion of pseudo-reality can be leveraged in the definition of a simulation-only protocol that would be able to tell, with reasonable confidence, which automatic design method to apply to the problem at hand and when is the most appropriate time to stop the design process.

5.5 Discussion on Future Research Directions

Swarm robotics is an appealing way of realizing a group of robots that should operate in environments where the risk of damaging or losing robots is high and establishing a reliable communication between robots and between them and a supervisory entity is unfeasible. Ideal applications of swarm robotics include surveillance, search and rescue, demining, and underwater or space exploration. Yet, the real-world application of swarm robotics is not imminent, which is essentially due to a lack of a general methodology to reliably program the individual robots so that the desired collective behavior emerges from their interactions.

In this chapter, we focused on what appears to be a promising approach to solve the complex problem of designing a robot swarm: automatic off-line design. In particular, we highlighted the results recently obtained with AutoMoDe, an automatic method that generates control software for robot swarms by assembling predefined software modules. AutoMoDe was specifically conceived to address the main challenge in the automatic off-line approach: produce control software that is robust to the so-called reality gap, that is, that attains in reality a performance that is comparable to the one displayed in the simulations of the design phase. The core idea of AutoMoDe is to restrain the representational power of the control architecture. By doing so, it reduces the risk that the control software produced overfits the peculiarities of the simulations and fails subsequently to generalize to reality. Although AutoMoDe produced satisfactory results, work remains to be done to gain a full understanding of the reality gap problem and conceive a reliable automatic design method. A number of specializations of AutoMoDe have been proposed so far that differ one from the other in some of their components, including the optimization algorithm and the architecture in which modules are assembled. The space of the possible alternatives is vast and the research conducted so far has only scratched the surface. Indeed, the use of two architectures has been investigated so far: probabilistic finite state machines and behavior trees. Other alternatives are worth being explored, such as executable Petri nets [63] and Boolean networks [6, 68]. Similarly, only three optimization algorithms have been investigated so far and a few are under analysis. Yet, many more exist or could be conceived specifically for being adopted in the context of AutoMoDe. Finally, we presented some results in the concurrent development of control software and configuration of the hardware. Although preliminary, these results are promising and clearly indicate that the principles of the automatic modular design of AutoMoDe are not restricted to the generation of control software but have more general applicability.

References

1. S. Amari, N. Murata, K.R. Müller, M. Finke, H.H. Yang, Statistical theory of overtraining - is cross-validation asymptotically effective?, in *NIPS'95: Advances in Neural Information Processing Systems*, ed. by D.S. Touretzky, M.C. Mozer, M.E. Hasselmo (MIT Press, Cambridge, MA, 1996), pp. 176–182
2. T. Bäck, D.B. Fogel, Z. Michalewicz, *Handbook of Evolutionary Computation* (IOP Publishing Ltd., Bristol, UK, 2000)
3. P. Balaprakash, M. Birattari, T. Stützle, Improvement strategies for the F-Race algorithm: Sampling design and iterative refinement, in *Hybrid Metaheuristics, 4th International Workshop, HM 2007*, vol. 4771. LNCS (Springer, Berlin, Germany, 2007), pp. 108–122
4. G. Baldassarre, V. Trianni, M. Bonani, F. Mondada, M. Dorigo, S. Nolfi, Self-organized coordinated motion in groups of physically connected robots. IEEE Trans. Syst. Man Cy. B **37**, 224–39 (2007). https://doi.org/10.1109/TSMCB.2006.881299
5. J. Beal, S. Dulman, K. Usbeck, M. Viroli, N. Correll, Organizing the aggregate: languages for spatial computing, in *Formal and Practical Aspects of Domain-Specific Languages: Recent Developments* (IGI Global, 2012), pp. 436–501. https://doi.org/10.4018/978-1-4666-2092-6.ch016
6. S. Benedettini, M. Villani, A. Roli, R. Serra, M. Manfroni, A. Gagliardi, C. Pinciroli, M. Birattari, Dynamical regimes and learning properties of evolved boolean networks. Neurocomputing **99**, 111–123 (2013). https://doi.org/10.1016/j.neucom.2012.05.023
7. S. Berman, V. Kumar, R. Nagpal, Design of control policies for spatially inhomogeneous robot swarms with application to commercial pollination, in *IEEE International Conference on Robotics and Automation – ICRA* (IEEE, Piscataway, NJ, 2011), pp. 378–385. https://doi.org/10.1109/ICRA.2011.5980440
8. M. Birattari, *Tuning Metaheuristics: A Machine Learning Perspective* (Springer, Berlin, Germany, 2009)
9. M. Birattari, B. Delhaisse, G. Francesca, Y. Kerdoncuff, Observing the effects of overdesign in the automatic design of control software for robot swarms, in *Swarm Intelligence – ANTS*, vol. 9882. LNCS, ed. by M. Dorigo, M. Birattari, X. Li, M. López-Ibáñez, K. Ohkura, C. Pinciroli, T. Stützle (Springer, Cham, Switzerland, 2016), pp. 45–57. https://doi.org/10.1007/978-3-319-44427-7_13
10. M. Birattari, A. Ligot, D. Bozhinoski, M. Brambilla, G. Francesca, L. Garattoni, D. Garzón Ramos, K. Hasselmann, M. Kegeleirs, J. Kuckling, F. Pagnozzi, A. Roli, M. Salman, T. Stützle, Automatic off-line design of robot swarms: a manifesto. Front. Robot. AI **6**, 59 (2019). https://doi.org/10.3389/frobt.2019.00059
11. M. Birattari, T. Stützle, L. Paquete, K. Varrentrapp, A racing algorithm for configuring metaheuristics, in *Proceedings of the Genetic and Evolutionary Computation Conference, GECCO*, ed. by W. Langdon, et al. (Morgan Kaufmann, San Francisco CA, 2002), pp. 11–18
12. M. Birattari, Z. Yuan, P. Balaprakash, T. Stützle, F-race and iterated f-race: an overview, in *Experimental Methods for the Analysis of Optimization Algorithms*, ed. by T. Bartz-Beielstein, M. Chiarandini, L. Paquete, M. Preuss (Springer, Berlin, Germany, 2010), pp. 311–336. https://doi.org/10.1007/978-3-642-02538-9_13
13. J.C. Bongard, Evolutionary robotics. Commun. ACM **56**(8), 74–83 (2013). https://doi.org/10.1145/2493883
14. D. Bozhinoski, D. Di Ruscio, I. Malavolta, P. Pelliccione, M. Tivoli, Flyaq: enabling non-expert users to specify and generate missions of autonomous multicopters, in *IEEE/ACM International Conference on Automated Software Engineering – ASE* (IEEE, Piscataway, NJ, 2015), pp. 801–806. https://doi.org/10.1109/ASE.2015.104
15. M. Brambilla, A. Brutschy, M. Dorigo, M. Birattari, Property-driven design for swarm robotics: a design method based on prescriptive modeling and model checking. ACM Trans. Auton. Adapt. Syst. **9**(4), 17.1–28 (2015). https://doi.org/10.1145/2700318

16. M. Brambilla, E. Ferrante, M. Birattari, M. Dorigo, Swarm robotics: a review from the swarm engineering perspective. Swarm Intell. **7**(1), 1–41 (2013). https://doi.org/10.1007/s11721-012-0075-2
17. N. Bredeche, E. Haasdijk, A. Prieto, Embodied evolution in collective robotics: a review. Front. Robot. AI **5**, 12 (2018). https://doi.org/10.3389/frobt.2018.00012
18. N. Bredeche, J.M. Montanier, W. Liu, A.F. Winfield, Environment-driven distributed evolutionary adaptation in a population of autonomous robotic agents. Math. Comput. Model. Dyn. Syst. **18**(1), 101–129 (2012)
19. R. Brooks, Artificial life and real robots, in *Proceedings of the First European Conference on Artificial Life Towards a Practice of Autonomous Systems* (MIT Press, Cambridge, MA, 1992), pp. 3–10
20. D. Brugali (Ed.), *Software Engineering for Experimental Robotics*, vol. 30 (Springer, 2007). https://doi.org/10.1007/978-3-540-68951-5
21. R. Caruana, S. Lawrence, C.L. Giles, Overfitting in neural nets: backpropagation, conjugate gradient, and early stopping, in *Advances in Neural Information Processing Systems 13*, ed. by T.K. Leen, T.G. Dietterich, V. Tresp (MIT Press, 2001), pp. 402–408
22. A.L. Christensen, M. Dorigo, Evolving an integrated phototaxis and hole-avoidance behavior for a swarm-bot, in *Arfiticial Life – ALIFE* (MIT Press, Cambridge, MA, 2006), pp. 248–254
23. W.J. Conover, *Practical Nonparametric Statistics*, 3rd edn. (Wiley, New York, NY, 1999)
24. D. Di Ruscio, I. Malavolta, P. Pelliccione, A family of domain-specific languages for specifying civilian missions of multi-robot systems, in *Proceedings of the 1st International Workshop on Model-Driven Robot Software Engineering – MORSE* (2014), pp. 13–26
25. M. Dorigo, M. Birattari, Swarm intelligence. Scholarpedia **2**(9), 1462 (2007). https://doi.org/10.4249/scholarpedia.1462
26. M. Dorigo, M. Birattari, M. Brambilla, Swarm robotics. Scholarpedia **9**(1), 1463 (2014). https://doi.org/10.4249/scholarpedia.1463
27. E. Ferrante, E. Duéñez Guzmán, A.E. Turgut, T. Wenseleers, Geswarm: Grammatical evolution for the automatic synthesis of collective behaviors in swarm robotics, in *Genetic and Evolutionary Computation – GECCO* (ACM, New York, NY, 2013), pp. 17–24. https://doi.org/10.1145/2463372.2463385
28. E. Ferrante, A. Turgut, E. Duéñez-Guzmán, M. Dorigo, T. Wenseleers, Evolution of self-organized task specialization in robot swarms. PLoS Comput. Biol. **11**(8), e1004,273 (2015). https://doi.org/10.1371/journal.pcbi.1004273
29. D. Floreano, P. Husbands, S. Nolfi, Evolutionary robotics, in *Handbook of Robotics* (2008), pp. 1423–1451
30. G. Francesca, A modular approach to the automatic design of control software for robot swarms: from a novel perspective on the reality gap to AutoMoDe. Ph.D. thesis, Université libre de Bruxelles (2017)
31. G. Francesca, M. Birattari, Automatic design of robot swarms: achievements and challenges. Front. Robot. AI **3**(29), 1–9 (2016). https://doi.org/10.3389/frobt.2016.00029
32. G. Francesca, M. Brambilla, A. Brutschy, L. Garattoni, R. Miletitch, G. Podevijn, A. Reina, T. Soleymani, M. Salvaro, C. Pinciroli, M. Birattari, AutoMoDe-Chocolate: automatic design of control software for robot swarms. Swarm Intell. **9**(2/3), 125–152 (2015). https://doi.org/10.1007/s11721-015-0107-9
33. G. Francesca, M. Brambilla, A. Brutschy, L. Garattoni, R. Miletitch, G. Podevijn, A. Reina, T. Soleymani, M. Salvaro, C. Pinciroli, V. Trianni, M. Birattari, An experiment in automatic design of robot swarms: AutoMoDe-Vanilla, EvoStick, and human experts, in *Swarm Intelligence - ANTS*, vol. 8667. LNCS (Springer, Berlin, Germany, 2014), pp. 25–37
34. G. Francesca, M. Brambilla, A. Brutschy, V. Trianni, M. Birattari, AutoMoDe: a novel approach to the automatic design of control software for robot swarms. Swarm Intell. **8**(2), 89–112 (2014). https://doi.org/10.1007/s11721-014-0092-4
35. A. Franzin, T. Stützle, Revisiting simulated annealing: a component-based analysis. Comput. Oper. Res. **104**, 191–206 (2019). https://doi.org/10.1016/j.cor.2018.12.015

36. L. Garattoni, M. Birattari, Autonomous task sequencing in a robot swarm. Sci. Robot. **3**(20) (2018). https://doi.org/10.1126/scirobotics.aat0430
37. L. Garattoni, G. Francesca, A. Brutschy, C. Pinciroli, M. Birattari, Software infrastructure for e-puck (and TAM). Technical Report TR/IRIDIA/2015-004, IRIDIA, Université libre de Bruxelles, Belgium (2015)
38. S. Geman, E. Bienenstock, R. Doursat, Neural networks and the bias/variance dilemma. Neural Comput. **4**(1), 1–58 (1992)
39. J. Gomes, P. Urbano, A. Christensen, Evolution of swarm robotics systems with novelty search. Swarm Intell. **7**, 115–144 (2013). https://doi.org/10.1007/s11721-013-0081-z
40. Á. Gutiérrez, A. Campo, M. Dorigo, J. Donate, F. Monasterio-Huelin, L. Magdalena, Open e-puck range & bearing miniaturized board for local communication in swarm robotics, in *IEEE International Conference on Robotics and Automation, ICRA*, ed. by K. Kosuge (IEEE, Piscataway, NJ, 2009), pp. 3111–3116
41. E. Haasdijk, N. Bredeche, A. Eiben, Combining environment-driven adaptation and task-driven optimisation in evolutionary robotics. PloS ONE **9**(6), e98,466 (2014)
42. H. Hamann, H. Wörn, A framework of space-time continuous models for algorithm design in swarm robotics. Swarm Intell. **2**(2–4), 209–239 (2008). https://doi.org/10.1007/s11721-008-0015-3
43. I. Harvey, P. Husband, D. Cliff, A. Thompson, N. Jakobi, Evolutionary robotics: the Sussex approach. Robot. Auton. Syst. **20**(2), 205–224 (1997)
44. K. Hasselmann, F. Robert, M. Birattari, Automatic design of communication-based behaviors for robot swarms, in *Swarm Intelligence, ANTS*, vol. 11172. LNCS, ed. by M. Dorigo, et al. (Springer, Cham, Switzerland, 2018), pp. 16–29
45. S. Hauert, J.C. Zufferey, D. Floreano, Evolved swarming without positioning information: an application in aerial communication relay. Auton. Robots **26**(1), 21–32 (2009). https://doi.org/10.1007/s10514-008-9104-9
46. N. Jakobi, P. Husbands, I. Harvey, Noise and the reality gap: the use of simulation in evolutionary robotics. LNAI **929**, 704–720 (1995). https://doi.org/10.1007/3-540-59496-_337
47. S. Kazadi, Model independence in swarm robotics. Int. J. Intell. Comput. Cybern. **2**(4), 672–694 (2009). https://doi.org/10.1108/17563780911005836
48. L. König, S. Mostaghim, Decentralized evolution of robotic behavior using finite state machines. Int. J. Intell. Comput. Cybern. **2**(4), 695–723 (2009). https://doi.org/10.1108/17563780911005845
49. S. Koos, J.B. Mouret, S. Doncieux, The transferability approach: crossing the reality gap in evolutionary robotics. IEEE Trans. Evol. Comput. **17**(1), 122–145 (2013). https://doi.org/10.1109/TEVC.2012.2185849
50. J. Kuckling, A. Ligot, D. Bozhinoski, M. Birattari, Behavior trees as a control architecture in the automatic modular design of robot swarms, in *Swarm Intelligence – ANTS*, vol. 11172. LNCS (Springer, Cham, Switzerland, 2018), pp. 30–43. https://doi.org/10.1007/978-3-030-00533-7_3
51. J. Kuckling, K. Ubeda Arriaza, M. Birattari, Simulated annealing as an optimization algorithm in the automatic modular design of robot swarms, in *Proceedings of the Reference AI & ML Conference for Belgium, Netherlands & Luxemburg, BNAIC/BENELEARN 2019*, vol. 2491. CEUR Workshop Proceedings, ed. by K. Beuls, B. Bogaerts, G. Bontempi, P. Geurts, N. Harley, B. Lebichot, T. Lenaerts, G. Louppe, P.V. Eecke (CEUR-WS.org, Aachen, Germany, 2019)
52. J.B. Lee, R.C. Arkin, Adaptive multi-robot behavior via learning momentum, in *IEEE/RSJ International Conference on Intelligent Robots and Systems, IROS*, ed. by C.S. George Lee (IEEE, Piscataway, NJ, 2003), pp. 2029–2036
53. S. Li, R. Batra, D. Brown, H.D. Chang, N. Ranganathan, C. Hoberman, D. Rus, H. Lipson, Particle robotics based on statistical mechanics of loosely coupledÂ components. Nature **567**(7748), 361–365 (2019). https://doi.org/10.1038/s41586-019-1022-9
54. A. Ligot, M. Birattari, On mimicking the effects of the reality gap with simulation-only experiments, in *Swarm Intelligence – ANTS*, vol. 11172. LNCS (Springer, Cham, Switzerland, 2018), pp. 109–122. https://doi.org/10.1007/978-3-030-00533-7_9

55. A, Ligot, M. Birattari, Simulation-only experiments to mimic the effects of the reality gap in the automatic design of robot swarms. Swarm Intell. pp. 1–24 (2019). https://doi.org/10.1007/s11721-019-00175-w
56. H. Lipson, Evolutionary robotics and open-ended design automation. Biomimetics **17**, 129–155 (2005). https://doi.org/10.1201/9781420037715.ch4
57. Y.K. Lopes, S.M. Trenkwalder, A.B. Leal, T.J. Dodd, R. Groß, Supervisory control theory applied to swarm robotics. Swarm Intell. **10**(1), 65–97 (2016). https://doi.org/10.1007/s11721-016-0119-0
58. M. López-Ibáñez, J. Dubois-Lacoste, L. Pérez Cáceres, M. Birattari, T. Stützle, The irace package: iterated racing for automatic algorithm configuration. Oper. Res. Perspect. **3**, 43–58 (2016)
59. D. Marocco, S. Nolfi, Emergence of communication in embodied agents evolved for the ability to solve a collective navigation problem. Connect. Sci. **19**(1), 53–74 (2007). https://doi.org/10.1080/09540090601015067
60. F. Mondada, M. Bonani, X. Raemy, J. Pugh, C. Cianci, A. Klaptocz, S. Magnenat, J.C. Zufferey, D. Floreano, A. Martinoli, The e-puck, a robot designed for education in engineering, in *Proceedings of the 9th Conference on Autonomous Robot Systems and Competitions*, ed. by P. Gonçalves, P. Torres, C. Alves (Instituto Politécnico de Castelo Branco, Portugal, 2009), pp. 59–65
61. N. Morgan, H. Bourlard, Generalization and parameter estimation in feedforward nets: some experiments, in *Advances in Neural Information Processing Systems 2, NIPS 1990*, ed. by D.S. Touretzky (Morgan Kaufmann, San Francisco, 1990), pp. 630–637
62. S. Nolfi, D. Floreano, *Evolutionary Robotics* (MIT Press, Cambridge, MA, 2000)
63. J.N. Pereira, P. Silva, P.U. Lima, A. Martinoli, Formalizing institutions as executable petri nets for distributed robotic systems, in *Advances in Artificial Life, ECAL 2011*, ed. by T. Lenaerts, M. Giacobini, H. Bersini, P. Bourgine, M. Dorigo, R. Doursat (MIT Press, Cambridge, MA, 2011), pp. 646–653
64. C. Pinciroli, G. Beltrame, Buzz: a programming language for robot swarms. IEEE Softw. **33**, 97–100 (2016). https://doi.org/10.1109/MS.2016.95
65. L. Prechelt, Early stopping – but when?, in *Neural Networks: Tricks of the Trade*, vol. 7000, 2nd edn., LNCS, ed. by G. Montavon, G.B. Orr, K.R. Müller (Springer, Berlin, Heidelberg, 2012), pp. 53–67. https://doi.org/10.1007/978-3-642-35289-8_5
66. M. Quinn, L. Smith, G. Mayley, P. Husbands, Evolving controllers for a homogeneous system of physical robots: structured cooperation with minimal sensors. Philos. Trans. R. Soc. A **361**, 2321–43 (2003). https://doi.org/10.1098/rsta.2003.1258
67. A. Reina, G. Valentini, C. Fernàndez-Oto, M. Dorigo, V. Trianni, A design pattern for decentralised decision making. PLoS ONE **10**(10), e0140,950 (2015). https://doi.org/10.1371/journal.pone.0140950
68. A. Roli, M. Manfroni, C. Pinciroli, M. Birattari, On the design of boolean network robots, in *Applications of Evolutionary Computation*, vol. 6624/5. LNCS (Springer, Berlin, Germany, 2011), pp. 43–52. https://doi.org/10.1007/978-3-642-20525-5_5
69. M. Rubenstein, A. Cornejo, R. Nagpal, Programmable self-assembly in a thousand-robot swarm. Science **345**(6198), 795–799 (2014). https://doi.org/10.1126/science.1254295
70. M. Salman, A. Ligot, M. Birattari, Concurrent design of control software and configuration of hardware for robot swarms under economic constraints. PeerJ Comput. Sci. **5**, (2019). https://doi.org/10.7717/peerj-cs.221
71. C. Schlegel, A. Lotz, M. Lutz, D. Stampfer, J.F. Inglés-Romero, C. Vicente-Chicote, Model-driven software systems engineering in robotics: covering the complete life-cycle of a robot. It-Inf. Technol. **57**(2), 85–98 (2015). https://doi.org/10.1515/itit-2014-1069
72. F. Silva, M. Duarte, L. Correia, S. Oliveira, A. Christensen, Open issues in evolutionary robotics. Evol. Comput. **24**(2), 205–236 (2016). https://doi.org/10.1162/EVCO_a_00172
73. F. Silva, P. Urbano, L. Correia, A.L. Christensen, odNEAT: an algorithm for decentralised online evolution of robotic controllers. Evol. Comput. **23**(3), 421–449 (2015)

74. I. Slavkov, D. Carrillo-Zapata, N. Carranza, X. Diego, F. Jansson, J. Kaandorp, S. Hauert, J. Sharpe, Morphogenesis in robot swarms. Sci. Robot. **3**, 25 (2018). https://doi.org/10.1126/scirobotics.aau9178
75. G. Spaey, M. Kegeleirs, D. Garzón Ramos, M. Birattari, Comparison of different exploration schemes in the automatic modular design of robot swarms, in *Proceedings of the Reference AI & ML Conference for Belgium, Netherlands & Luxemburg, BNAIC/BENELEARN 2019*, vol. 2491. CEUR Workshop Proceedings, ed. by K. Beuls, B. Bogaerts, G. Bontempi, P. Geurts, N. Harley, B. Lebichot, T. Lenaerts, G. Louppe, P.V. Eecke (CEUR-WS.org, Aachen, Germany, 2019)
76. V. Trianni, *Evolutionary Swarm Robotics* (Springer, Berlin, Germany, 2008)
77. V. Trianni, Evolutionary robotics: model or design? Front. Robot. AI **1**, 13 (2014). https://doi.org/10.3389/frobt.2014.00013
78. V. Trianni, M. López-Ibáñez, Advantages of task-specific multi-objective optimisation in evolutionary robotics. PLoS ONE **10**(8), e0136,406 (2015). https://doi.org/10.1371/journal.pone.0136406
79. V. Trianni, S. Nolfi, Self-organizing sync in a robotic swarm: a dynamical system view. IEEE Trans. Evol. Comput. **13**(4), 722–741 (2009). https://doi.org/10.1109/TEVC.2009.2015577
80. E. Tuci, An investigation of the evolutionary origin of reciprocal communication using simulated autonomous agents. Biol. Cybern. **101**(3), 183–99 (2009). https://doi.org/10.1007/s00422-009-0329-2
81. M. Waibel, L. Keller, D. Floreano, Genetic team composition and level of selection in the evolution of multi-agent systems. IEEE Trans. Evol. Comput. **13**, 648–660 (2009). https://doi.org/10.1109/TEVC.2008.2011741
82. R. Watson, S.G. Ficici, J. Pollack, Embodied evolution: distributing an evolutionary algorithm in a population of robots. Robot. Auton. Syst. **39**, 1–18 (2002). https://doi.org/10.1016/S0921-8890(02)00170-7
83. J. Werfel, K. Petersen, R. Nagpal, Designing collective behavior in a termite-inspired robot construction team. Science **343**(6172), 754–758 (2014). https://doi.org/10.1126/science.1245842
84. A. Winfield, M. Erbas, On embodied memetic evolution and the emergence of behavioural traditions in robots. Memetic Comput. **3**(4), 261–270 (2011). https://doi.org/10.1007/s12293-011-0063-x
85. D. Wolpert, On bias plus variance. Neural Comput. **9**, 1211–1243 (1997). https://doi.org/10.1162/neco.1997.9.6.1211
86. H. Xie, M. Sun, X. Fan, Z. Lin, W. Chen, L. Wang, L. Dong, Q. He, Reconfigurable magnetic microrobot swarm: Multimode transformation, locomotion, and manipulation. Sci. Robot. **4**(28) (2019). https://doi.org/10.1126/scirobotics.aav8006
87. G.Z. Yang, J. Bellingham, P.E. Dupont, P. Fischer, L. Floridi, R. Full, N. Jacobstein, V. Kumar, M. McNutt, R. Merrifield, B. Nelson, B. Scassellati, M. Taddeo, R. Taylor, M. Veloso, Z. Lin Wang, R. Wood, The grand challenges of science robotics. Sci. Robot. **3**(14), eaar7650 (2018). https://doi.org/10.1126/scirobotics.aar7650
88. J. Yu, B. Wang, X. Du, Q. Wang, L. Zhang, Ultra-extensible ribbon-like magnetic microswarm. Nat. Commun. **9**, 1 (2018). https://doi.org/10.1038/s41467-018-05749-6

Chapter 6
A Cross-Domain Method for Generation of Constructive and Perturbative Heuristics

Christopher Stone, Emma Hart, and Ben Paechter

Abstract Hyper-heuristic frameworks, although intended to be cross-domain at the highest level, usually rely on a set of domain-specific low-level heuristics which exist below the domain-barrier and are manipulated by the hyper-heuristic itself. However, for some domains, the number of available heuristics can be very low, while for novel problems, no heuristics might exist at all. We address this issue by describing two general methods for the automated production of constructive and perturbative low-level heuristics. Grammatical evolution is used to evolve low-level heuristics that operate on an "intermediate" graph-based representation built over partial permutations. As the same grammar can be applied to multiple application domains, assuming they follow this representation, the grammar can be viewed as a cross-domain. The method is evaluated on two domains to indicate generality (the Travelling Salesman Problem and Multidimensional Knapsack Problem). Empirical results indicate that the approach can generate both constructive and perturbative heuristics that outperform well-known heuristic methods in a number of cases and are competitive with specialised methods for some instances.

6.1 Introduction

Hyper-heuristics, "heuristics to choose heuristics", were first introduced in an attempt to raise the generality at which search methodologies operate [4], searching over the space of solvers rather than solutions (as in typical meta-heuristics). Their development was motivated by a desire to produce a method that was cheaper to implement

C. Stone (✉)
University of St Andrews, St Andrews, Scotland
e-mail: cls29@st-andrews.ac.uk

E. Hart · B. Paechter
Edinburgh Napier University, Edinburgh, Scotland
e-mail: e.hart@napier.ac.uk

B. Paechter
e-mail: b.paechter@napier.ac.uk

N. Pillay and R. Qu (eds.), *Automated Design of Machine Learning and Search Algorithms*, Natural Computing Series,
https://doi.org/10.1007/978-3-030-72069-8_6

and easier to use than problem-specific, customised methods while producing solutions of acceptable quality to an end-user in an appropriate time-frame. Specifically, it aimed to address a concern that the practical impact of search-based optimisation techniques in commercial and industrial organisations had not been as great as might have been expected, due to the prevalence of problem-specific or knowledge-intensive techniques, which were inaccessible to the non-expert or expensive to implement.

The canonical hyper-heuristic framework introduces a *domain-barrier* that separates a general algorithm to choose heuristics from a set of low-level heuristics that are specific to a domain, i.e. a particular application class of problem such as bin packing or vehicle routing. The over-riding idea is that switching domains only require a change in the set of low-level heuristics, with no change to the controlling high-level hyper-heuristic. Clearly, the success of the high-level heuristic is strongly influenced by the number and the quality of the low-level heuristics available. Low-level heuristics incorporating problem-specific knowledge are often designed by hand, relying on intuition or human-expertise [4]. In general, they are also tied to a specific problem representation, given that they either modify an existing solution (in the case of perturbative heuristics) or create a solution from scratch (in the case of constructive heuristics). Therefore, it is unlikely that low-level heuristics from one domain transfer well (or at all) to another. As a result, when tackling a new domain, a new low-level heuristic set for the domain must be created. This can be often supplied by experts, or in cases where no heuristics are available, it has been shown that new heuristics can be evolved, for example using Genetic Programming (GP) [2]. However, the latter approach requires an in-depth understanding of a domain in order to select appropriate function and terminal nodes that can be used by the genetic programming algorithm to evolve a heuristic. As such, although at a conceptual level, GP can be used to evolve heuristics for any domain, it has to be individually customised to a domain each time it is used.

For new problem domains that do not map well to well-studied domains in the literature, developing an appropriate set of low-level heuristics remains a challenging problem. In this study, we aim to address this challenge by introducing a method of creating new heuristics that is *cross-domain* in the sense that the *generating* method can be used without modification to create heuristics in multiple domains; the heuristics created as a result, however, are specialised to an individual domain. In other words, we describe a cross-domain generation method of generating domain-specific heuristics.

A cross-domain generation approach must necessarily utilise a common problem representation. We adopt a graph-based representation as it enables a broad spectrum of practical problems to be represented. While this includes obvious applications such as routing and scheduling [26] which have natural representations as graphs, it can also be applied in many less obvious ones including packing problems [22] and utility maximisation in complex negotiations [24] through appropriate manipulation.

We describe two approaches that use grammatical-evolution to generate low-level heuristics for any domain that is represented in a graph form. Each method can be used *without modification* to generate heuristics for multiple domains. The first approach generates constructive heuristics while the second uses a modified version of the grammar to generate perturbative heuristics. The research lays the foundation for a paradigm shift in designing heuristics for combinatorial optimisation domains in which no heuristics currently exist or those domains in which hyper-heuristic methods would benefit from additional low-level heuristics. The approach significantly reduces the burden on human experts, as it only requires that the problem can be represented as a graph, with no further specialisation, and does not require a large database of training examples. The method is not expected to compete with domain-specific approaches that have been customised to the idiosyncrasies of a given domain; rather it is intended as a straightforward way of creating new heuristics that have acceptable performance when no other heuristics are available and the expert knowledge need to create them is lacking. The vast majority of hyper-heuristic research is focussed on generating algorithms that operate above the domain-barrier—in keeping with the original philosophy of creating generalised methods. In contrast, our approach operates "under" the domain-barrier. However, in keeping with the spirit of hyper-heuristics, our approach is also generalisable, in being able to create low-level heuristics for a diverse range of domains.

The article provided brings together research previously described in detail in [29, 30]. It provides a synthesised overview of the previous work, while providing some examples of results selected from the original papers to illustrate the salient points. The reader is referred to the original papers for more complete results and more detailed description of the methods.

6.2 Related Work

While the majority of initial work in the field of hyper-heuristics focussed on development of the high-level controlling heuristics [4], more recent attention has focussed on the role of the low-level heuristics themselves. Low-level heuristics fall into two categories [4]. *Constructive* heuristics build a solution from scratch, adding an element at a time, e.g. [26] and have been applied in a variety of domains such as personnel scheduling, job-shop problem [31], education timetabling [23] and packing [27]. On the other hand, *perturbative* heuristics modify an existing solution, e.g. re-ordering elements in a permutation [7] or modifying genes [4].

Typical methods to generate constructive heuristics include Genetic Programming (GP) [16] and Grammatical Evolution (GE) [20]. GP constructs trees that, for example, output a number representing an item priority, e.g. for vehicle routing [26], job-shop scheduling [12] and TSP [14]. GE is a form of grammar-based genetic programming developed for the automatic generation of programs. Different from GP, it does not apply the evolutionary process directly to a program but on a variable length genome. A mapping process then turns the genome into a program by following grammar rules specified using Backus Naur Form [20]. This approach ensures the creation of syntactically correct programs that then are executed and their fitness function evaluated. GE has already been applied to construct heuristics for the capacitated vehicle routing problem and for the bin packing problem [25]. With respect to generation of *perturbative* heuristics, GP approaches are also common, e.g. for generating novel local-search heuristics for satisfiability testing [4]. Grammatical Evolution was applied to evolve new local-search heuristics for 1d-bin packing in [4, 18].

Despite some success in the areas just described, we note that in each case, the function and terminal nodes used in GP or the grammar specification in GE are specifically tailored to a single domain. While clearly specialisation is likely to be beneficial, it can require significant expertise and investment in algorithm design. For a practitioner, such knowledge is unlikely to be available, and for new domains, this may be time-consuming even for an expert. Therefore, we are motivated to design a general-purpose method that is capable—without modification—of producing heuristics in multiple domains. While we do not expect such a generator to compete with specialised heuristics or meta-heuristics, we evaluate whether the approach can be used as a "quick and dirty" method of generating a heuristic that produces an acceptable quality solution in multiple domains.

6.3 Evaluation Domains and Their Representation as Graphs

In the proposed system, we encode all the properties of the problems into a graph embedded in some arbitrary space. Whenever possible, we convert properties into some spatial concept to which we can associate some arbitrary metric. We select two evaluation domains. The first is the *Travelling Salesman Problem* (TSP) [17], one of the most studied problems in combinatorial optimisation, in which a tour passing through exactly n points once must be *minimised*. Due to the fact that it is naturally encoded as an ordering problem represented by a graph in which the cities to visit can be trivially encoded as vertices in 2-D Euclidean space, it provides a straightforward baseline for our experiments. The second domain chosen is the *Multidimensional Knapsack Problem* (MKP). This is also well studied with applications in budgeting, packing and cutting problems. In the typical version, the profit from items selected among a collection must be *maximised* while respecting the constraints of a knapsack. In contrast to TSP, knapsack solvers do not typically use a graph-based representation of the problem [6]. However, it can be re-represented in a graph-based formulation as follows.

Assume there is one vertex corresponding to each object and one vertex for the knapsack. The properties of the vertex can be interpreted as coordinates that determine the location of the vertices in some constraint-profit space. A geometric interpretation of the problem can be intuitively described as follows: when an object is chosen (connected to the knapsack vertex), the properties of the object are added to the knapsack and it is moved in the constraint-profit space. The amount of motion is equal to the values of the object's vector in constraint space and in the direction of

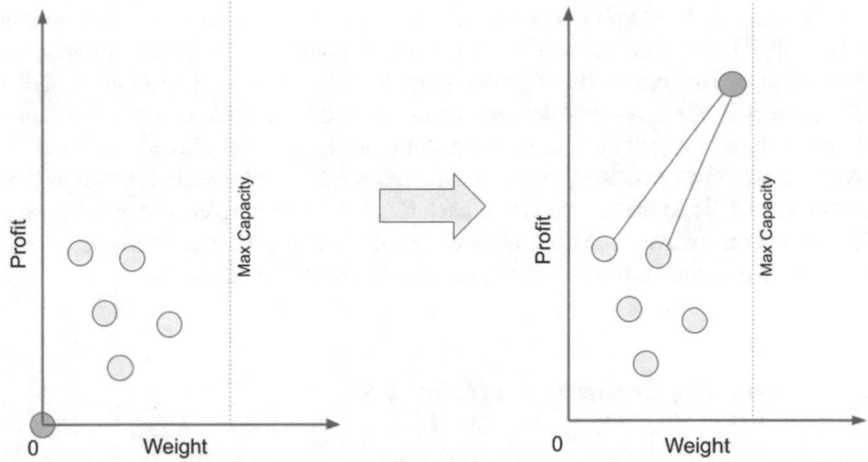

Fig. 6.1 Geometric interpretation of the knapsack problem simplified to two dimensions (weight constraint and profit). On the left, the knapsack at initialisation has 0 weight and 0 profit. As objects are connected to the knapsack, it is moved of an amount equivalent to the vectors defined by the sum of the objects

the profit space. The configuration of objects connected to the knapsack that move the knapsack the furthest in profit space without the knapsack crossing the line corresponding to its maximum capacity in any of its constraint dimensions is the best configuration. An example with just one constraint (weight) is drawn in Fig. 6.1.

6.4 Using Grammatical Evolution to Evolve Low-Level Heuristics

Grammatical Evolution [19], is a population-based approach developing a program through manipulating an integer string (the genotype) which is subsequently mapped to a program (or similar) through the use of a grammar. Given a grammar defined in Backus Naur Form (BNF) containing a terminal Set $< T >$, a non-terminal set $< N >$ and a set of production rules $< P >$ and a start point, an integer sequence can be used to specify a program (a function) by selecting production rules and their expansions (see [19] for a full description). The role of the evolutionary process is then to search the space of integers to find a suitable program.

Here we use the PonyGE3[1] Python implementation of GE [10] to evolve grammars that create constructive and perturbative heuristics. This uses a linear genome representation encoding a list of integers (codons). The mapping between the genotype and the phenotype is actuated by the use of the modulus operator on the value

[1] https://github.com/PonyGE/PonyGE2.

of the codon, i.e. *Selected node* $= c \bmod n$, where c is the integer value of the codon to be mapped and n is the number of options available in the specific production rule. Offsprings are created through one-point crossover followed by a mutation that substitutes a single randomly selected codon with a new, randomly chosen value. Then we employ a generational replacement strategy with the elitism of size 1. To evolve constructive heuristics, we use a grammar rich in geometric operations that allows a heuristic to make a choice at each step based on measures over the graph. To evolve perturbative heuristics, we use a grammar that performs three operations: cuts, inversions and permutations. These are described in detail below.

6.4.1 Evolving Constructive Heuristics

To evolve a new constructive heuristic that builds a solution from scratch, GE is used to evolve a ranking function that ranks candidate vertices. The ranking function is iteratively applied to select the next vertex to be added to the partial solution. Assuming there are n available vertices for a domain, then in the TSP case, exactly $k = n$ vertices must be selected, while in the knapsack domain, $k < n$ are selected.

In the case of a TSP solution, each successive vertex defines the next city to visit. In the case of MKP, each successive vertex of the chain is used to select the next item to be placed in the knapsack as shown in Fig. 6.2.

The set of production rules used is given in Fig. 6.3. Definitions of the terminal nodes used to define nodes can be found in [28]. Note that the same *grammar* is used to generate constructive heuristics for both the TSP and Knapsack domains.

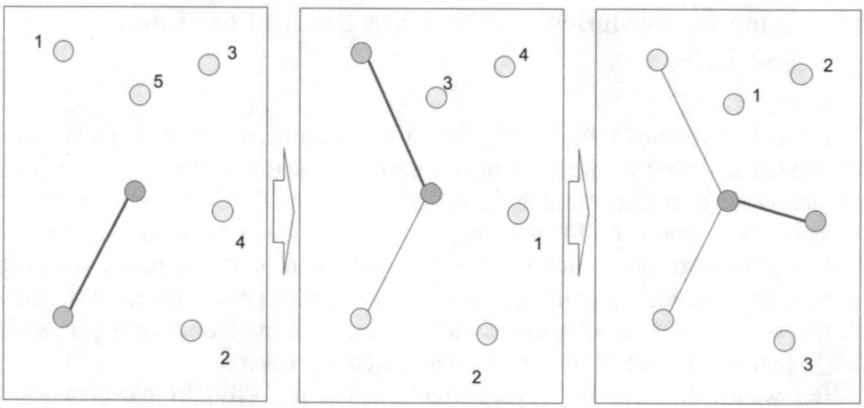

Fig. 6.2 Constructing a solution for the MKP. Blue node is the knapsack. Green node is the last appended vertex

```
<exp> → <exp><arithmetic_op><exp> |
        protected_division(<exp>,<exp>) |
        root(<exp>) |
        log(<exp>) |
        <c><c>.<c><c>|
        <trig> |
        <graph_function> |
        <info> |
        <constant>
<c> →   0 | 1 | 2 | 3 | 4 | 5 | 6 | 7 | 8 | 9
<arithmetic_op>  → + | * | -
<trig> → sine(<exp>) |
         cosine(<exp>) |
         tangent(<exp>)

<graph_function> → distance(vertex, <metric>) |
                   kd_angle_leg(vertex) |
                   estimated_graph_complexity |
                   hull_area
                   longest_edge |
                   distance_to_v0(vertex, <metric>) |
                   vec_max(<vector>) |
                   vec_min(<vector>) |
                   elements_sum(<vector>)
<vector>   →   v0_difference(vertex) |
               chain_delta_vectorsum |
               v0
<metric>   →   euclidean | cosine distance
<constant> →   π | ε
<info>     →   chain_length | vertices_num
```

Fig. 6.3 Complete grammar for generation of *constructive* heuristics

6.4.2 Evolving Perturbative Heuristics

In this case, we use GE to evolve a Python program that takes a sequence (i.e. a permutation) as an input and returns a modified version of the same sequence (permutation) with the same length. The production rules of the grammar are shown in Fig. 6.4. As above, the PonyGE2 implementation is used to evolve a program,

```
<op>                 →   addCut(<loci_ref>,<distance>)
                         <c>
                         <ExtraCuts>
                         Iteration_effect(<motion>,<loci_computation>)
                         permutation(<perm_behaviour>)
                         inversions(<inv_behaviour>)
<ExtraCuts>          →   ∅ | <c> | <c><c> | <c><c><c>
<c>                  →   addCut(<loci_ref>,<distance>)
                         isInverted(<invert>)
                         permutationFactor(<r>)
<motion>             →   'random' | 'oscillate' | 'steps' | 'none'
<loci_ref>           →   'none' | 'left' | 'right' | 'limit'
<distance>           →   'linear' | 'negative_binomial',(<r>,<p>)
<r>                  →   1 | 2 | 3 | 4 | 5 | 6 | 7 | 8 | 9 | 10
<p>                  →   0.1 | 0.2 | 0.3 | 0.4 | 0.5 | 0.6 | 0.7
<loci_computation>   →   'once' | 'always'
<perm_behaviour>     →   'fixed' | 'random'
<inv_behaviour>      →   'fixed' | 'random'
<invert>             →   0 | 1
```

Fig. 6.4 Complete grammar for generation of *perturbative* heuristics which in this case modifies an existing solution. Definitions of the terminal nodes used in the production rules can be found in [30].

The operator constructed by the grammar can be thought of as a form of k-opt [13] that is configurable and includes extra functions that determine where to break a sequence. However, the formulation and implementation are *vertex* centric rather than *edge* centric. The mechanics of the algorithm are as follows:

Number of cuts: This determines in how many places a sequence will be cut creating $(k-1)$ subsequences where k is the number of cuts. The number of possible loci of the cuts is equal to $n+1$, where n is the number of vertices (the sequence can be cut both before the first element and after the last element).

Location of cuts: The grammar associates a strategy to each cut that will determine the location of the specific cut. A strategy may contain a reference location such as the ends of the sequence or subsequence, a specific place in the sequences or a random location. The reference can be used together with a probability distribution that determines the chances of any given location to be the place of the next cut. These probability distributions *de facto* regulate the length of each subsequence. Two probability distributions can be selected by the grammar: a discretised triangular distribution and a negative binomial distribution. An example can be seen in Fig. 6.5a, b.

After the cutting phase, the subsequences are given symbols with S being always the leftmost subsequence and E being the rightmost subsequence such as in Fig. 6.5c. The start and end sequences (S, E) are never altered by the evolved operator which

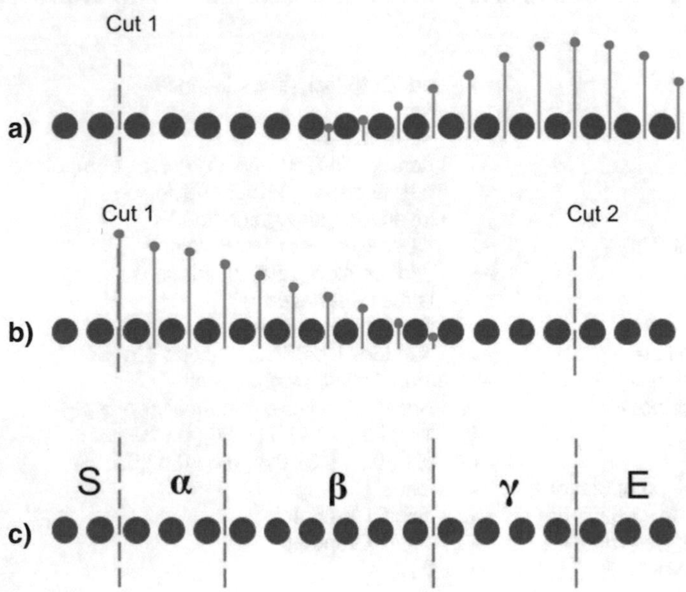

Fig. 6.5 **a** Example of a sequence with one cut and a probability mass function that will decide the loci of the second cut. **b** Both cuts now shown **c** Final set of subsequences after k-cuts

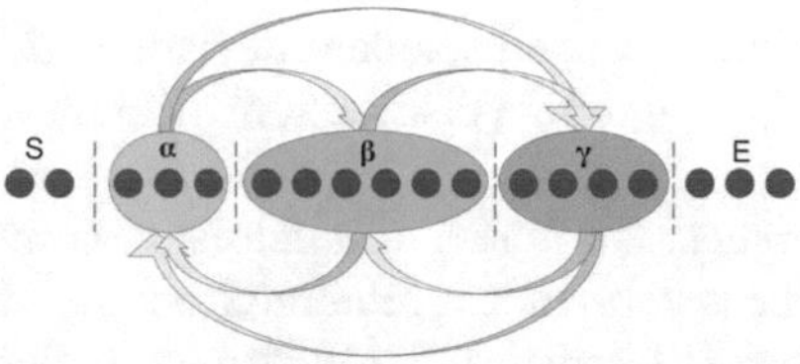

(a) Subsequence permutation

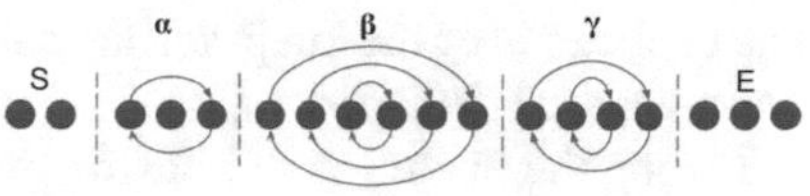

(b) Subsequence inversion

Fig. 6.6 Example perturbations of the subsequences produced by the grammar

only acts on the sequences labelled α-β in Fig. 6.5c. Note that subsequences may be empty. This can happen if the leftmost cut is on the left of the first element (leaving S empty), if the rightmost cut is after the last element (leaving E empty) or if two different cuts are applied in the same place.

Permutation of the subsequence: After cutting the sequence ,the subsequences become the units of a new sequence. The grammar can specify if the subsequence will be reordered to a specific permutation (including the identity, i.e. no change) or to a random permutation. An example can be seen in Fig. 6.6a.

6.5 Methodology

We conduct experiments in the two domains described above. An experiment consists of two phases: a *training* phase in which GE is used to evolve a heuristic on a small training set of randomly generated instances. This is followed by a *test* phase in which heuristics evolved from multiple runs of the GE algorithm are evaluated on a test set of benchmark instances taken from the literature. The next two sections describe the procedures by which the training data is generated for both constructive and perturbative approaches and provide the details of the experimental setup in each case.

6.5.1 Training Phase

A set of 10 random instances is synthesised in order to train the heuristic generator in each case. The reader is referred to [29, 30] for an exact description of each synthesiser and the associated parameters in each domain; however, a brief outline is repeated here.

For TSP, a set of instances each containing n cities are generated using a uniform-random distribution on a 2-D plane. For MKP, instances have m objects with k constraints each. Each constraint is a sample from a uniform-random distribution with a specified range o. The profits of each object are taken from a normal distribution with a mean equal to the sum of the constraints and fixed standard deviation sd_p. The constraints of the knapsack are sampled from a normal distribution[2] with mean c and standard deviation sd_c.

During the evolution of constructive heuristics, the fitness of a heuristic on the training set in both domains is calculated as the *median* fitness returned from the set of training instances. When evolving perturbative heuristics, the fitness evaluation consists of applying the heuristics as the move-operator within a hill-climbing algorithm to each of the training instances starting from an randomly initialised solution. The hill-climber runs for x iterations with an improvement-only acceptance criteria. The fitness at the end-point is averaged over the 5 instances and assigned to the heuristic.

All experiments are repeated in each domain 10 times, with a new set of training instances generated for each run. All parameters of the PonyGE algorithm to evolve the heuristics using the specified grammars can be found in [29, 30]. The best performing heuristic from each run is retained, creating an ensemble of 10 heuristics as a result to be used in the test phase.

6.5.2 Test Phase

For the purposes of evaluating the evolved heuristics, we select an indicative set of benchmarks from each domain. The evolved heuristics are compared to well-known approaches from the literature in each case. The work in [29, 30] provides extensive evaluation results over large numbers of benchmarks. In this chapter for clarity, we select representative results for presentation.

In the TSP domain, we provide results on 5 benchmarks instances taken from the TSPLib.[3] In the case of *constructive* heuristics, we compare results to the known optimal, as well as two well-known constructive heuristics from the literature, the nearest-neighbour heuristic [17] and the MST heuristic [17]. Both these heuristics are deterministic. For evaluation of the perturbative heuristics, we use the same instances and compare them to the best known perturbative heuristic 2-opt [8], using the R TSPLIB implementation.[4] As this is a stochastic method, it is repeated 50 times.

In the MKP domain, constructive heuristics are compared to a greedy depth first search algorithm [15] which also constructs solutions. As the vast majority of published results in this domain use meta-heuristic approaches, there are no obvious heuristic methods to use a comparison. Therefore, we compare with two meta-heuristic approaches from [5], the Chaotic Binary Particle Swarm Optimisation with Time-Varying Acceleration Coefficient (CBPSO) and an improved version of this algorithm that includes a self-adaptive check and repair operator (SACRO CBPSO),

---

[2] We recognise that real-instances are unlikely to be uniformly distributed: our implementation therefore represents the worst-case scenario in which the system can be evolved.

[3] http://comopt.ifi.uni-heidelberg.de/software/TSPLIB95/.

[4] https://cran.r-project.org/web/packages/TSP/TSP.pdf.

the most recent and highest-performing methods in MKP optimisation. Both algorithms use problem-specific knowledge: a penalty function in the former, and a utility ratio estimation function in the latter, with a binary representation for their solution. Both are allocated a considerably larger evaluation budget than our experiments. The heuristics evolved using our approach would not be expected to outperform these approaches—however, we wish to investigate whether the approach can produce solutions within a reasonable range of known optima that would be acceptable to a practitioner requiring a quick solution.

In all testing experiments, the 10 heuristics in the ensemble created in the training phase are applied to each test instance. In the constructive case, each heuristic is applied once to each test instance to construct a solution. In the perturbative domain, each of the 10 evolved heuristics are applied 5 times to a randomly initialised solution using an improvement-only acceptance criteria (hill-climber). We record the average performance of each heuristic over 5 runs, as well as the best and the worst. These values were selected following a minimal amount of empirical investigation, motivated by the desire to develop a system that could quickly generate a set of new heuristics (hence the choice of a small ensemble) and quickly provide a reasonable estimate of heuristic fitness (hence a small number of replications).

6.6 Results

We present the results first for the experiments in which constructive heuristics were evolved, followed by those for the evolution of perturbative heuristics. Recall from above that two grammars are specified, one for constructive heuristics and one for perturbative heuristics. The constructive grammar is used without modification to generate heuristics for two distinct domains (TSP and MKP). Similarly, the perturbative grammar is also used without modification in both domains.

6.6.1 Constructive Heuristics

The results in Table 6.1 show a comparison of the best, worse and median fitness of the evolved heuristics on each of the TSP test instances. As explained above, these are compared to the deterministic values obtained from a single run of the human-designed heuristics. The best evolved heuristic is better than both human heuristics in all 5 cases, while in 3 out of 5 instances, the median performance of the evolved heuristics is better than both the simple human heuristics.

The results for the MKP tests are shown in Table 6.2 which compares the performance of the evolved heuristics to a greedy constructive heuristic (run 10 times), where the heuristic tries to fit each object in the knapsack if there is sufficient space using a different ordering each time and to random construction. The best of evolved heuristics outperforms the greedy (deterministic) heuristic in 4 out of 7 instances. It

Table 6.1 Results obtained from generating reusable constructive heuristics for the TSP domain

Instance name	Optima	NN	MST	Constructive-GE		
				Median	Best	Worst
berlin52	7542	8868	10404	9196	**8452**	*10515*
ch130	6110	7575	8277	**7501**	**6942**	*8469*
eil101	629	826	846	**803**	**736**	897
eil51	426	521	605	547	**451**	*620*
eil76	538	700	739	**652**	**603**	678

Table 6.2 Results obtained from generating reusable constructive heuristics for the MKP domain

Instance	optima	Rand			Greedy			Constructive-GE		
		Worst	Median	Best	Worst	Median	Best	Worst	Median	Best
mknap1-1	3800	100	1700	3100	1200	2700	**3800**	**1800**	**3300**	**3800**
mknap1-2	8706.1	1482.1	5059	8687.5	4340.7	6504.8	8650.1	4212.4	**7059.8**	**8706.1**
mknap1-3	4015	985	2235	2860	1895	**3325**	**3765**	**2390**	2480	3725
mknap1-4	6120	1320	3240	5820	2460	**3525**	5390	**2480**	3020	**5640**
mknap1-5	12400	3770	7770	10340	**7590**	**8990**	**11550**	6855	8150	10510
mknap1-6	10618	4286	6566	9770	**7400**	**8032**	**10345**	7238	7641	9352
mknap1-7	16537	5661	9509	12769	**8770**	**12363**	15330	8335	10887	**15668**

is also of note that in 2 cases, the global optima is obtained by the best heuristics. The worst performing evolved heuristics outperform the greedy heuristic in 3 out of 7 instances. Statistical analysis using a Wilcoxon rank test fails to reject the null hypothesis that constructiveGE produces the same results as the greedy construction method at a significance level of 0.05 for all instances.

6.7 Results: Perturbative Heuristics

Table 6.3 shows the best, worst and median performance of the evolved heuristics and the two-opt-based algorithm for TSP. The median result obtained by the evolved heuristic improved on 2-opt in each case, with the evolved heuristics finding the best single result on 4 out of 5 instances. A Wilcoxon Rank sum test applied to compare the two treatments on each instance enables us to reject the null hypothesis in each case, i.e. improvements are statistically significant at the 5% level.

In Table 6.4, we present results in the MKP instances. The table compares the Average Success Rate (ASR) across all instances grouped by dataset against the results presented by [5] on 2 versions of SACRO algorithms and an additional fish-swarm method. The results given in the table are taken directly from this paper. In [5], ASR is calculated as the number of times the global optima was found for each instance divided by the number of trials. For *perturbativeGE*, we define a trial as

Table 6.3 Results obtained from generating perturbative heuristics for use in the TSP domain

	perturbativeGE			2-opt			Rank sum p-value
	Best	**Worst**	**Median**	**Best**	**Worst**	**Median**	
berlin52	7793	8825	**8170**	**7741**	9388	8310	0.0033
ch130	**6418**	7108	**6722**	6488	7444	6984	0.0030
eil101	**674**	739	**702**	680	749	709	0.0073
eil51	**435**	484	**456**	442	494	473	$\ll 0.001$
eil76	**563**	616	**593**	583	628	611	$\ll 0.001$

Table 6.4 Comparison of results obtained from the perturbativeGE algorithm with the latest specialised meta-heuristics from the literature: a fish-swarm algorithm IbAFSA and the two most recent SACRO algorithms, results taken directly from [5]. *na* indicates that no results were provided in [5] on this dataset

Problem set	Instances	Average success rate			
		IbAFSA	BPSO–TVAC	CBPSO–TVAC	**perturbativeGE**
Sento	2	1.000	0.9100	0.9100	0.90
Weing	8	0.7875	0.7825	0.7838	0.80
Weish	30	0.9844	0.9450	0.9520	0.907
Hp	2	0.9833	0.8000	0.8600	1.00
Pb	6	1.000	0.9617	0.9517	0.967
Pet	6	*na*	*na*	*na*	1.00

successful if at least one of the 10 heuristics found the optima in the trial and repeat this 5 times. Despite the fact that our new perturbative heuristics have no domain-specific information and are simplistic compared to the specialised methods we compare to, it can be seen that the results are comparable to those of specialised algorithms. In fact, perturbativeGE outperforms the specialised methods on the Weing dataset.

6.8 Discussion

In this article, we set out a method of tackling the issue of generating new low-level heuristics that could be used across the domain-barrier in a hyper-heuristic. Unlike previous approaches to low-level heuristic generation that are customised to a particular domain, the results presented above show that a *single grammar* can be used to generate heuristics for two different domains, without modification.[5]

[5] Note that different grammars are required depending on whether one wishes to generate constructive or perturbative heuristics.

```
a) psqrt(distance_to_v0(vertex,'cosine'))-
sin(plog(exp(distance_osms(vertex,'cosine'))))

b)distance_osms(vertex,'euclidean')-
exp(cos(distance_to_v0(vertex,'euclidean')))
```

Fig. 6.7 Examples of evolved constructive heuristics for **a** MKP and **b** TSP domain. Each heuristic returns a priority for a vertex; the vertex with the highest priority is chosen. For example, the MKP heuristic is interpreted as '*The priority of the current vertex is equal to the root of the cosine distance between the current vertex and the container vertex minus the sine of the distance between the last vertex of the chain and the current vertex*', etc

This is made possible by assuming a common representation of a problem, in this case as a graph. While this may appear somewhat restrictive, it is clear that many practical problems can be represented in this form. In fact several renowned industrial applications have used graph representations such as Google's page rank algorithm [21], Amazon and Netflix recommendation system [3], Drug Discovery [1], General Electric's power distribution system [9] and GSM mobile phone network frequency assignment [11].

Motivated by the general challenge of designing heuristics for new domains in which few examples of instances are available, we trained the two heuristic generators (one for constructive heuristics, one for perturbative heuristics) on very small training sets containing randomly synthesised instances. Despite this, the evolved heuristics are shown capable of outperforming well-known simple heuristics on many benchmark instances in the TSP domain and finding comparable results to specialised meta-heuristics in the MKP domain. Therefore, it is reasonable to consider the method *cross-domain* for the set of problem domains that can be represented in graph form. The grammar used to evolve the heuristics is exclusively composed of geometric properties and functions that are not tied to any specific problem domain, and we only implement graph-manipulation techniques. Figure 6.7 shows examples of a constructive heuristic evolved in each of the two domains that returns a priority for each vertex (with the highest priority vertex then being added to the solution). The heuristics exploit the geometric properties of the graphs. For instance, in the MKP domain, the *cosine* distance appears in 97% of evolved heuristics with the *Euclidean* distance measure only appearing in 17%: in contrast, in TSP, the *Euclidean* distance metric appears in 100% of evolved heuristics, with the *cosine* metric only appearing in 12%.

Clearly, there remains considerable scope for training using much larger instance sets or non-random instances. In this respect, our results are representative of the worst-case performance of the system. As noted at the start, the motivation behind the research is not to develop heuristics that outperform very specialised methods—

there will always be a trade-off between specialist and generalist heuristics in terms of performance. However, to be useful, heuristics should have acceptable performance. The results presented clearly demonstrate that this is the case.

6.9 Conclusion

The article has presented a method that demonstrates it is possible to go below the hyper-heuristic domain-barrier and use a cross-domain grammar, without modification, to generate new heuristics for each of two separate domains. The generation method is cross-domain, while the heuristics it produces are specialised to each individual domain considered. The article synthesises previous work which was reported in [29, 30] where expanded results and analysis can be found. Given that a graph-based representation enables a rich and diverse set of application domains to be represented, the approach augments existing hyper-heuristic methods, particularly in being able to provide a source of low-level heuristics for new types of problem classes for which low-level heuristics are unavailable. Importantly, it removes the need for expertise in either heuristic design or the domain itself. While of course domain-expertise will result in the creation of high-quality heuristics, we have demonstrated that in fact our approach is able to generate high-performing heuristics that are comparable to (and occasionally better than) existing methods.

Many improvements are possible to the method itself. This includes expanding the components of the grammar that currently uses only a fraction of the possible geometric information derivable from a graph and extensive tuning of the parameters of the approach. The ability to generate new heuristics for a domain also opens up the ability of improving existing hyper-heuristic methods that operate *above* the domain-barrier by extending the set of heuristics available for selection.

References

1. J.M. Amigó, J. Gálvez, V.M. Villar, A review on molecular topology: applying graph theory to drug discovery and design. Naturwissenschaften (2009)
2. M. Bader-El-Den, R. Poli, Generating sat local-search heuristics using a gp hyper-heuristic framework, in *International Conference on Artificial Evolution (Evolution Artificielle)* (Springer, 2007), pp. 37–49
3. T. Bogers, Movie recommendation using random walks over the contextual graph, in *Proceedings of the 2nd International Workshop on Context-Aware* (2010)
4. E.K. Burke, M. Gendreau, M. Hyde, G. Kendall, G. Ochoa, E. Özcan, R. Qu, Hyper-heuristics: a survey of the state of the art. J. Oper. Res. Soc. **64**(12), 1695–1724 (2013)
5. M. Chih, Self-adaptive check and repair operator-based particle swarm optimization for the multidimensional knapsack problem. Appl. Soft Comput. **26**, 378–389 (2015)
6. P.C. Chu, J.E. Beasley, A genetic algorithm for the multidimensional knapsack problem. J. Heuristics **4**(1), 63–86 (1998)

7. P. Cowling, G. Kendall, E. Soubeiga, A hyperheuristic approach to scheduling a sales summit, in *International Conference on the Practice and Theory of Automated Timetabling* (Springer, 2000), pp. 176–190
8. G.A. Croes, A method for solving traveling-salesman problems. Oper. Res. **6**(6), 791–812 (1958)
9. O.I. Elgerd, H.H. Happ, Electric Energy Systems Theory: An Introduction. IEEE Transactions on Systems, Man, and (1972)
10. M. Fenton, J. McDermott, D. Fagan, S. Forstenlechner, E. Hemberg, M. O'Neill, PonyGE2, in *Proceedings of the Genetic and Evolutionary Computation Conference Companion on - GECCO '17* (ACM Press, New York, New York, USA, 3 2017), pp. 1194–1201
11. A. Gamst, Application of graph theoretical methods to GSM radio network planning, in *Circuits and Systems, 1991., IEEE International* (1991)
12. E. Hart, K. Sim, A hyper-heuristic ensemble method for static job-shop scheduling. Evol. Comput. **24**(4), 609–635 (2016)
13. K. Helsgaun, General k-opt submoves for the lin-kernighan tsp heuristic. Math. Program. Comput. **1**(2–3), 119–163 (2009)
14. R.E. Keller, R. Poli, Linear genetic programming of parsimonious metaheuristics, in *2007 IEEE Congress on Evolutionary Computation* (IEEE, 9 2007), pp. 4508–4515
15. D.E. Knuth, *The Art of Computer Programming: Sorting and Searching*, vol. 3 (Pearson Education, 1998)
16. J.R. Koza, *Genetic Programming: on the Programming of Computers by Means of Natural Selection* (1992)
17. G. Laporte, A concise guide to the traveling salesman problem. J. Oper. Res. Soc. **61**(1), 35–40 (2010)
18. F. Mascia, M. López-Ibánez, J. Dubois-Lacoste, T. Stützle, From grammars to parameters: automatic iterated greedy design for the permutation flow-shop problem with weighted tardiness, in *International Conference on Learning and Intelligent Optimization* (Springer, 2013), pp. 321–334
19. M. O'Neill, C. Ryan, Grammatical evolution. IEEE Trans. Evol. Comput. **5**(4), 349–358 (2001)
20. M. O'Neill, C. Ryan, *Grammatical Evolution: Evolutionary Automatic Programming in an Arbitrary Language* (Springer, 2003)
21. L. Page, S. Brin, R. Motwani, T. Winograd, The PageRank citation ranking: bringing order to the web (1999)
22. U. Pferschy, J. Schauer, The knapsack problem with conflict graphs. J. Graph Algorithms Appl. **13**(2), 233–249 (2009)
23. N. Pillay, W. Banzhaf, A study of heuristic combinations for hyper-heuristic systems for the uncapacitated examination timetabling problem. Eur. J. Oper. Res. **197**(2), 482–491 (2009)
24. V. Robu, D.J.A. Somefun, J.A. La Poutré, Modeling complex multi-issue negotiations using utility graphs, in *Proceedings of the fourth international joint conference on Autonomous agents and multiagent systems* (ACM, 2005), pp. 280–287
25. N.R. Sabar, M. Ayob, G. Kendall, R. Qu, Grammatical evolution hyper-heuristic for combinatorial optimization problems. IEEE Trans. Evol. Comput. **17**(6), 840–861 (2013)
26. K. Sim, E. Hart, A combined generative and selective hyper-heuristic for the vehicle routing problem, in *Proceedings of the 2016 on Genetic and Evolutionary Computation Conference* (ACM, 2016), pp. 1093–1100
27. K. Sim, E. Hart, B. Paechter, A hyper-heuristic classifier for one dimensional bin packing problems: improving classification accuracy by attribute evolution, in *International Conference on Parallel Problem Solving from Nature* (Springer, 2012), pp. 348–357
28. C. Stone, E. Hart, B. Paechter, Automatic generation of constructive heuristics for multiple types of combinatorial optimisation problems with grammatical evolution and geometric graphs, in *International Conference on the Applications of Evolutionary Computation (EvoStar)* (Springer, 2018), pp. 578–593
29. C. Stone, E. Hart, B. Paechter, Automatic generation of constructive heuristics for multiple types of combinatorial optimisation problems with grammatical evolution and geometric graphs, in

Applications of Evolutionary Computation, ed. by K. Sim, P. Kaufmann (Springer International Publishing, 2018), pp. 578–593

30. C. Stone, E. Hart, B. Paechter, On the synthesis of perturbative heuristics for multiple combinatorial optimisation domains, in *International Conference on Parallel Problem Solving from Nature* (Springer, 2018), pp. 170–182
31. J.C. Tay, N.B. Ho, Evolving dispatching rules using genetic programming for solving multi-objective flexible job-shop problems. Comput. Ind. Eng. **54**(3), 453–473 (2008)

Chapter 7
Hyper-heuristics: Autonomous Problem Solvers

Mustafa Mısır

Abstract Algorithm design is a general task for any problem-solving scenario. For Search and Optimization, this task becomes rather challenging due to the immense algorithm design space. Those existing design options are usually traversed to devise algorithms by the human algorithm development experts together with the specialists on the target problem domains. The resulting algorithms are mostly problem-specific as they are unable to solve a different problem than the current target. Unlike the traditionally developed algorithms, Hyper-heuristics are known as problem-independent solvers pursuing the grand goal of generality. Generality, in this context, means that effectively solving different problems with a single algorithm under varying experimental conditions. This generality element is chased by performing a high-level search across the algorithm space differently than the majority of the algorithms directly operating on the solution space. In that respect, by design, a hyper-heuristic can be applied to any problem with a search space of quantifiable solutions. This flexibility coming from their easy-to-use nature has been validated in various academic and real-world applications. The present chapter provides a general overview of hyper-heuristics while discussing their shortcomings and recipes for future hyper-heuristic research.

7.1 Introduction

Autonomy is a trait to perform certain tasks without or limited human intervention while giving dynamic decisions [54]. The goal is to reduce the required resources for carrying out those tasks while elevating and standardizing the quality of the outcome.

M. Mısır (✉)
Department of Computer Engineering, Istinye University, Topkapı Campus, Maltepe Mah. Edirne Çırpıcı Yolu, No: 9, 34010 Zeytinburnu, Istanbul, Turkey
e-mail: mustafa.misir@istinye.edu.tr

Duke Kunshan University, Duke Avenue No: 8, 215316 Kunshan, Jiangsu, China

N. Pillay and R. Qu (eds.), *Automated Design of Machine Learning and Search Algorithms*, Natural Computing Series,
https://doi.org/10.1007/978-3-030-72069-8_7

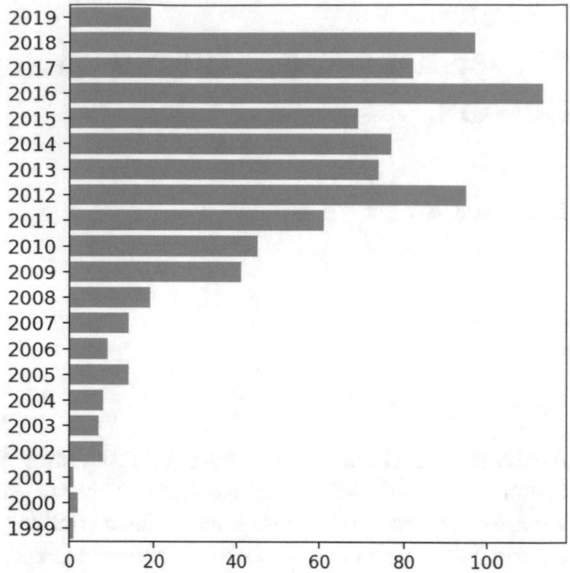

Fig. 7.1 The number of the published hyper-heuristic papers per year (from http://mustafamisir.github.io/hh.html)

Algorithms have been benefiting from autonomy as well, referring to *Autonomous Search* [147] or *Automated Algorithm Design* (AAD) [67]. This field is popular specifically in Machine Learning as *meta-learning* [142] and *Automated Machine Learning* (AutoML)[1] [60].

Hyper-heuristics (HHs)[2] [20, 43, 112] are a family of algorithms directly focusing on the autonomy in algorithm development. Generality in problem-solving [99] plays a critical role in the autonomy of HHs, as a consequence of their self-behaving characteristics. The generality implies being able to solve a variety of problems using a single algorithm. Their success and easy development nature promote them as the popular techniques in the literature. This popularity can be quantified, considering that the number of the published papers reaching up to ∼900 (Fig. 7.1) within 2019. Due to the naming resemblance, it is likely to confuse HHs with *Meta-heuristics* (MHs) [50]. While MHs are also referred generally applicable approaches, a MH requires a developer who should shape it accordingly such that it can deliver acceptable performance on a new problem or even on the different instances of the exact same problem. Thus, MHs can be denoted as universal algorithmic frameworks that need to be tailored to a given target problem. In other words, each MH happens to be a problem-specific variant of a particular MH type.

HHs differ from MHs by strictly separating the algorithm and problem parts, leading to completely problem-independent methods. This entails that, unlike MHs, there is no need for the problem-focused customization of HHs. That's why while HHs search across the heuristic/algorithm search space, MHs do their search directly

[1] https://www.automl.org/.

[2] A hyper-heuristic bibliography: http://mustafamisir.github.io/hh.html.

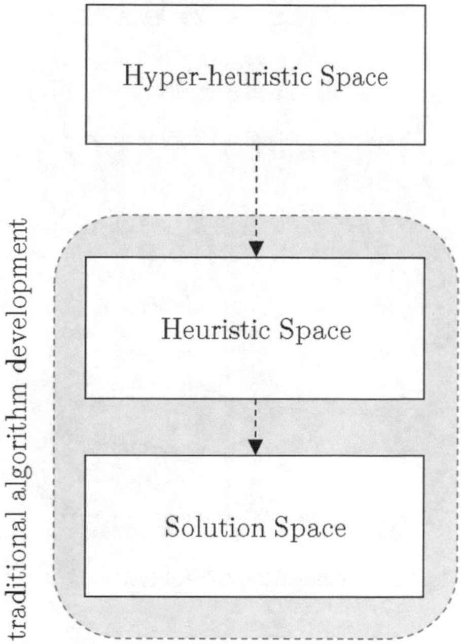

Fig. 7.2 Hyper-heuristic versus traditional algorithms' search space

on the solution space, as shown in Fig. 7.2. The discriminator between algorithm and problem for HHs is termed as the *domain barrier*. Although the phrase sounds too restrictive, the options for the problem-related yet independent data to be used by the HH component are relatively large [137]. Nevertheless, in terms of HHs versus MHs, it should be noted that HHs can also be portrayed as problem-independent MHs while most MHs are expressed as problem-dependent or problem-specific. Besides that, despite this difference between HHs and MHs, MHs are widely employed as HHs or HH components in a problem-independent form.

The HH literature starts with the *Selection HHs* (SHHs) [22, 43]. A SHH is concerned with managing multiple heuristics by determining and applying the most appropriate ones at each decision step, e.g., an iteration. These heuristics are named as *Low-Level Heuristics* (LLHs). They directly operate on the solution space, i.e., low-level, with the role of either constructing or manipulating solutions. This process is motivated by benefiting from the heuristics' strengths instead of relying on a single one. Although heuristics generally mean move operators that can make small changes on a solution, complete solvers can also be a part of such a candidate algorithm pool for SHHs [49, 74]. At this point, it should be noted that SHHs aren't the only algorithms taking advantage of multiple heuristics. MHs like *Variable Neighborhood Search* (VNS) [55] and *Iterated Local Search* (ILS) [83] have already been doing that. Moving to Evolutionary Computation (EC) [13], almost all the algorithms in that family utilize multiple operators, e.g., crossover and mutation for Genetic Algorithms (GAs) [37, 144]. Yet, the aforementioned domain barrier of SHHs ensures that the problem-related data used by SHHs doesn't contain any problem-specific

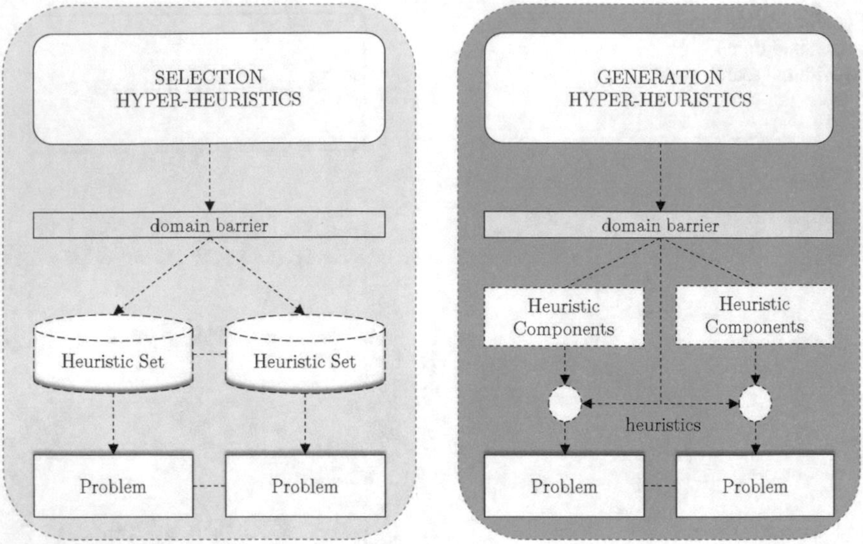

Fig. 7.3 Traditional hyper-heuristics

details while MHs do not have such an obligation. Following SHHs, *Generation HHs* (GHHs) [19] arose as a core HH alternative. Unlike SHHs that operate on a suite of heuristics, GHHs aim at generating heuristics, targeting a given problem or even a specific problem instance. Figure 7.3 visualizes the general setting for the SHHs and GHHs [20, 23]. A SHH application is carried out on a suite of heuristics which are dedicated to solve a specific problem. A GHH, however, focuses on a single heuristic design that can be used to solve a target problem. For the generation approach, a set of components or a template that can be used to build heuristics is essential.

The present chapter offers an overview of the existing HH studies while revealing their deficiencies. In the remainder of the chapter, Sect. 7.2 discusses the underlying motivation behind HHs. Section 7.3 provides a review of the existing HH studies as well as the relevant research trends. The challenges faced by HHs are argued in Sect. 7.4, disclosing the current research gaps with the poor practices. The chapter is finalized with a summary and suggestions to the HH community in Sect. 7.5.

7.2 Motivation and Claims

Algorithm design is usually carried out targeting a specific problem scenario. Thus, it naturally necessitates the problem domain expertise as well as the algorithm development capabilities. Yet, the design space tends to be extremely large, resulting in sub-optimal algorithms which are soon outperformed by the new, follow-up methods. As a consequence, the human-designed algorithms are doomed to be defective.

Still, it should be noted that an expert-developed algorithm can also be effective and good-enough for a problem. However, as mentioned, this comes with the cost of having the related specialists while substantial development time. Moreover, algorithm development is a gradual process, needing continuous modifications, leading to varying algorithm versions. In other words, conventional algorithm design is time-consuming and not resource-friendly. Furthermore, considering the problem-specific nature of such algorithms, it is rather difficult to use the developed algorithms for solving other problems.

HHs are mainly motivated by their problem-independent nature that also supports their easy applicability to a wide range of problems. In relation to that, HHs were initially denoted as methods to reach *good-enough*, *soon-enough*, and *cheap-enough* solutions [22]. In other words, HHs were proposed as a family of problem-solving techniques allowing quick algorithm development requiring comparatively limited computational budget and expertise while offering reasonably well performance. These promises lead to *multi-purpose algorithms* such that different problems can be tackled without any modification effort by those algorithms. All these claims were attacked by limiting the algorithm accessibility. This limitation is achieved by the aforementioned domain barrier that strictly separates the algorithm—so the main HH component—and the problem itself with all the relevant elements.

Linked with the idea of multi-purpose algorithms, one unique and critical aspect of HHs is *generality*. The common generality claim is to offer effective performance across multiple problem domains. However, this can be challenging referring to the *No Free Lunch Theorem* (NFLT) [145]. The NFLT states that all thc algorithms perform the same on average, considering all the possible problems—so their solution spaces. HHs are already shown to have free lunches despite the NFLT [115]. Additional theoretical studies also provide evidences supporting the effectiveness of HHs [57, 72, 80]. Those theoretical works mostly discuss the benefits of using multiple heuristics while providing runtime analysis linked to the HHs' design choices with their parameter settings. Since the scenario stated in the NFLT is rather extreme, in practice, the problem domain space happens to be comparatively limited. However, still, even on a single problem, it is quite rare to find an algorithm performing strictly and significantly better than its competitors, under the fair experimental conditions.

Additionally, there exist challenges directly on the problem instance level, motivating the HH research. A *search/fitness landscape* [114] concerning a problem instance can be hard to explore. Figure 7.4 exemplifies a synthetic solution space, referring to an optimization problem. The given circles refer to the solutions of a given problem instance. Assuming that the problem is a minimization problem, the goal is to seek the best solution placed at the lower levels of the given imaginary landscape. Thus, the black circle is the best solution for the given search region. Let's consider the search is currently at the second circle from the left. This means that the responsible algorithm or the search method needs to find a way to jump over the hill next to that solution to reach the black one. There are specially developed methods or criteria for this purpose—*exploration*—such as restarting [41] and accepting worsening solutions [25]. A certain type of HHs, i.e., Selection Hyper-heuristics (SHHs) which are detailed in the subsequent section, deals with this task implicitly

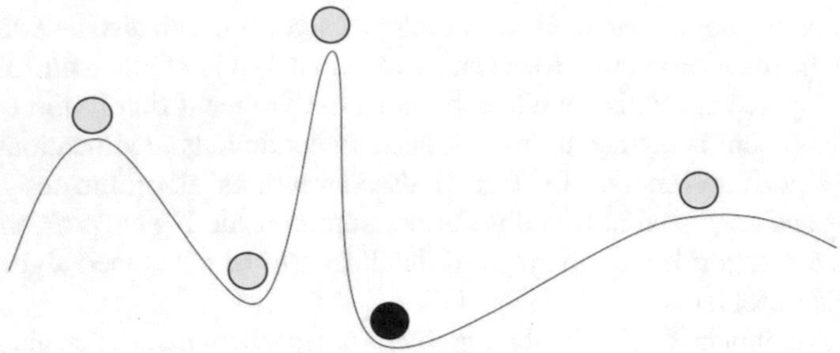

Fig. 7.4 An example solution space—imaginary landscape—for a minimization problem with 5 specified extreme solutions, each denoted by a colored circle

by simply switching heuristics. Switching heuristics actually means that changing the search landscape as heuristics take the role of neighborhood operators, connecting the solutions. The second-left gray solution might be located at the place of the third-left solution. Then, it will be easy to explore the black solution as the search region in-between is monotonically increasing, offering a smooth search. Considering the changing search requirements both at the problem level regarding the varying instance specifications and the solution level in terms of the search space, generating heuristics automatically can be highly practical. Generation Hyper-heuristics (GHHs) are present as the other HH type for automatically building heuristics.

7.3 Background

Hyper-heuristics (HHs) have been successfully applied to a large set of computationally challenging problems. These problems can be grouped as scheduling, timetabling, cutting and packing, and routing problems, as specified in Table 7.1. Besides these widely investigated problems, HHs have been applied to other domains such as software engineering [38, 62, 135, 152], game playing [10, 90], robot planning [148, 149], and machine learning [103, 122]. These problems largely fall in the category of single-objective optimization. Yet, there are also a considerable amount of HH studies focusing on the multi-objective optimization [31, 73, 146, 152].

As mentioned earlier, Selection HHs (SHHs) and Generation HHs (GHHs) are the two basic HH genres. Further sub-categories can be specified as the HHs that need to run prior to the actual problem-solving stage and during problem-solving. The earlier case is named as *Offline* while the latter option is denoted as *Online*. Online happens to be a more popular option than Offline for SHHs as it doesn't require any training process. All the decisions regarding the relevant high-level search are given on on-the-fly, while a problem instance is being solved. For GHHs, however, the research was carried out mostly for the Offline scenarios. The Offline aspect of GHHs tends to be more challenging and resource demanding than SHH as there has

Table 7.1 Problems studied with hyper-heuristics

Type	Problems
Scheduling	Flow-shop scheduling [77, 78], Job Shop scheduling [56, 109], Project scheduling [29, 79], Nurse rostering [15, 113], Patient admission scheduling [15], Home care scheduling [96], Maintenance personnel scheduling [98], Task scheduling [117], Fixture scheduling [51], Sales summit scheduling [34]
Timetabling	School timetabling [66], Course timetabling [111, 118, 131], Exam timetabling [46, 111, 118, 119]
Routing	Traveling salesman [45, 63], Vehicle routing [31, 71, 125], Arc routing [6, 81], Query routing [58], Location routing [36, 73, 151], Urban transit routing [3, 4]
Cutting and packing	Bin packing [9, 52, 126], Strip packing [16, 42], Set packing [30, 30], Knapsack [1, 44], Stock cutting [39]

been a heuristic generation process that can be considered in the form of *expensive optimization* [139]. In particular, generation is usually an iterative process such that a generated complete heuristic is aimed to be improved. Thus, the generation heuristics need to be consistently evaluated in order to check their current qualities.

Besides this extension on the HH taxonomy, the other classification comes from the type of the heuristics, either *constructive* or *perturbative/improvement*. The first type is concerned with building a complete solution after a series of steps. During this procedure, heuristics are progressively built. The heuristics with the perturbative nature follows a different path by manipulating already constructed complete solutions. The constructive variants are exceptionally practical for the solution initialization. There are also problems like Bin Packing (BP) [24] which are highly popular for deriving new solutions via pure construction. The following sub-sections will further elaborate both on SHHs and GHHs.

7.3.1 Selection Hyper-heuristics

Figure 7.5 illustrates a basic Selection Hyper-heuristic (SHH) structure. A SHH is usually composed of two mechanisms including a *Heuristic Selection* (HS) method and *Move Acceptance* (MA) criterion. As its name suggests, the heuristic selection deals with the main selection task of utilizing the heuristics from a given heuristic set. The latter element acts like an adviser who decides which solutions to keep and which ones to discard where the solutions are explored by the selected heuristics.

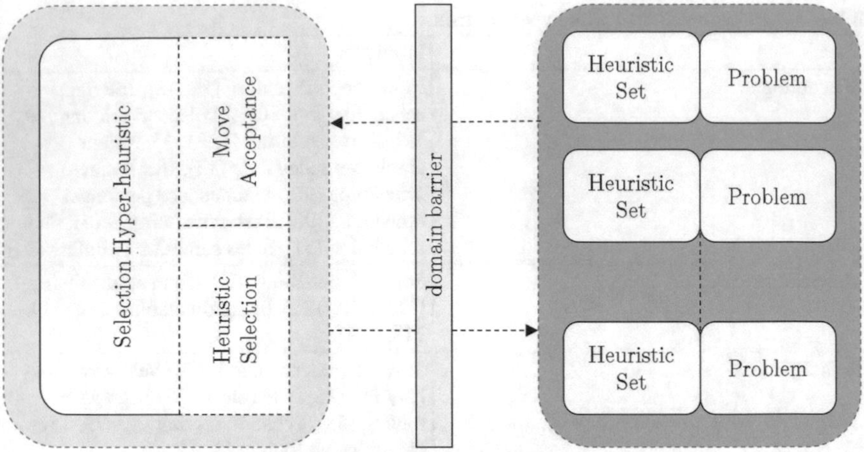

Fig. 7.5 A traditional selection hyper-heuristic

In terms of HS, learning is usually a critical feature. A strong HS approach needs to understand the behavior of the heuristics as well as their interactions. Then, the outcome is more of a system resembling the action-selection policies induced in *Reinforcement Learning* (RL) [136]. While such a policy can be state-dependent, e.g., for an easy search region use exploitation (improvement) oriented heuristics more often than the ones with the exploration nature, it is not always necessary to explicitly define states for HHs [97]. This policy step can be carried out either *Offline* or *Online*. The first option deals with the task by deciding on a policy prior to starting to solve the target problem (∼instance). Thus, there happens to be a training step, meaning extra computational cost. For the Online variant, the learning occurs while solving a problem instance so giving more of deciding how to choose heuristics dynamically. Choice Function (CF) [32, 33, 74] is a well-known and popular HS performing Online selection, considering both exploration and exploitation. CF operates solely based on the Online performance of the underlying heuristics and their speed. Learning Automata (LA) [75, 97] was incorporated as a stateless RL approach like CF. In [108], RL was used as a strategy combining varying reward schemes and selection criteria. Case-based Reasoning (CBR) [26] achieves this task in an Offline manner by matching the new problem-solving case with the historically saved problem-solution pairs.

The learning-based nature of these above-mentioned HS methods does not necessarily mean that an effective HS method needs intelligent components [5]. In that respect, there are also simple yet effective HS techniques especially under the specific test conditions. Simple Random (SR) [33] is a prime example as it simply performs uniform random selection. Considering the optimization problems, improving a low-quality solution tends to be much easier than improving near-optimal solutions. Thus, it is likely to encounter that well-performing heuristics during the early stages of an optimization task show rather poor performance when the search gets closer to the search regions with near-optimal solutions. From a learning point of view, after a while, it will look like the improvement capabilities of all the heuristics become similar due to the improvement hardness. In such cases, giving random choices or forgetting the historical performance of the heuristics can be a good idea. This supports that SR can be as effective as or even better than a highly learning-oriented HS method. Besides that, having long runtime budgets, allowing millions of iterations or optimization steps, will give a large space to make mistakes. Thus, picking up poor heuristics won't hurt the overall performance much. Of course, all these depend on the complete design of SHHs. For instance, ignoring the heuristics' past performance over time might be a bad or unnecessary choice for a SHH with restarting.

The HS element isn't a concept solely belonging to SHHs. A similar idea has been in consideration for Evolutionary Algorithms (EAs) [12] as they utilize multiple operators, one for each operator type, i.e., crossover and mutation. Although most of the EA studies use one fixed operator for each type, there are studies having multiple operators of a specific type. In such a setting, EAs are also responsible for determining which operators to use during which generation. Adaptive Operator Selection (AOS) [35, 140] is the term used to deal with this task. Considering the similarity between HS and AOS, AOS has also been used as HSs for SHHs [105, 130, 143].

As a complimentary part, MAs have been also considered as a critical component yet more limited work as the main contribution compared to HS. MA could offer two main characteristics including *exploration* and *exploitation*. This is essentially the same characteristics provided by HS. This can give us a hint about which HS and MA work better depending on their exploration and exploitation characteristics. MAs deliver these behaviors based on whether it is allowed to accept worsening solutions and how often. It is possible to incorporate this behavior in an offline form, suggesting fixed behavior. For instance, Simulated Annealing (SA) [68] is a good example of having pre-determined policies on their diversification activities. Yet, this algorithmic aspect does not need to be strict as it might depend on online or dynamic data [15, 25]. There are other SA-like MAs such as Great Deluge [108, 127], Record-to-Record Travel (RRT) [64], Late Acceptance [40], and Adaptive Iteration Limited Threshold Accepting (AILTA) [100]. Beyond these methods, as in HS, there are rather simple MA options including All Moves (AM) [33], Improving or Equal (IE) [33], Only Improving (OI) [33], and Naive Acceptance [18]. Although such MAs aren't necessarily effective by themselves, they can still be useful depending on the target problem and its given heuristic set together with the runtime budget. This is true especially when at least one of the following scenarios occur: the utilized HS is exploitation directed, the heuristic set involves mostly improving oriented operators and short execution time. In those cases, visits to the worsening solutions tend to be limited, which makes the use of MA insignificant. Thus, it is possible to reach effective performance even with such ordinary MAs.

Referring to the earlier discussion on HHs and Meta-heuristics (MHs), MHs have been also successfully used as the HH components by securing the problem-independent characteristics. To name a few, Simulated Annealing (SA) [21], Tabu Search (TS) [150], Ant Colony Optimization (ACO) [11], Particle Swarm Optimiza-

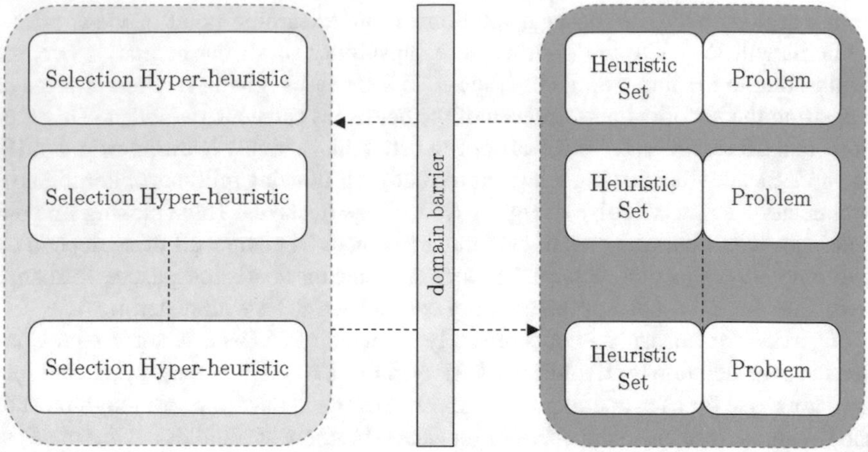

Fig. 7.6 The general structure of HyFlex as a selection hyper-heuristic framework

tion (PSO) [69], Memetic Algorithm (MeA) [14], and Cuckoo Search (CS) [116] can be listed besides the ones using multiple MHs in a hybridized manner [129].

For the sake of implementing new SHHs, HyFlex [104] was introduced as a practical library for SHHs. As visualized in Fig. 7.6, it is composed of two parts including SHH and the problem domain. Domain barrier is the contract between those parts for ensuring the problem-independent aspect of SHHs. The problem domain involves the problem definition concerning a solution space regarding a problem instance. In addition to that, a set of heuristics, a.k.a. Low-Level Heuristics (LLHs), is needed, largely as a problem-specific element. HyFlex permits both single-point search and population-based implementations yet frequently used for the SHHs of keeping one main solution.

Regarding the application domains, all kinds of problems addressed by HHs have been targeted by SHHs. Thus, there is no specific application domain widely preferred for SHHs. However, with the success of SHHs on the traditional problems, now the applications are happening more on the structured or complex problems. Each of these problems composed of more than one sub-problem like the workforce routing and rostering problem [98].

7.3.2 Generation Hyper-heuristics

Although Generation Hyper-heuristics (GHHs) were introduced rather later than SHHs, the general strategy for heuristic generation isn't new. Their underlying idea relies on the program generation that is concerned with automatically building programs. These programs are mostly at the function level, so dealing with rather simple tasks in terms of the action to be taken. The general and most commonly used method

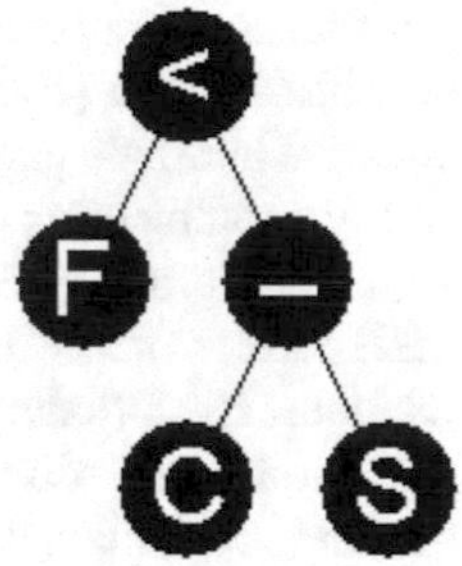

Fig. 7.7 A GP generated 1D bin packing heuristic [24]

in that respect is *Genetic Programming* (GP) [70]. A traditional GP is concerned with deriving algorithms, functions, or rules in the form of trees. A tree is composed of different components, usually picked up from a pre-determined set, used as the leaf and non-leaf nodes. While the non-leaf nodes denote functions, the leaf nodes are essentially variables or constants, fed to a function or used as additional elements. Figure 7.7 shows a simple heuristic generated by GP, for the Bin Packing (BP) problem. In this example, the produced tree constructs a rule that checks whether an item of size S can fit to a bin of size C, already involving F amount of items. In other words, if there is enough space in a bin, then the corresponding item is placed inside that bin, otherwise, keep checking other bins until finding one with enough space. This traditional application of GP is called as Tree-based GP (TGP), named after its solution representation. Besides this traditional implementation of GP as GHH [8, 29, 59, 61, 111, 141], there are other GP variants utilized as GHH, like Tree-based Grammar-Guided GP (T-GGGP) [132] and Context-free Grammar GP (CFG-GP) [92, 93].

Grammatical Evolution (GE) [106] is another strategy, yet still based on GP, only without Code Bloat of GP [85]. Although GPs offer more flexibility in terms of the design complexity referring to its search space, GEs follow a general template, named as the production rules. In other words, GEs widely perform a search across the design choices for each component of a template. In that respect, it is safe to say that GEs perform generation more of a parameter tuning way [89]. The pure GE has almost reached the popularity of TGP for GHH as exemplified in [7, 8, 48, 76, 92, 133, 134]. Its success has led to new GE variants, especially replacing the search element, that is basically Genetic Algorithms (GAs), with other meta-heuristics. Grammatical Swarm (GS) [133] and Grammatical Differential Evolution (GDE) [107] are two successful examples of those variants. In addition to these two most popular GHH methods, there are other, alternative algorithmic approaches used for generation. Scatter Programming (SP) [124], Iterated Local Search (ILS) [102], Parameter Tuning [82, 89], and Mathematical Programming [101] are the existing alternatives. The general philosophy is to model the generation jobs as the optimization problems. Thus, in principle, any search and optimization technique can be employed as GHHs.

Majority of these referred GHHs aim at building heuristics or algorithms Offline. Among the limited Online GHH studies, hybridization is a viable generation option.

The idea is simply calling more than one heuristics together—consecutively—as if a new heuristic. In [100], this idea is called *relay hybridization* that is able to explore effective heuristic pairs.

For implementing GHHs, EvoHyp[3] [110] can be regarded as a handy environment while also granting SHH development. The major difference to HyFlex that is a SHH framework is that EvoHyp specifically accommodates the population-based methods, Evolutionary Algorithms (EAs), i.e., GAs and GPs. EvoHyp additionally offers a chance to directly benefit from multiple computation entities like clusters by its distributed characteristics.

The application domains of GHHs tend to be more focused than SHHs. In particular, cutting and packing problems are the popular domains for a heuristic generation. Additionally, a rather large literature is present for deriving dispatching rules of varying production scheduling problems [17]. Besides these generation tasks of rather simple heuristics as move operators, there have been studies building complete solvers [47, 84, 88, 89, 91, 93]. Further generation applications cover the construction of the SHH components [120, 121]—GHHs for SHHs.

7.4 Challenges, Research Gaps, and Poor Practices

Despite generality is at the center of Hyper-heuristics (HHs), the majority of the HH studies focus on single problem-solving. The main aim here is to show that SHHs can provide comparable or better performance against other, mostly problem-specific algorithms. Thus, although HHs are problem-independent, they have been widely used in a rather problem-specific manner, solving one problem only. In those applications, it is also likely to see some problem-specific tweaking, i.e., playing with their hyper-parameters or design choices for the sake of improved performance. Besides that, especially for Selection HHs (SHHs), the effects of such problem-specific applications can be apparent from the heuristic sets. Mostly, they are designed more carefully or specifically for those target problem instances, so become even test-set specific. Still, the specialization levels of those HH variants aren't as drastic as MHs.

Although both SHHs and Generation HHs (GHHs) are problem-independent, they still require to implement certain problem-specific elements. From the SHH perspective, this aspect is mainly on the heuristic sets. For each target problem, it is desired to come up with an effective heuristic set. This process can be handled either by collecting strong heuristic designs from the literature or implementing the new ones. Yet, it should be noted putting up a group of strong heuristics does not necessarily refer to strong performance at the end. If the heuristics are unsuitable to work together, then poor performance is inevitable. As a counter-example, a group of weak heuristics on their own may even outperform the heuristic sets with strong heuristics if those weak ones are better as a team. Essentially, this point is referred

[3] http://titancs.ukzn.ac.za/EvoHyp.aspx.

to as algorithm portfolios in Algorithm Selection (AS) [65]. In a way, AS is actually a special case of SHHs. It basically specifies which algorithm to apply for solving a given problem (∼instance). Those algorithms, however, are mostly complete problem solvers while SHHs usually work with more like operators which do minor changes on solutions during the problem-solving stage. Still, there are studies titled SHHs working with the complete solvers [53, 86, 87, 138]. Going back to the original discussion on what lacks for SHHs is the step to build a heuristic set in the first place. Although there are studies aiming at automating the process of choosing those heuristic (sub-)sets [28, 100, 128], they are unable to make the SHHs *human-independent*. Considering the case where poor heuristics are used in a heuristic set, a heuristic set solely composed of simple heuristics can also offer high performance. In that respect, it is possible to say that SHHs can also effectively operate as *expert-independent*. Yet, expert knowledge, particularly in the problem domain, can be highly valuable.

For GHHs, although the story is different, the effect is mainly the same. To be able to perform a certain type of heuristic generation, a suite of heuristic building blocks need to be specified. This means that GHHs also need human intervention. Since GHHs operate Offline in most of the cases, they require a training set which also requires someone who understands the target task. If the training set differs from the test or target set at a certain level, then the performance might fail to meet the expectations. This is a valid and general concern also in Machine Learning (ML).

From a broader view, generality is usually neglected even though it is frequently mentioned with HHs. The ones emphasizing generality investigate generality from a narrow perspective. Generality, from a larger perspective, can be considered through 3 main criteria [99] including (1) across multiple problems, (2) distinct heuristic sets, (3) under varying experimental conditions, as also visualized in Fig. 7.8.

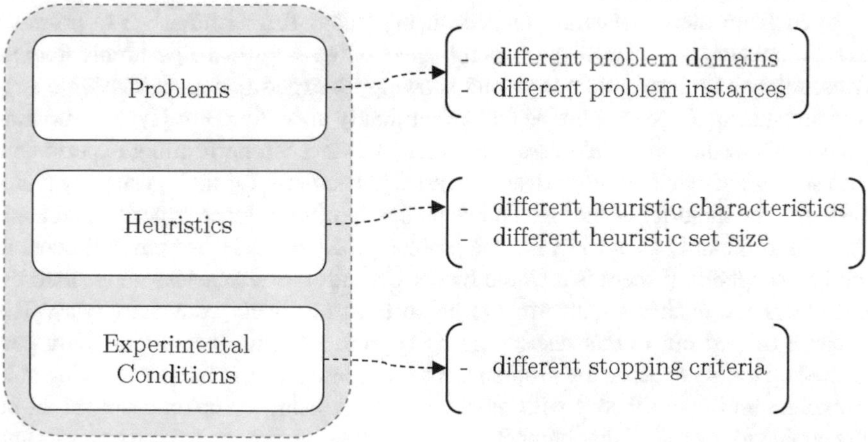

Fig. 7.8 Hyper-heuristic generality elements

Performance across different problems sounds like a straightforward paradigm. However, different problems do not necessarily mean different challenges. Essentially, it is possible to see that the instances of different problems show similar characteristics [94]. This suggests that it is vital to determine a diverse instance set coming from varying problem domains. This is specifically critical beyond the HH community as such empirical comparisons have been usually done on the corresponding widely accepted benchmark sets. Yet, their diversity can be a question, requiring a more thorough analysis of the diversity. In that respect, performance variations of a suite of algorithms can be considered as a practical measure to evaluate the instance set diversity [95]. The first Cross-domain Heuristic Search Challenge (CHeSC 2011),[4] performed on HyFlex, is a fine example with reasonable instance diversity [94].

Regarding the heuristic set condition, the evaluation needs to be considered in terms of both the nature of the heuristics and the set size. To be able to deliver generality, Selection HHs (SHHs) require to be capable of dealing with heuristics of varying behavior. The behavior can be denoted as the solutions explored by the selected heuristics, e.g., often improve a solution, and its speed like heuristic A takes $0.2 \times n$ seconds where n is the problem instance size. As SHHs benefit from multiple heuristics, even with relatively simple and poor heuristics, it might be possible to reach a high-performance level. This is likely, if, of course, those heuristics are effective together despite their weak standalone performance. The size of the heuristic set is another aspect that needs to be taken into account for generality. A SHH should be able to deal with large or small heuristic sets. Varying experimental conditions also need to be in consideration for the sake of high generality. In particular, different time limits can be provided to evaluate the behavior of SHHs. That being said, a specific HH can focus on a certain suite of generality criteria instead of achieving all the generality standards. Then, it is important to stress the generality level of HHs so that the HH users can be aware of the limitations of those HHs prior to using them.

Apart from these issues in practice, theory needs further attention to promote HHs. The theory is generally the missing aspect of the empirical algorithmic studies. Thus, solely offering an algorithm and showing its experimental success on a specific test setting alone may not be that scientifically appealing. For Hyper-heuristics (HHs), this issue can be addressed to a certain extent via performing experiments with somewhat extensive empirical test cases, particularly for their generality claim [99]. Yet, the majority of the HH studies incline to offer reduced experimental analysis, predominantly as one HH for one problem. Still, one HH-one problem scheme can be acceptable if there is a viable theory behind it. Nevertheless, those theoretical works are unable to solve this issue, at least in a truly convincing way. The research carried out in that respect, going beyond HHs, has been commonly performed on highly specific toy problems. The reasoning here is mostly on being able to explain and relate theory with practice. Indeed, using complex cases might be flawed due to the increasing number of factors affecting the theoretical analysis and its conclusiveness. Although those studies are highly appreciated as they provide

[4] http://www.asap.cs.nott.ac.uk/external/chesc2011/.

interesting insights, their practicality is still an open question. Thus, theory needs to move toward more realistic scenarios so that the gap between theory and practice can be minimized. When theory is already ignored, then the only option for HHs is to deliver an experimental analysis offering more than the one HH-one problem matching.

Furthermore, in connection with the theory facet to a certain extent, interpretability or explainability is essential for the algorithmic studies. Especially, for the so-called intelligent algorithms where some level of learning is incorporated, it makes even more sense. As algorithms give certain decisions, the underlying logic would be understandable, in particular for the follow-up algorithm designs. This subject is getting popular in ML itself, mostly for DL [123] these days. This is critical for the applications preferring accuracy over robustness such as in healthcare [27]. The same aspect needs to be considered for HHs to tell why and under which conditions certain HHs perform well, vice versa. Thus, the reported results need to go beyond some performance-related numbers but compelling arguments, matching the HH designs with their performance or behavior.

7.5 Conclusion

Hyper-heuristics (HHs) are effective search and optimization techniques. Their main notable trait is being problem-independent such that a HH can be applied to any problem with no modification at the HH design level. This characteristic designates HHs as general solvers contrary to the algorithms tweaked to address a particular problem or even a specific instance set of a problem. In other words, HHs were born as the methods chasing generality. The existing HH studies showed that HHs are effective methods beyond their initial claim of good-enough, soon-enough, and cheap-enough. Their effectiveness exhibited at the computational level through empirical studies was supported by theory as well. However, as discussed in Sect. 7.4, HHs have their own obstacles in which some of them are also valid for the other algorithmic studies. These challenges shed light on the research gaps while requiring common practices that need to be considered in the incoming HH papers.

Beyond the discussion in Sect. 7.4 targeting the individual HH researchers and practitioners, the HH community also has some responsibilities. In particular, widely accepted, open-source libraries should be built and released. HyFlex [104] is a prime example of a such a contribution. Although HyFlex is currently need-to-be-used as a benchmark environment for any SHH, it has its own limits as it is closed-source. Despite its closed-source nature, HyFlex has been independently used by other researchers to extend the framework [2]. These extensions aren't integrated into HyFlex but they are just offered as external implementations on HyFlex. That's why those new problems tend to stay away from the public attention. On the subject of this practice, new papers are coming without considering those new problem domains even though they are available. Thus, a HH consortium needs to come together to offer an open-source HH framework. Also, many studies perform HH in a standalone manner, without relying on a framework like HyFlex. Thus, the methods in such studies presumably stay local or hidden and are ignored, for comparison specifically. It is likely to see comparative methods against those studies, only by the same authors as the modified versions of those methods. This fact causes having many papers with limited or zero practical contribution to the HH literature, similarly for non-HH algorithms.

Acknowledgements This study was supported by the 2232 Reintegration Grant from the Scientific and Technological Research Council of Turkey (TUBITAK) under Project 119C013.

References

1. N. Acevedo, C. Rey, C. Contreras-Bolton, V. Parada, Automatic design of specialized algorithms for the binary knapsack problem. in *Expert Systems with Applications* (2019), p. 112908
2. S. Adriaensen, G. Ochoa, A. Now'e, A benchmark set extension and comparative study for the hyflex framework, in *IEEE Congress on Evolutionary Computation (CEC)* (IEEE, 2015), pp. 784–791
3. L. Ahmed, P. Heyken-Soares, C. Mumford, Y. Mao, Optimising bus routes with fixed terminal nodes: comparing hyper-heuristics with nsgaii on realistic transportation networks, in *Proceedings of the Genetic and Evolutionary Computation Conference (GECCO)* (ACM, 2019), pp. 1102–1110
4. L. Ahmed, C. Mumford, A. Kheiri, Solving urban transit route design problem using selection hyper-heuristics. Eur. J. Oper. Res. **274**(2), 545–559 (2019)
5. F. Alanazi, P.K. Lehre, Runtime analysis of selection hyper-heuristics with classical learning mechanisms, in *IEEE Congress on Evolutionary Computation (CEC)* (IEEE, 2014), pp. 2515–2523
6. M.A. Ardeh, Y. Mei, M. Zhang, Transfer learning in genetic programming hyper-heuristic for solving uncertain capacitated arc routing problem, in *2019 IEEE Congress on Evolutionary Computation (CEC)* (IEEE, 2019), pp. 49–56
7. F. Assunçao, N. Lourenço, P. Machado, B. Ribeiro, Automatic generation of neural networks with structured grammatical evolution, in *IEEE Congress on Evolutionary Computation (CEC)* (San Sebastian, Spain, 2017), pp. 1557–1564
8. F. Assunção, N. Lourenço, P. Machado, B. Ribeiro, Using gp is neat: evolving compositional pattern production functions, in *European Conference on Genetic Programming* (Springer, 2018), pp. 3–18
9. S. Asta, E. Özcan, A.J. Parkes, CHAMP: creating heuristics via many parameters for online bin packing. Expert Syst. Appl. **63**, 208–221 (2016)
10. I. Azaria, A. Elyasaf, M. Sipper, Evolving artificial general intelligence for video game controllers, in *Genetic Programming Theory and Practice XIV* (Springer, 2018), pp. 53–63
11. Z.A. Aziz, Ant colony hyper-heuristics for travelling salesman problem. Procedia Comput. Sci. **76**, 534–538 (2015)
12. T. Back, *Evolutionary Algorithms in Theory and Practice: Evolution Strategies, Evolutionary Programming, Genetic Algorithms* (Oxford University Press, 1996)
13. T. Bäck, D.B. Fogel, Z. Michalewicz, *Evolutionary Computation 1: Basic Algorithms and Operators* (CRC press, 2018)
14. M. Beyaz, T. Dokeroglu, A. Cosar, Robust hyper-heuristic algorithms for the offline oriented/non-oriented 2d bin packing problems. Appl. Soft Comput. **36**, 236–245 (2015)
15. B. Bilgin, P. Demeester, M. Mısır, W. Vancroonenburg, G. Vanden Berghe, One hyperheuristic approach to two timetabling problems in health care. J. Heuristics **18**(3), 401–434 (2012)

16. I. Borgulya, A parallel hyper-heuristic approach for the two-dimensional rectangular strip-packing problem. *CIT. J. Comput. Inf. Technol.* **22**(4), 251–265 (2014)
17. I. Borgulya, A parallel hyper-heuristic approach for the two-dimensional rectangular strip-packing problem. *CIT. J. Comput. Inf. Technol.***22**(4), 251–265 (2014)
18. E. Burke, T. Curtois, M. Hyde, G. Kendall, G. Ochoa, S. Petrovic, J.A. Vázquez-Rodrıguez, M. Gendreau, Iterated local search vs. hyper-heuristics: towards general-purpose search algorithms, in *Proceedings of the IEEE Congress on Evolutionary Computation (CEC)* (Barcelona, Spain, July 18–23 2010), pp. 3073–3080
19. E.K. Burke, M.R. Hyde, G. Kendall, G. Ochoa, E. Ozcan, J.R. Woodward, Exploring hyper-heuristic methodologies with genetic programming, in *Computational Intelligence* (Springer, 2009), pp. 177–201
20. E.K. Burke, M.R. Hyde, G. Kendall, G. Ochoa, E. Özcan, J.R. Woodward, A classification of hyper-heuristic approaches: revisited, in *Handbook of Metaheuristics* (Springer, 2019), pp. 453–477
21. E.K. Burke, G. Kendall, M. Mısır, E. Özcan, Monte carlo hyper-heuristics for examination timetabling. Ann. Oper. Res. **196**(1), 73–90 (2012)
22. E.K. Burke, E. Hart, G. Kendall, J. Newall, P. Ross, S. Schulenburg, Hyper-heuristics: an emerging direction in modern search technology, in *Handbook of Meta-Heuristics* (Kluwer Academic Publishers, 2003), pp. 457–474
23. E.K. Burke, M. Hyde, G. Kendall, G. Ochoa, E. Ozcan, J.R. Woodward, A classification of hyper-heuristic approaches, in *Handbook of Metaheuristics* (2010), pp. 449–468
24. E.K. Burke, M.R. Hyde, G. Kendall, Evolving bin packing heuristics with genetic programming, in *Proceedings of the 9th International Conference on Parallel Problem Solving from Nature (PPSN)*, vol. 4193. LNCS, ed. by T.P. Runarsson, H.-G. Beyer, E. Burke, J.J. Merelo-Guervos, L.D. Whitley, X. Yao (Springer, Reykjavik, Iceland, September 9–13 2006), pp. 860–869
25. E.K. Burke, G. Kendall, M. Mısır, E. Özcan, Monte carlo hyper-heuristics for examination timetabling. Ann. Oper. Res. **196**(1), 73–90 (2012)
26. E.K. Burke, S. Petrovic, R. Qu, Case based heuristic selection for timetabling problems. J. Sched. **9**(2), 115–132 (2006)
27. F. Cabitza, R. Rasoini, G.F. Gensini, Unintended consequences of machine learning in medicine. Jama **318**(6), 517–518 (2017)
28. K. Chakhlevitch, P. Cowling, Choosing the fittest subset of low level heuristics in a hyper-heuristic framework, in *Proceedings of the 5th European Conference on Evolutionary Computation in Combinatorial Optimization (EvoCOP)*, vol. 3448. LNCS, ed. by G.R. Raidl, J. Gottlieb (Springer, 2005), pp. 23–33
29. S. Chand, Q. Huynh, H. Singh, T. Ray, M. Wagner, On the use of genetic programming to evolve priority rules for resource constrained project scheduling problems. Inf. Sci. **432**, 146–163 (2018)
30. S.N. Chaurasia, D. Jung, H.M. Lee, J.H. Kim, An evolutionary algorithm based hyper-heuristic for the set packing problem, in *Harmony Search and Nature Inspired Optimization Algorithms* (Springer, 2019), pp. 259–268
31. B. Chen, Q. Rong, R. Bai, W. Laesanklang, A hyper-heuristic with two guidance indicators for bi-objective mixed-shift vehicle routing problem with time windows. Appl. Intell. **48**(12), 4937–4959 (2018)
32. S.S. Choong, L.-P. Wong, C.P. Lim, An artificial bee colony algorithm with a modified choice function for the traveling salesman problem, in *IEEE International Conference on Systems, Man, and Cybernetics (SMC)* (IEEE, 2017)
33. P. Cowling, G. Kendall, E. Soubeiga, A hyperheuristic approach to scheduling a sales summit, in *PATAT'00: Selected papers from the Third International Conference on Practice and Theory of Automated Timetabling III* (Springer, London, UK, 2001), pp. 176–190
34. P. Cowling, G. Kendall, E. Soubeiga, A parameter-free hyperheuristic for scheduling a sales summit, Ii *Proceedings of 4th Metahuristics International Conference (MIC)* (Porto, Portugal, July 16–20 2001), pp. 127–131

35. L. Da Costa, A. Fialho, M. Schoenauer, M. Sebag, Adaptive operator selection with dynamic multi-armed bandits, in *Proceedings of Genetic and Evolutionary Computation Conference (GECCO)* (Atlanta, Georgia, USA, 2008), pp. 913–920
36. K. Danach, S. Gelareh, R.N. Monemi, The capacitated single-allocation p-hub location routing problem: a lagrangian relaxation and a hyper-heuristic approach, in *EURO Journal on Transportation and Logistics* (2019), pp. 1–35
37. L. Davis, in *Handbook of Genetic Algorithms* (1991)
38. J. de Andrade, L. Silva, A. Britto, R. Amaral, Solving the software project scheduling problem with hyper-heuristics, in *International Conference on Artificial Intelligence and Soft Computing* (Springer, 2019), pp. 399–411
39. J. de Armas, G. Miranda, C. León, Hyperheuristic encoding scheme for multi-objective guillotine cutting problems, in *Proceedings of the 13th Annual Conference on Genetic and Evolutionary Computation* (ACM, 2011), pp. 1683–1690
40. P. Demeester, B. Bilgin, P. De Causmaecker, G. Vanden Berghe, A hyperheuristic approach to examination timetabling problems: benchmarks and a new problem from practice. J. Sched. **15**(1) (2012)
41. T. Dokeroglu, A. Cosar, A novel multistart hyper-heuristic algorithm on the grid for the quadratic assignment problem. Eng. Appl. Artif. Intell. **52**, 10–25 (2016)
42. D. Domović, T. Rolich, M. Golub, Evolutionary hyper-heuristic for solving the strip-packing problem, in *The Journal of The Textile Institute* (2019), pp. 1–11
43. J.H. Drake, A. Kheiri, E. Özcan, E.K. Burke, Recent advances in selection hyper-heuristics, in *European Journal of Operational Research* (2019)
44. J.H. Drake, E. Özcan, E.K. Burke, A case study of controlling crossover in a selection hyper-heuristic framework using the multidimensional knapsack problem. Evol. Comput. **24**(1), 113–141 (2016)
45. G. Duflo, E. Kieffer, M.R. Brust, G. Danoy, P. Bouvry, A gp hyper-heuristic approach for generating tsp heuristics, in *2019 IEEE International Parallel and Distributed Processing Symposium Workshops (IPDPSW)* (IEEE, 2019), pp. 521–529
46. A. Elhag, E. Özcan, A grouping hyper-heuristic framework: application on graph colouring. Expert Syst. Appl. **42**(13), 5491–5507 (2015)
47. I. Fajfar, J. Puhan, Á. Burmen, Evolving a nelder-mead algorithm for optimization with genetic programming. Evolutionary computation (2016)
48. V.D. Fontoura, A.T.R. Pozo, R. Santana, Automated design of hyper-heuristics components to solve the psp problem with hp model, in *IEEE Congress on Evolutionary Computation (CEC)* (IEEE, 2017), pp. 1848–1855
49. A. Garcia-Villoria, S. Salhi, A. Corominas, R. Pastor, Hyper-heuristic approaches for the response time variability problem. Eur. J. Oper. Res. **1**, 160–169 (2011)
50. M. Gendreau, J.-Y. Potvin, in *Handbook of Metaheuristics* (Springer, 2019)
51. J. Gibbs, G. Kendall, E. Ozcan Scheduling english football fixtures over the holiday period using hyper-heuristics, in *Proceedings of the 9th International Conference on Parallel Problem Solving from Nature (PPSN)*, vol. 6238. LNCS, ed. by R. Schaefer, C. Cotta, J. Kolodziej, G. Rudolph (Springer, Krakow, Poland, September 11–15 2010), pp. 496–505
52. J.C. Gomez, H. Terashima-Marín, Evolutionary hyper-heuristics for tackling bi-objective 2d bin packing problems. Genet. Program. Evolvable Mach. **19**(1–2), 151–181 (2018)
53. J. Grobler, A.P. Engelbrecht, G. Kendall, V.S.S. Yadavalli, Heuristic space diversity control for improved meta-hyper-heuristic performance. Inf. Sci. **300** (2015)
54. G.D. Hager, D. Rus, V. Kumar, H. Christensen, Toward a science of autonomy for physical systems (2016). arXiv:1604.02979
55. P. Hansen, N. Mladenović, J. Brimberg, J.A. Moreno Pérez, Variable neighborhood search, in *Handbook of metaheuristics* (Springer, 2019), pp. 57–97
56. E. Hart, K. Sim, A hyper-heuristic ensemble method for static job-shop scheduling. Evol. Comput. **24**(4), 609–635 (2016)
57. J. He, F. He, H. Dong, Pure strategy or mixed strategy? - an initial comparison of their asymptotic convergence rate and asymptotic hitting time, in *Proceedings of the 12th European*

Conference on Evolutionary Computation in Combinatorial Optimisation (EvoCOP), vol. 7245. LNCS, ed. by J.-K. Hao, M. Middendorf (2012), pp. 218–229
58. P. Hernandez, C. Gomez, L. Cruz, A. Ochoa, N. Castillo, G. Rivera, Hyperheuristic for the parameter tuning of a bio-inspired algorithm of query routing in p2p networks, in *the 10th Mexican International Conference on Artificial Intelligence (MICAI*, vol. 7095. Advances in Soft Computing, LNAI, ed. by I. Batyrshin, G. Sidorov (Springer, Berlin/Heidelberg, 2011), pp. 119–130
59. L. Hong, J.H. Drake, J.R. Woodward, E. Özcan, A hyper-heuristic approach to automated generation of mutation operators for evolutionary programming. Appl. Soft Comput. **62**, 162–175 (2018)
60. F. Hutter, L. Kotthoff, J. Vanschoren, in *Automated Machine Learning - Methods, Systems, Challenges* (Springer, 2019)
61. J. Jacobsen-Grocott, Y. Mei, G. Chen, M. Zhang, Evolving heuristics for dynamic vehicle routing with time windows using genetic programming, in *IEEE Congress on Evolutionary Computation (CEC)* (San Sebastian, Spain, 2017)
62. H.L. Jakubovski Filho, T.N. Ferreira, S.R. Vergilio, Incorporating user preferences in a software product line testing hyper-heuristic approach, in *IEEE Congress on Evolutionary Computation (CEC)* (IEEE, 2018), pp. 1–8
63. G. Kendall, J. Li, Competitive travelling salesmen problem: a hyper-heuristic approach. J. Oper. Res. Soc. (2012)
64. G. Kendall, M. Mohamad, Channel assignment optimisation using a hyper-heuristic, in *Proceedings of the IEEE Conference on Cybernetics and Intelligent Systems (CIS)* (Singapore, December 1–3 2004), pp. 790–795
65. P. Kerschke, H.H. Hoos, F. Neumann, H. Trautmann, Automated algorithm selection: survey and perspectives, in *Evolutionary Computation* (2018), pp. 1–47
66. A. Kheiri, Ed. Keedwell, A hidden markov model approach to the problem of heuristic selection in hyper-heuristics with a case study in high school timetabling problems. Evol. Comput. **25**(3), 473–501 (2017)
67. A.R. KhudaBukhsh, L. Xu, H.H. Hoos, K. Leyton-Brown, Satenstein: automatically building local search sat solvers from components, in *Proceedings of the 21th International Joint Conference on Artifical Intelligence (IJCAI'09)* (2009), pp. 517–524
68. S. Kirkpatrick, C.D. Gelatt, M.P. Vecchi, Optimization by simulated annealing. Science **220**, 671–680 (1983)
69. G. Koulinas, L. Kotsikas, K. Anagnostopoulos, A particle swarm optimization based hyper-heuristic algorithm for the classic resource constrained project scheduling problem. Inf. Sci. **277**, 680–693 (2014)
70. J.R. Koza, *Genetic Programming: On the Programming of Computers by Means of Natural Selection*, vol. 1 (MIT press, 1992)
71. R. Lahyani, A.-L. Gouguenheim, L.C. Coelho, A hybrid adaptive large neighbourhood search for multi-depot open vehicle routing problems. Int. J. Prod. Res., pp. 1–14 (2019)
72. P.K. Lehre, E. Özcan, A runtime analysis of simple hyper-heuristics: to mix or not to mix operators, in *Proceedings of the 12th Workshop on Foundations of Genetic Algorithms (FOGA)* (ACM, 2013), pp. 97–104
73. L. Leng, Y. Zhao, Z. Wang, J. Zhang, W. Wang, C. Zhang, A novel hyper-heuristic for the biobjective regional low-carbon location-routing problem with multiple constraints. Sustainability **11**(6), 1596 (2019)
74. W. Li, E. Ozcan, R. John, Multi-objective evolutionary algorithms and hyper-heuristics for wind farm layout optimisation. Renew. Energy **105**, 473–482 (2017)
75. W. Li, E. Ozcan, R. John, A learning automata based multiobjective hyper-heuristic, in *IEEE Transactions on Evolutionary Computation* (2018)
76. J.A.P. Lima, S.R. Vergilio, et al., Automatic generation of search-based algorithms applied to the feature testing of software product lines, in *Proceedings of the 31st Brazilian Symposium on Software Engineering* (ACM, 2017), pp. 114–123

77. J. Lin, Backtracking search based hyper-heuristic for the flexible job-shop scheduling problem with fuzzy processing time. Eng. Appl. Artif. Intell. **77**, 186–196 (2019)
78. J. Lin, Z.-J. Wang, X. Li, A backtracking search hyper-heuristic for the distributed assembly flow-shop scheduling problem. Swarm Evol. Comput. **36**, 124–135 (2017)
79. J. Lin, L. Zhu, K. Gao, A genetic programming hyper-heuristic approach for the multi-skill resource constrained project scheduling problem, in *Expert Systems with Applications* (2019), pp. 112915
80. A. Lissovoi, P.S. Oliveto, J.A. Warwicker, On the time complexity of algorithm selection hyper-heuristics for multimodal optimisation, in *Proceedings of the AAAI Conference on Artificial Intelligence*, vol. 33 (2019), pp. 2322–2329
81. Y. Liu, Y. Mei, M. Zhang, Z. Zhang, Automated heuristic design using genetic programming hyper-heuristic for uncertain capacitated arc routing problem, in *the 18th Annual Conference on Genetic and Evolutionary Computation (GECCO)* (Berlin, Germany, 2017)
82. M. López-Ibánez, M.-E. Kessaci, T. Stützle, Automatic design of hybrid metaheuristics from algorithmic components. Technical report (2017)
83. H.R. Lourenço, O.C. Martin, T. Stützle, Iterated local search: framework and applications, in *Handbook of metaheuristics* (Springer, 2019), pp. 129–168
84. N. Lourenço, F. Pereira, E. Costa, Evolving evolutionary algorithms, in *Proceedings of the 14th Annual Conference Companion on Genetic and Evolutionary Computation* (ACM, 2012), pp. 51–58
85. S. Luke, *Issues in scaling genetic programming: breeding strategies, tree generation, and code bloat*. Ph.D. thesis, research directed by Dept. of Computer Science.University of Maryland, College Park (2000)
86. M. Maashi, G. Kendall, E. Özcan, Choice function based hyper-heuristics for multi-objective optimization. Appl. Soft Comput. **28**, 312–326 (2015)
87. M. Maashi, E. Ozcan, G. Kendall, A multi-objective hyper-heuristic based on choice function. Expert Syst. Appl. **41**(9) (2014)
88. T. Mariani, G. Guizzo, S.R. Vergilio, A.T.R. Pozo, Grammatical evolution for the multi-objective integration and test order problem, in *Proceedings of the 2016 on Genetic and Evolutionary Computation Conference* (ACM, 2016), pp. 1069–1076
89. F. Mascia, M. López-Ibáñez, J. Dubois-Lacoste, T. Stützle, Grammar-based generation of stochastic local search heuristics through automatic algorithm configuration tools. Comput. Oper. Res. (2014), pp. 190–199
90. A. Mendes, A. Nealen, J. Togelius. Hyperheuristic general video game playing, in *Proceedings of the IEEE Computational Intelligence and Games (CIG)* (2016)
91. P.B. Miranda, R.B. Prudêncio, GEFPSO: a framework for pso optimization based on grammatical evolution, in *Proceedings of the Annual Conference on Genetic and Evolutionary Computation (GECCO)* (ACM, 2015), pp. 1087–1094
92. P.B.C. Miranda, R.B.C. Prudencio, Generation of particle swarm optimization algorithms: an experimental study using grammar-guided genetic programming. Appl. Soft Comput. **60**, 281–296 (2017)
93. P.B.C. Miranda, R.B.C. Prudêncio, G.L. Pappa, H3AD: a hybrid hyper-heuristic for algorithm design, in *Information Sciences* (2017)
94. M. Mısır, Matrix factorization based benchmark set analysis: a case study on HyFlex, in *the 11th International Conference on Simulated Evolution and Learning (SEAL)*, vol. 10593. LNCS (Springer, 2017), pp. 184–195
95. M. Mısır, M. Sebag, ALORS: an algorithm recommender system. Artif. Intell. **244**, 291–314 (2017)
96. M. Mısır, K. Verbeeck, P. De Causmaecker, G. Vanden Berghe, Hyper-heuristics with a dynamic heuristic set for the home care scheduling problem, in *Proceedings of the IEEE Congress on Evolutionary Computation (CEC)* (Barcelona, Spain, 18–23 2010), pp. 2875–2882
97. M. Mısır, T. Wauters, K. Verbeeck, G. Vanden Berghe, A hyper-heuristic with learning automata for the traveling tournament problem, in *Metaheuristics: Intelligent Decision*

Making, the 8th Metaheuristics International Conference (MIC) - Post Conference Volume (Springer, 2011)
98. M. Mısır, P. Smet, G.V. Berghe, An analysis of generalised heuristics for vehicle routing and personnel rostering problems. J. Oper. Res. Soc. **66**(5), 858–870 (2015)
99. M. Mısır, K. Verbeeck, P. De Causmaecker, G.V. Berghe, An investigation on the generality level of selection hyper-heuristics under different empirical conditions. Appl. Soft Comput. **13**(7), 3335–3353 (2013)
100. M. Mısır, K. Verbeeck, P. De Causmaecker, G.V. Berghe, A new hyper-heuristic as a general problem solver: an implementation in HyFlex. J. Sched. **16**(3), 291–311 (2013)
101. A. Mitsos, J. Najman, I.G. Kevrekidis, Optimal deterministic algorithm generation (2016). arXiv:1609.06917
102. S. Nguyen, M. Zhang, M. Johnston, K.C. Tan, Automatic programming via iterated local search for dynamic job shop scheduling. IEEE Trans. Cybern. **45**(1), 1–14 (2015)
103. B. Nikpour, H. Nezamabadi-pour, HTSS: a hyper-heuristic training set selection method for imbalanced data sets. Iran J. Comput. Sci. pp. 1–20 (2018)
104. G. Ochoa, M. Hyde, T. Curtois, J.A. Vazquez-Rodriguez, J. Walker, M. Gendreau, G. Kendall, B. McCollum, A.J. Parkes, S. Petrovic, E.K. Burke, Hyflex: a benchmark framework for cross-domain heuristic search, in *European Conference on Evolutionary Computation in Combinatorial Optimisation(EvoCOP)*, vol. 7245. *LNCS* (Springer, Berlin, 2012), pp. 136–147
105. G. Ochoa, J. Walker, M. Hyde, T. Curtois, Adaptive evolutionary algorithms and extensions to the HyFlex hyper-heuristic framework, in *Proceedings of the 12th International Conference on Parallel Problem Solving from Nature (PPSN)*, vol. 7492. *LNCS*, ed. by C.A. Coello Coello, V. Cutello, K. Deb, S. Forrest, G. Nicosia, M. Pavone (Springer, 2012), pp. 418–427
106. M. O'Neil, C. Ryan, *Grammatical Evolution: Evolutionary Automatic Programming in an Arbitrary Language* (Springer, 2003)
107. M. O'Neill, A. Brabazon, Grammatical differential evolution, in *IC-AI* (2006), pp. 231–236
108. E. Özcan, M. Mısır, G. Ochoa, E.K. Burke, A reinforcement learning - great-deluge hyper-heuristic for examination timetabling. Int. J. Appl. Metaheuristic Comput. **1**(1), 39–59 (2010)
109. J. Park, S. Yi Mei, G.C. Nguyen, M. Zhang, An investigation of ensemble combination schemes for genetic programming based hyper-heuristic approaches to dynamic job shop scheduling. Appl. Soft Comput. **63**, 72–86 (2018)
110. N. Pillay, D. Beckedahl, EvoHyp - a java toolkit for evolutionary algorithm hyper-heuristics, in *IEEE Congress on Evolutionary Computation (CEC)* (San Sebastian, Spain, 2017)
111. N. Pillay, E. Özcan, Automated generation of constructive ordering heuristics for educational timetabling. Ann. Oper. Res. **275**(1), 181–208 (2019)
112. N. Pillay, Q. Rong, *Hyper-Heuristics: Theory and Applications*. Natural Computing Series (Springer, 2018)
113. N. Pillay, R. Qu, Nurse rostering problems, in *Hyper-Heuristics: Theory and Applications* (Springer, 2018), pp. 61–66
114. E. Pitzer, M. Affenzeller, A comprehensive survey on fitness landscape analysis, in *Recent Advances in Intelligent Engineering Systems* (Springer, 2012), pp. 161–191
115. R. Poli, M. Graff, There is a free lunch for hyper-heuristics, genetic programming and computer scientists, in *the 12th European Conference on Genetic Programming (EuroGP)* (Tubingen, Germany, 2009)
116. C.B. Pop, V.R. Chifu, N. Dragoi, I. Salomie, E.S. Chifu, Recommending healthy personalized daily menus–a cuckoo search-based hyper-heuristic approach, in *Applied Nature-Inspired Computing: Algorithms and Case Studies* (Springer, 2020), pp. 41–70
117. S.M. Pour, J.H. Drake, E.K. Burke, A choice function hyper-heuristic framework for the allocation of maintenance tasks in danish railways. Comput. Oper. Res. **93**, 15–26 (2018)
118. R. Qu, E.K. Burke, Hybridizations within a graph-based hyper-heuristic framework for university timetabling problems. J. Oper. Res. Soc. **60**(9), 1273–1285 (2009)
119. Q. Rong, N. Pham, R. Bai, G. Kendall, Hybridising heuristics within an estimation distribution algorithm for examination timetabling. Appl. Intell. **42**(4) (2015)

120. N.R. Sabar, M. Ayob, G. Kendall, R. Qu, Automatic design of a hyper-heuristic framework with gene expression programming for combinatorial optimization problems. IEEE Trans. Evol. Comput. **19**(3), 309–325 (2015)
121. N.R. Sabar, M. Ayob, G. Kendall, R. Qu, A dynamic multiarmed bandit-gene expression programming hyper-heuristic for combinatorial optimization problems. IEEE Trans. Cybern. **45**(2), 217–228 (2015)
122. N.R. Sabar, A. Turky, A. Song, A. Sattar, An evolutionary hyper-heuristic to optimise deep belief networks for image reconstruction. Appl. Soft Comput. pp. 105510 (2019)
123. W. Samek, T. Wiegand, K.-R. Müller, Explainable artificial intelligence: understanding, visualizing and interpreting deep learning models (2017). arXiv:1708.08296
124. W. Shi, X. Song, J. Sun, Automatic heuristic generation with scatter programming to solve the hybrid flow shop problem. Adv. Mech. Eng. **7**(2) (2015)
125. K. Sim, E. Hart, A combined generative and selective hyper-heuristic for the vehicle routing problem, in *Proceedings of Genetic and Evolutionary Computation Conference (GECCO)* (ACM, 2016), pp. 1093–1100
126. K. Sim, E. Hart, B. Paechter, A lifelong learning hyper-heuristic method for bin packing. Evol. Comput. **23**(1), 37–67 (2015)
127. E.S. Sin, N.S.M. Kham, Hyper heuristic based on great deluge and its variants for exam timetabling problem. Int. J. Artif. Intell. Appl. **3**(1), 149–162 (2012)
128. J.A. Soria-Alcaraz, G. Ochoa, M.A. Sotelo-Figeroa, E.K. Burke, A methodology for determining an effective subset of heuristics in selection hyper-heuristics. Eur. J. Oper. Res. **260**(3), 972–983 (2017)
129. J.A. Soria-Alcaraz, G. Ochoa, M.A. Sotelo-Figueroa, M. Carpio, H. Puga, Iterated vnd versus hyper-heuristics: Effective and general approaches to course timetabling, in *Nature-Inspired Design of Hybrid Intelligent Systems* (Springer, 2017), pp. 687–700
130. J.A. Soria-Alcaraz, G. Ochoa, J. Swan, M. Carpio, H. Puga, E.K. Burke, Effective learning hyper-heuristics for the course timetabling problem. Eur. J. Oper. Res. **238**(1) (2014)
131. J.A. Soria-Alcaraz, E. Özcan, J. Swan, G. Kendall, M. Carpio, Iterated local search using an add and delete hyper-heuristic for university course timetabling. Appl. Soft Comput. **40**, 581–593 (2016)
132. A. Sosa-Ascencio, G. Ochoa, H. Terashima-Marin, S.E. Conant-Pablos, Grammar-based generation of variable-selection heuristics for constraint satisfaction problems, Genet. Program. Evolvable Mach. **17**(2), 119–144 (2016)
133. M.A. Sotelo-Figueroa, H.J.P. Soberanes, J.M. Carpio, H.J.F. Huacuja, L.C. Reyes, J.A.S. Alcaraz, A. Espinal, Generating bin packing heuristic through grammatical evolution based on bee swarm optimization, in *Nature-Inspired Design of Hybrid Intelligent Systems* (Springer, 2017), pp. 655–671
134. C. Stone, E. Hart, B. Paechter, Automatic generation of constructive heuristics for multiple types of combinatorial optimisation problems with grammatical evolution and geometric graphs, in *International Conference on the Applications of Evolutionary Computation* (Springer, 2018), pp. 578–593
135. A. Strickler, J.A. Prado Lima, S.R. Vergilio, A.T.R. Pozo, Deriving products for variability test of feature models with a hyper-heuristic approach. Appl. Soft Comput. **49**, 1232–1242 (2016)
136. R.S. Sutton, A.G. Barto, *Reinforcement Learning: An Introduction* (MIT press, 2018)
137. J. Swan, P. De Causmaecker, S. Martin, E. Ozcan, A re-characterization of hyper-heuristics, in *Recent Developments of Metaheuristics*, ed. by L. Amodeo, E-G. Talbi, F. Yalaoui (Springer, 2018), pp. 75–89
138. F. Tao, L. Bi, Y. Zuo, A.Y.C. Nee, Partial/parallel disassembly sequence planning for complex products. J. Manuf. Sci. Eng. **140**(1), 011016 (2018)
139. Y. Tenne, C.-K. Goh, *Computational Intelligence in Expensive Optimization Problems*, vol. 2 (Springer Science & Business Media, 2010)
140. D. Thierens, Adaptive strategies for operator allocation. Parameter Setting Evol. Algorithms **54**, 77–90 (2007)

141. R.R.S. van Lon, J. Branke, T. Holvoet, Optimizing agents with genetic programming: an evaluation of hyper-heuristics in dynamic real-time logistics, in *Genetic Programming and Evolvable Machines* (2017), pp. 1–28
142. J. Vanschoren, Meta-learning, in *Automated Machine Learning* (Springer, 2019), pp. 35–61
143. J.D. Walker, G. Ochoa, M. Gendreau, E.K. Burke, Vehicle routing and adaptive iterated local search within the HyFlex hyper-heuristic framework, in *Proceedings of the 6th Learning and Intelligent OptimizatioN Conference (LION)*, vol. 7219. LNCS, ed. by Y. Hamadi, M. Schoenauer (Springer, 2012), pp. 265–276
144. D. Whitley, Next generation genetic algorithms: a users guide and tutorial, in *Handbook of Metaheuristics* (Springer, 2019), pp. 245–274
145. D.H. Wolpert, W.G. Macready, No free lunch theorems for optimization. IEEE Trans. Evol. Comput. **1**, 67–82 (1997)
146. Y. Yao, Z. Peng, B. Xiao, Parallel hyper-heuristic algorithm for multi-objective route planning in a smart city. IEEE Trans. Veh. Technol. **67**(11), 10307–10318 (2018)
147. H. Youssef, E. Monfroy, F. Saubion, *Autonomous Search* (Springer, New York, 2012)
148. S. Yu, A. Song, A. Aleti, Collective hyper-heuristics for self-assembling robot behaviours, in *Pacific Rim International Conference on Artificial Intelligence* (Springer, 2018), pp. 499–507
149. S. Yu, A. Song, A. Aleti, A study on online hyper-heuristic learning for swarm robots, in *IEEE Congress on Evolutionary Computation (CEC)* (IEEE, 2019), pp. 2721–2728
150. K.Z. Zamli, B.Y. Alkazemi, G. Kendall, A tabu search hyper-heuristic strategy for t-way test suite generation. Appl. Soft Comput. **44**, 57–74 (2016)
151. C. Zhang, Y. Zhao, L. Leng, A hyper heuristic algorithm to solve the low-carbon location routing problem. Algorithms **12**(7), 129 (2019)
152. Y. Zhang, M. Harman, G. Ochoa, G. Ruhe, S. Brinkkemper, An empirical study of meta- and hyper-heuristic search for multi-objective release planning. ACM Trans. Softw. Eng. Methodol. (TOSEM) **27**(1), 3 (2018)

Chapter 8
Toward Real-Time Federated Evolutionary Neural Architecture Search

Hangyu Zhu and Yaochu Jin

Abstract Neural architecture search (NAS) is an important research topic of automated machine learning, which aims to automatically search for neural network architectures that can efficiently learn for a given task. Furthermore, there is an increasing demand for deploying computationally efficient NAS systems that can be used on edge devices that have limited computational powers. In particular, federated learning is an online distributed machine learning scheme that requires online and federated search of neural architectures involving edge devices. However, most exiting NAS methods are naturally not well suited for distributed real-time systems, due to high computational and communication costs. This chapter provides a brief introduction to methods for reducing computational cost in NAS, followed by a presentation of two evolutionary frameworks we recently developed for real-time federated NAS.

8.1 Introduction

Neural architecture search (NAS) is one of the hottest research topics in automated machine learning. Instead of designing the architecture of neural networks by a human expert, NAS aims to accomplish this task automatically. A plethora of research on NAS has been done in recent years, empirically demonstrating that NAS is able to find neural network models better than human experts.

Reinforcement learning (RL) is one of the most commonly used search strategies for NAS [1, 36, 39, 40]. The general framework of this approach contains an agent

H. Zhu · Y. Jin (✉)
Department of Computer Science, University of Surrey, Guildford GU2 7XH, UK
e-mail: yaochu.jin@surrey.ac.uk

H. Zhu
e-mail: hangyu.zhu@surrey.ac.uk

N. Pillay and R. Qu (eds.), *Automated Design of Machine Learning and Search Algorithms*, Natural Computing Series,
https://doi.org/10.1007/978-3-030-72069-8_8

(controller) and an environment. The controller is used to sample and generate a model from a pre-defined architecture pool, and then this model can be trained by gradient descent methods [26] on real training data. After that, the trained model will send a reward back to the controller based on its performance upon the validation data for updating the parameters of the controller. By repeating this process, the enhanced controller is able to sample a model architecture with expected better performance.

Unlike RL based methods that only optimize one objective (the reward), evolutionary algorithms (EAs), as a class of population-based search methods, can more elegantly deal with multi-objective NAS problems [18, 20, 24, 25, 29, 38] by using multi-objective evolutionary algorithms (MOEAs) [6, 7]. At one generation of evolutionary optimization, a population of offspring solutions, each representing a new architecture, are generated using genetic operators such as crossover and mutation from existing architectures (a population of parent solutions). Usually, all these newly generated architectures need to be trained to calculate the value of the objective function. If NAS is formulated to be an optimization problem containing more than one objective, such as maximization of accuracy and minimization of model complexity, the Pareto dominance relationships between these solutions are usually used to determine whether a solution can survive and become the parent solutions of the next generation. After the evolution of several generations, a set of Pareto optimal solution models will be found.

Although NAS algorithms can search for an optimized neural structure automatically and achieve state-of-the-art model performance, it usually requires substantial computation resources and the whole procedure of NAS by training neural network models from scratch is computationally prohibitive. Thus, even though some researchers have made the code for their algorithms public, it remains challenging to reproduce their results for others who may not have the same computational resources. For instance, Zoph et al. [39] present some early work on NAS using reinforcement learning, which needs around 1500 GPUs per day for training. In addition, not all potential users of NAS can afford such huge computational resources. So developing lightweight and computationally efficient NAS frameworks has become a high demand for NAS research.

All aforementioned NAS methods are developed for a centralized learning environment, which requires storing all training data on a single powerful server for training. This requirement may cause concerns about privacy leakage. Therefore, a distributed learning approach called federated learning [3] was proposed to mitigate this issue by enabling multiple local devices to collaboratively train a shared global model. Specifically, every connected client can train and update their model parameters on their own data, and upload the trained model parameters or gradients to the server where all the uploads will be aggregated to generate a new shared global model. In this framework, the central server has no access to the private raw data and thus the client privacy is protected to a certain degree.

However, existing search strategies for NAS are not well suited for distributed machine learning such as federated learning for the following reasons.

1. Most deep learning models contain batch normalization layers [14] which is used to calibrate the statistics of layer outs for training mini-batch data. The batch normalization layer is used to normalize the outputs of hidden layers in the neural network, e.g., by subtracting the mean and then dividing the variance among feature channels. However, it becomes unclear if the moving statistic of batch normalization is still correct or not after the global model aggregation in the central server. And incorrect statistics of batch normalization will definitely cause severe divergence of the global model.
2. Many current search strategies focus on improving the model performance without paying much attention to the model size and computation cost. Edge devices like mobile phones cannot afford computationally intensive model training and bandwidth restrictions do not allow very large models to be transmitted frequently between the server and clients.
3. Almost all the NAS methods are offline optimization schemes. That is, model architecture search and model training are performed in sequence but not at the same time. Consequently, the searched model needs to be trained from scratch to achieve the final stand-alone result. However, it is not applicable in federated learning, since this kind of model training is expensive and consumes additional communication resources.
4. The training data on clients in federated learning are always non-independent and identically distributed (non-IID) while all the NAS systems are built on IID dataset. For instance, datasets on every client share the same feature space but different spaces in samples. Non-IID may lead to unexpected impact for federated NAS optimization.

In order to address the problems above, it is necessary to develop a real-time approach to enable NAS in a federated environment. In addition, we believe federated NAS is also a multi-objective task, where the model performance should be maximized and the communication cost needs to be minimized.

8.2 Computationally Efficient Neural Architecture Search

Most NAS aims to find an optimal repeated cell (a module or sub-network) to construct the whole neural network model, while the number of total cells and the linking method among these cells are always fixed. And each cell is represented by a directed acyclic graph (DAG) where each node denotes one model operation (i.e., convolutional operation) and each directed edge means a connection between two nodes. However, early methods for NAS [39] are computationally expensive and training the whole procedure from scratch needs approximately one month for one GPU. Fortunately, many researchers have already recognized this as a big issue in NAS and developed lightweight and computationally efficient NAS methods, which are divided into the following four categories:

1. Parameter sharing. The idea of parameter sharing was first proposed by Pham et al. [23] to represent the whole NAS search space using a DAG, in which the nodes represent the local computations and the edges represent the flow of information. Thus, a model architecture can be derived by sampling a subgraph of the DAG and the model parameters of each node are trained or updated when the node is activated. In other words, the search progress only changes the connection method among the individual nodes in a DAG, while all the node operations remain unchanged during the NAS. Recently, this parameter sharing technique has been widely used in [5, 9, 10, 19, 28, 32, 35], because it can avoid model reinitialization for sampled subgraphs which can significantly shrink the training time used in NAS.
2. Proxy models. Proxy models can reduce both computational time and memory consumption for training. A proxy [5] model approach aims to reduce the computation load during the search progress of NAS and the main idea is to do structure search on a smaller model (e.g, models with less cells). The searched cell structure can be transferred into a much larger model which will be trained from scratch to achieve the final stand-alone model performance. However, this method is very likely to bring in search biases and it is uncertain if the architecture found in the proxy model still works or not in the final model [28].
3. Surrogate-assisted optimization. Surrogate-assisted evolutionary optimization [15] has been very popular in data-driven surrogate-assisted evolutionary optimization, where cheap machine learning models (surrogates) are built to replace in part the expensive fitness evaluations. Thus, surrogate-assisted NAS methods [30], Bayesian optimization [16, 31] or Bayesian evolutionary optimization [37] can be used to accelerate model evaluations by using cheap approximated models to replace the time-consuming training of deep neural networks. Here, the already trained neural architectures and their corresponding performances are used to train the surrogate model. Then in the evolutionary search, this surrogate model is used to quickly predict the performance when a new model architecture is generated.
4. Gradient-based method. Gradient-based methods are currently the fastest class of NAS methods. It was originally introduced in DARTS [19], where all the available operations and connections within a cell are re-parameterized and summed together. Thus, this also utilizes the idea of parameter sharing and architecture search can be performed directly by a very fast gradient descent algorithm [26] that reduces the training time to 1.5 GPU days. Subsequent research enhancement [9, 32] has been done on DARTS to further reduce the computation time to 4 GPU hours. One shortcoming of the gradient-based methods is that these methods need much more hardware memory than other NAS approaches because all the model paths in a cell are computed simultaneously, which is equivalent to training several neural networks at the same time.
5. One-shot method. One-shot method is a lightweight approach to NAS. A sampling strategy called one-shot NAS [2, 11] is adopted in which only one or two paths (a path is a sub-network connecting the inputs and outputs) are sampled from a supernet for training. One layer of the supernet is another kind of DAG (also called choice block) containing several branches and each branch represents a

pre-defined combination of operations. Since only one or two paths are sampled during the structure search, this one-shot NAS method uses much less computation memory compared to the gradient-based one. In addition, it still implements the idea of parameter sharing and the model parameters of each sampled subnet do not need to be re-initialized and is directly inherited from the supernet.

To sum up, parameter sharing can effectively accelerate NAS procedures by avoiding training sampled neural networks from scratch and this technique is widely used in efficient NAS research work nowadays. The proxy model method is also widely used in NAS, since it can significantly reduce the computation load in the model search procedure. However, it may bring in unexpected search biases. Gradient-based methods have the fastest search speed although it utilizes the largest hardware memories. Finally, the one-shot NAS approach achieves a good trade-off between computation speed and hardware memory usage, which has become the mainstream technique used in efficient NAS [10, 35].

8.3 Evolutionary Optimization of One-Shot Neural Architecture Search

In this section, we would like to introduce the basic idea of 'two-stage' evolutionary one-shot NAS [11], which will be modified and further extended to our proposed real-time federated evolutionary NAS framework.

For the one-shot NAS approach, only one path of the supernet is sampled to construct a subgraph for model evaluation, which saves plenty of hardware memory compared to the gradient-based methods. On the other hand, sampled subnets always share the same model parameters. Thus, the parameter sharing technique can be also used here for accelerating the computation speed.

8.3.1 Training the Supernet

The first stage is to train the supernet. A typical structure of the supernet is shown in Fig. 8.1, which contains a total of L layers and each layer is a so-called choice block consisting of several branches that are pre-defined operation blocks, e.g., residual block used in ResNet [12]. The stem layer is a fixed combination of operations, e.g., convolution followed by batch normalization [14], and the tail layer is always a fully connected layer.

The training strategy for the supernet is as follows. For each min-batch data training iteration, a subnet is randomly generated from the supernet by sampling one path (branch) of the choice block for all L layers. When the search space is large, the training can easily cover all operations, and this is why this single path training strategy works. The pseudocode is shown in Algorithm 6.

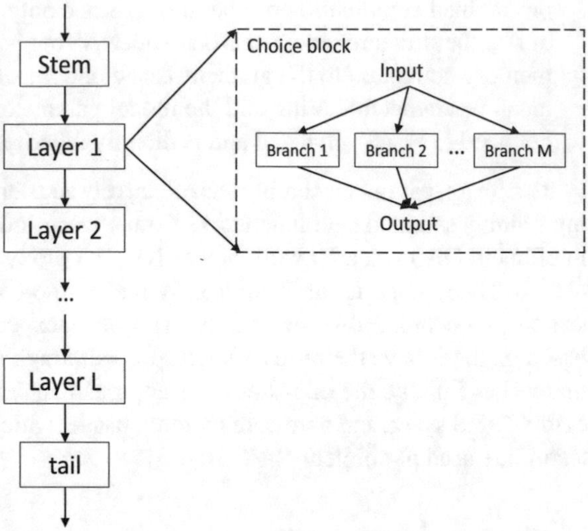

Fig. 8.1 A typical structure of supernet, where the stem and tail are fixed layers and other layers represent multi-branch choice blocks sampled during the training

---

Algorithm 6 Single path supernet training, where N is the total number of training epochs, D is the training data, L is the number of total layers, M is the number of total branches per layer, and $L \times M$ supernet parameters $\Theta(L, M)$.

Initialize parameters of the supernet $\Theta(L, M)$
for $i = 1$ to N **do**
    for $data, labels$ in D **do**
        for each layer $l \in L$ **do**
            Uniformly sample one branch of the choice block $\theta_l^{m_l}$
            where $m_l \in M$ is a random sampled branch for layer l
        Build $subnet = (\theta_1^{m_1}, \theta_2^{m_2}, ..., \theta_L^{m_L})$
        Calculate the gradients of subnet, $\nabla\theta_1^{m_1}, \nabla\theta_2^{m_2}, ..., \nabla\theta_L^{m_L}$
        Update the subnet
Output supernet $\Theta(L, M)$

8.3.2 *Evolutionary Architecture Search*

The second stage to conduct the model architecture search. Efficient NAS is naturally a multi-objective optimization problem since it always needs to deals with at least two objectives, for example, the model accuracy and its floating-point operations per second (FLOPs).

The elitist non-dominated sorting genetic algorithm (NSGA-II) [8] is a very popular multi-objective evolutionary algorithm (MOEA) widely used in evolutionary NAS [11, 18, 20, 24, 25, 29]. The overall framework by using NSGA-II for searching model solutions upon the previously trained supernet is summarized as follows.

1. Initialize N parent model architectures and generate N offspring models by applying crossover and mutation on parents.

2. Combine parent and offspring populations and sample all the subnets from the trained supernet in the whole population.
3. Calculate the objective values for each network. Typically, the accuracy of each sampled subnetworks serves as one objective and the FLOPS or the number of parameters serves as the other objective.
4. Perform fast non-dominated sorting and calculate the crowding distance for individuals on the same front based on their objective values.
5. Select the best N individuals as the new parents.
6. Repeat from step (2) to step (5) until the maximum number of generations is reached.

Finally, all subnet models should be trained from scratch to achieve their final stand-alone model performances.

8.3.3 One-Shot NAS in Federated Learning

One-shot NAS is more suited for federated learning compared to other NAS methods. First, it intrinsically applies parameter sharing techniques to avoid model reinitialization for newly sampled subnets, significantly reducing the communication rounds in federated learning. Thus, using the one-shot NAS model in federated learning can save more communication resources. Second, this method is more suited for client device computation since only one path is sampled for model training and evaluation.

However, conventional evolutionary optimization of one-shot NAS is not a real-time framework, because it does not satisfy the requirement of optimizing the architecture and training the model parameters simultaneously. And this method should be adapted to a real-time scheme for federated learning.

8.4 Real-Time Federated Evolutionary Neural Architecture Search

In this section, the aforementioned evolutionary optimization of one-shot NAS is adjusted at first to satisfy the requirement of real-time evolutionary NAS. And then the structure of the supernet model and the overall procedure of real-time federated evolutionary NAS will be introduced.

8.4.1 Real-Time Evolutionary Neural Architecture Search

Conventional evolutionary one-shot NAS is not appropriate for real-time search, because the training of the supernet and evolutionary search stages are undertaken in sequence while a real-time NAS framework requires optimizing the architecture and train the model parameters at the same time. Apart from this, all the subnets consisting of the found architectures must usually be trained from scratch in the stand-alone environment, which makes it unsuited for real-time NAS.

Different from the one-shot evolutionary NAS described above, we are going to present a real-time method for training the supernet at each generation. That is to say, only the subnets sampled from the parent or offspring individuals will be trained, making it possible that some paths or branches in the supernet may never be trained during the evolutionary optimization. This will lead to a large bias in training the supernet compared to the method used in the previous section.

Once the whole optimization process is complete, we will obtain the trained supernet and a population of subnets from the previous generation. And the final model performances of each subnet can be directly evaluated from the sampled supernet on the validation data.

The above procedure enables us to train the model parameters when optimizing the architecture of the neural networks and there is no need to re-train the optimized subnets from scratch. However, this real-time approach also has some limitations. Since paths of the supernet derived from the parent or offspring individuals can be trained and updated, the architecture search gets more easily trapped in local minima.

8.4.2 Real-Time Federated Evolutionary Neural Architecture Search

The structure of the supernet model used here is similar to the one presented in Fig. 8.1, where a convolutional block ('stem' block), 4×3 choice blocks (total 12 'Layer' block), and a fully connected layer ('tail' block) are linked to build a supernet. Specifically, each choice block has four paths or branches, namely identity block, residual block [12], inverted residual block [27], and depthwise separable block [13]. Thus, in total 4^{20} possible single path subnets can be sampled from a supernet.

We use NSGA-II to optimize both model FLOPs and the accuracy of each sampled subnet (more objectives can be injected, we just use these two objectives as an example here) for the real-time evolutionary federated NAS framework. The overall framework can be divided into the following stages.

1. Initialize the global (master) model. Generate the initial N parent choice keys (each choice key is an encoding number representing one specific subnet) and sample N one-shot model from a master model based on the parent choice keys. Sample m connected clients for each individual in parents without replacement. That is, each client should be sampled only once.
2. Download the subnet of each parent individual to the m selected clients and train it using the data on the clients. Once the training is completed, upload the m local submodels to the server for aggregation, thereby updating the master model.

3. Generate N offspring choice keys using genetic operators and sample N subnets based. Download the subnet of each offspring individual to m randomly sampled participating clients and train it on these clients. After that, these m updated subnetworks will be collected by the server for the maser model aggregation.
4. Download the master model together with the choice keys of all parents and offspring to all clients to evaluate the validation errors and FLOPs. Upload the validation errors and FLOPs to the server and calculate the weighted averaging of validation errors for each individual.
5. Select N best individuals from a combination N parent and N offspring individuals to generate N new parents for the next generation. This whole progress should be repeated until the maximum number of generations is reached.

Note that the whole master model is downloaded to each of the m participating clients for calculating validation errors (the server cannot contain any data in federated learning). Thus, only the offspring choice keys need to be downloaded from the second generation and sampling subnets is done on the client side as the master model has already been downloaded to the client at the last generation.

Model averaging aggregation of this proposed federated NAS method is not easy, as all the locally trained subnets have different model structures. Fortunately, all the m submodels are sampled from the same master supernet model and they can be embedded into m supernets before averaging the model parameters.

8.5 Steady State Evolutionary Federated Neural Architecture Search

At each generation, the method proposed above generates N (which is the population size) new subnets and then randomly allocates these subnets to all connected clients for model training. Therefore, the whole population may vary a lot between two generations, which makes evolutionary optimization unstable.

Different from generational MOEAs where all parents are replaced by offspring at each generation, steady-state MOEAs [4, 33, 34] immediately re-sort the whole population as long as one new offspring is created. Therefore, steady-state MOEAs are relatively more stable and the whole population does not change a lot between two adjacent generations.

In addition, it is inefficient to use generational MOEAs under the parallel computing environment, because generation methods can only start sorting individuals of the whole population until all fitness values are collected. Just as mentioned before, steady-state MOEAs update the whole population once a new offspring comes which can save a lot of waiting time for parallel computing.

Apart from it, tournament selection is often used in steady-state MOEAs. It aims to select the fittest candidates from the current generation to the next generation. For a K-way tournament selection, k individuals would be selected and only the best candidate among these selected candidates can be chosen for the next generation.

For example, we can select the individual located at the Pareto front in k individuals. This technique can potentially enhance the probability of selecting good solutions in steady-state MOEAs.

When a steady-state MOEA is adopted for federated NAS, only one choice key and one related subnet are generated from the parent choice keys. In this case, there is no need to do client sampling from the second generation onward, and just one choice key (or one sampled subnet in the first generation) is downloaded to every connected client for local training. It should be noticed that we still need to sample clients and perform local training for all N sampled subnets in the first generation.

This steady-state MOEA can accelerate the convergence speed at the early stage, since all the connected clients just train one sampled subnet model. However, it may aggravate the problem of biased training of the master supernet and is easier to get trapped into a local minimum in architecture search.

8.6 Illustrative Empirical Results

8.6.1 Experimental Settings

In the following, we are going to present some empirical results comparing the two approaches to real-time evolutionary NAS described in the previous sections. The population size of the NSGA-II is set to 10 and the number of generations to 300. The probability of crossover and mutation are set to 0.9 and 0.1, respectively.

For federated learning settings, the number of connected clients for each communication round is 20, and each local subnet is only trained for one epoch with a batch size of 50. Moreover, the initial learning rate is 0.1 with a learning rate decay of 0.995 and the learning momentum is 0.5 here. Both learnable parameters and moving statistics are disabled in the supernet.

8.6.2 Dataset

We use three datasets in our simulations: CIFAR10 [17], CIFAR100 [17] and SVHN [21]. All these datasets are 32×32 RGB images for image classification tasks.

CIFAR10 dataset contains 50000 training and 10000 test data with 10 different kinds of objects, and CIFAR100 has the same number of data compared to CIFAR10 but with 100 different kinds of objects. SVHN has 73257 training digits and 26032 testing digits ranging from 1 to 10.

For IID federated simulations, all training image data are evenly and randomly distributed to each local client without overlaps. For experiments on non-IID data, each client has images with only five (50 for CIFAR100 dataset) different kinds of objects. No extra data augmentation [22] is used in our simulation, since the server cannot do any operations on the client data in federated learning.

8.6.3 Real-Time Performances Between NSGA-II and Steady-State NSGA-II

ResNet18 [12] is the baseline model used in our simulations. Without the learnable parameters of all batch normalization layers, it has a FLOPs (MAC) of $0.5587G$ on CIFAR10, CIFAR100, and SVHN dataset and it contains 11.16(M) learnable parameters.

In this simulation, we use the CIFAR10 dataset and set validation error and model FLOPs as two objectives. The real-time performances of two Pareto optimal models found by both two evolutionary NAS algorithms (NSGA-II and steady-state NSGA-II), one is the model having the highest validation accuracy and the other is the knee solution of the Pareto front. The results are plotted in Fig. 8.2. It is clear to see that ResNet18 converges much faster than all models found by the evolutionary search method at the early stages for both IID and non-IID datasets. However, both Pareto optimal models found by the two algorithms outperform ResNet18 at the end of the communication rounds.

It is clear to observe that the two Pareto optimal models found by NSGA-II have better model performances than the steady-state one for both IID and non-IID data. However, the performances of both models evolved by SS-NSGA-II steadily enhance over the generations and there is no big difference in performance between the knee point model and the one with the highest accuracy obtained by the steady-state method.

The model FLOPs of the four solutions are also shown in Fig. 8.2c, d, which are much smaller than that of the original ResNet18.

8.6.4 Real-Time Performances on Different Datasets

Except CIFAR10 dataset, CIFAR100 and SVHN are also evaluated in our simulations. In addition, we inject the number of model parameters as an additional objective to extend the previous experiments into a three-objective optimization problem. Instead of tracking the real-time validation accuracies among communication rounds, only the final test results are listed here in Table 8.1.

For the CIFAR100 dataset, models having the highest test accuracy and the knee points of the Pareto optimal front perform much better than the default ResNet model and contain much less learnable model parameters and FLOPs for both IID and non-IID datasets. Apart from this, it is surprising to see that ‘High’ solution evolved by IID data is not expected to have higher final test accuracy than that evolved by non-

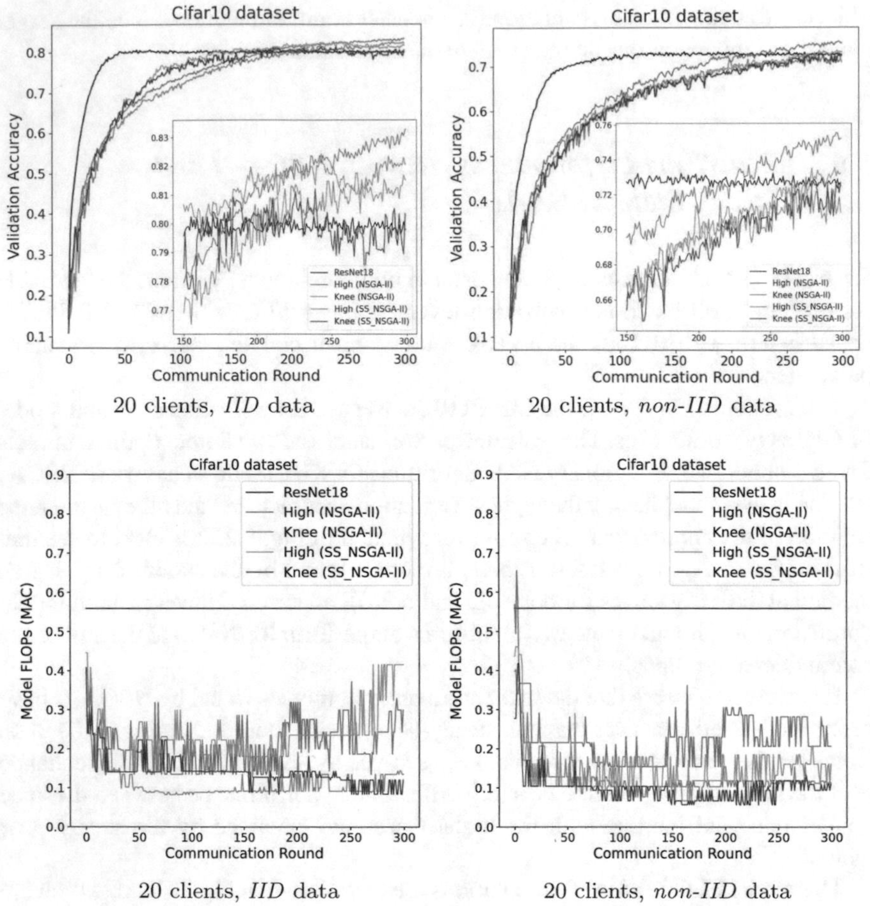

Fig. 8.2 Validation accuracies and the model FLOPs of the best model and the knee solution at each generation of the evolutionary search. Here, NSGA-II denotes the models obtained by the real-time NSGA-II algorithm, whereas SS-NSGA-II denotes the models found by the steady-state NSGA-II

IID data. One reason is that there are some randomness in the search procedure and the other one is model training is hard to converge for this data under the federated environment.

For SVHN dataset, our searched results also show feasible performances compared to the default model. However, the default ResNet model performs slightly better than the searched solutions on non-IID data, while it has a much larger number of parameters and FLOPs.

Table 8.1 Comparison between ResNet and NSGA-II evolved two pareto solutions. # of params means the number of trainable model parameters

Model	Dataset	IID	Test accuracy (%)	FLOPs (MAC)	# of params
ResNet	CIFAR100	Yes	46.15	0.5576G	11.21M
High	CIFAR100	Yes	**52.72**	0.2251G	2.84M
Knee	CIFAR100	Yes	51.39	**0.2112G**	**2.10M**
ResNet	CIFAR100	No	46.35	0.5576G	11.21M
High	CIFAR100	No	**52.86**	0.1560G	2.07M
Knee	CIFAR100	No	50.8	**0.1182G**	**1.60M**
ResNet	SVHN	Yes	94.19	0.5575G	11.16M
High	SVHN	Yes	**94.33**	0.3148G	3.67M
Knee	SVHN	Yes	94.09	**0.1758G**	**2.39M**
ResNet	SVHN	No	**94.07**	0.5575G	11.16M
High	SVHN	No	93.12	0.2219G	2.85M
Knee	SVHN	No	92.89	**0.1287G**	**2.53M**

8.7 Conclusion

This chapter introduces the most recent work on efficient NAS and discusses why these NAS methods are not suited for federated NAS. A real-time evolutionary federated NAS framework is proposed so that NAS can be used in a federated environment. This is made possible by sampling both the master supernet and the connected clients. This approach ensures that the supernet is trained together with the architecture search and therefore, no extra communication costs are needed when evolutionary optimization is adopted for real-time neural architecture search. In addition, a steady-state multi-objective approach is also introduced for federated neural architecture search.

Much work remains to be done for future work. Although the two approaches presented in this chapter perform well for federated learning when the data is horizontally partitioned, they are expected to work properly when the data is vertically partitioned. Another issue is that the risk of privacy leakage cannot fully avoid using the federated learning approach, in particular when the data is vertically partitioned. Thus, homomorphic encryption and other secure multi-party computation techniques must be incorporated into the federated learning framework to make machine learning more secure and trustworthy.

References

1. B. Baker, O. Gupta, N. Naik, R. Raskar, Designing neural network architectures using reinforcement learning (2016). arXiv:1611.02167
2. G. Bender, Understanding and simplifying one-shot architecture search (2019)
3. H. Brendan McMahan, E. Moore, D. Ramage, S. Hampson, B. Agüera y Arcas, Communication-efficient learning of deep networks from decentralized data (2016). arXiv:1602.05629
4. M. Buzdalov, I. Yakupov, A. Stankevich, Fast implementation of the steady-state nsga-ii algorithm for two dimensions based on incremental non-dominated sorting, in *Proceedings of the 2015 Annual Conference on Genetic and Evolutionary Computation* (2015), pp. 647–654
5. H. Cai, L. Zhu, S. Han, Proxylessnas: direct neural architecture search on target task and hardware (2018). arXiv:1812.00332
6. C. Coello Coello, A comprehensive survey of evolutionary-based multiobjective optimization techniques. Knowl. Inf. Syst. **1**(3), 269–308 (1999)
7. C. Coello Coello, Evolutionary multiobjective optimization: open research areas and some challenges lying ahead. Complex Intell. Syst. **6**(2), 221–236 (2020)
8. K. Deb, A. Pratap, S. Agarwal, T.A.M.T. Meyarivan, A fast and elitist multiobjective genetic algorithm: Nsga-ii. IEEE Trans. Evol. Comput. **6**(2), 182–197 (2002)
9. X. Dong, Y. Yang, Searching for a robust neural architecture in four gpu hours, in *Proceedings of the IEEE Conference on Computer Vision and Pattern Recognition* (2019), pp. 1761–1770
10. X. Dong, Y. Yang, Nas-bench-102: extending the scope of reproducible neural architecture search (2020). arXiv:2001.00326
11. Z. Guo, X. Zhang, H. Mu, W. Heng, Z. Liu, Y. Wei, J. Sun, Single path one-shot neural architecture search with uniform sampling (2019). arXiv:1904.00420
12. K. He, X. Zhang, S. Ren, J. Sun, Deep residual learning for image recognition, in *Proceedings of the IEEE Conference on Computer Vision and Pattern Recognition* (2016), pp. 770–778
13. A.G. Howard, M. Zhu, B. Chen, D. Kalenichenko, W. Wang, T. Weyand, M. Andreetto, H. Adam, Mobilenets: efficient convolutional neural networks for mobile vision applications (2017). arXiv:1704.04861
14. S. Ioffe, C. Szegedy, Batch normalization: Accelerating deep network training by reducing internal covariate shift (2015). arXiv:1502.03167
15. Y. Jin, H. Wang, T. Chugh, D. Guo, K. Miettinen, Data-driven evolutionary optimization: an overview and case studies. IEEE Trans. Evol. Comput. **23**(3), 442–458 (2019)
16. K. Kandasamy, W. Neiswanger, J. Schneider, B. Poczos, E.P. Xing, Neural architecture search with Bayesian optimisation and optimal transport, in *Advances in Neural Information Processing Systems* (2018), pp. 2016–2025
17. A. Krizhevsky, V. Nair, G. Hinton, Cifar-10 (canadian institute for advanced research) (2010). http://www.cs.toronto.edu/kriz/cifar.html
18. H. Liu, K. Simonyan, O. Vinyals, C. Fernando, K. Kavukcuoglu, Hierarchical representations for efficient architecture search (2017). arXiv:1711.00436
19. H. Liu, K. Simonyan, Y. Yang, Darts: differentiable architecture search (2018). arXiv:1806.09055
20. Z. Lu, I. Whalen, V. Boddeti, Y. Dhebar, K. Deb, E. Goodman, W. Banzhaf, A multi-objective genetic algorithm for neural architecture search, Nsga-net (2018)
21. Y. Netzer, T. Wang, A. Coates, A. Bissacco, B. Wu, A.Y. Ng, Reading digits in natural images with unsupervised feature learning (2011)
22. L. Perez, J. Wang, The effectiveness of data augmentation in image classification using deep learning (2017). arXiv:1712.04621
23. H. Pham, M.Y. Guan, B. Zoph, Q.V. Le, J. Dean, Efficient neural architecture search via parameter sharing (2018). arXiv:1802.03268
24. E. Real, A. Aggarwal, Y. Huang, Q.V. Le, Regularized evolution for image classifier architecture search, in *Proceedings of the aaai Conference on Artificial Intelligence*, vol. 33 (2019), pp. 4780–4789

25. E. Real, S. Moore, A. Selle, S. Saxena, Y. Leon Suematsu, J. Tan, Q.V. Le, A. Kurakin, Large-scale evolution of image classifiers, in *Proceedings of the 34th International Conference on Machine Learning*, vol. 70 (JMLR. org, 2017), pp. 2902–2911
26. S. Ruder, An overview of gradient descent optimization algorithms (2016). arXiv:1609.04747
27. M. Sandler, A. Howard, M. Zhu, A. Zhmoginov, L.-C. Chen, Mobilenetv2: inverted residuals and linear bottlenecks, in *Proceedings of the IEEE Conference on Computer Vision and Pattern Recognition* (2018), pp. 4510–4520
28. C. Sciuto, K. Yu, M. Jaggi, C. Musat, M. Salzmann, Evaluating the search phase of neural architecture search (2019). arXiv:1902.08142
29. M. Suganuma, S. Shirakawa, T. Nagao, A genetic programming approach to designing convolutional neural network architectures, in *Proceedings of the Genetic and Evolutionary Computation Conference* (2017), pp. 497–504
30. Y. Sun, H. Wang, B. Xue, Y. Jin, G.G. Yen, M. Zhang, Surrogate-assisted evolutionary deep learning using an end-to-end random forest-based performance predictor. IEEE Trans. Evol. Comput. **24**(2), 350–364 (2020)
31. C. White, W. Neiswanger, Y. Savani, BANANAS: bayesian optimization with neural architectures for neural architecture search (2019). arXiv:1910.11858
32. Y. Xu, L. Xie, X. Zhang, X. Chen, G.-J. Qi, Q. Tian, H. Xiong, Pc-darts: partial channel connections for memory-efficient architecture search, in *International Conference on Learning Representations* (2019)
33. I. Yakupov, M. Buzdalov, Improved incremental non-dominated sorting for steady-state evolutionary multiobjective optimization, in *Proceedings of the Genetic and Evolutionary Computation Conference* (2017), pp. 649–656
34. I. Yakupov, M. Buzdalov, On asynchronous non-dominated sorting for steady-state multiobjective evolutionary algorithms, in *Proceedings of the Genetic and Evolutionary Computation Conference Companion* (2018), pp. 205–206
35. A. Zela, J. Siems, F. Hutter, Nas-bench-1shot1: benchmarking and dissecting one-shot neural architecture search (2020). arXiv:2001.10422
36. Z. Zhong, J. Yan, W. Wu, J. Shao, C.-L. Liu, Practical block-wise neural network architecture generation, in *Proceedings of the IEEE Conference on Computer Vision and Pattern Recognition* (2018), pp. 2423–2432
37. Y. Zhou, Y. Jin, J. Ding, Surrogate-assisted evolutionary search of spiking neural architectures in liquid state machines. Neurocomputing (2020)
38. H. Zhu, Y. Jin, Multi-objective evolutionary federated learning. IEEE Trans. Neural Netw. Learn. Syst. **31**(4), 1320–1322 (2020)
39. B. Zoph, Q.V. Le, Neural architecture search with reinforcement learning (2016). arXiv:1611.01578
40. B. Zoph, V. Vasudevan, J. Shlens, Q.V. Le, Learning transferable architectures for scalable image recognition, in *Proceedings of the IEEE Conference on Computer Vision and Pattern Recognition* (2018), pp. 8697–8710

Chapter 9
Knowledge Transfer in Genetic Programming Hyper-heuristics

Yi Mei, Mazhar Ansari Ardeh, and Mengjie Zhang

Abstract Genetic Programming Hyper-heuristics (GPHHs) have been successfully applied in various problem domains for automatically designing heuristics such as dispatching rules in scheduling and routing policies in vehicle routing. In the real world, it is normal to encounter related problem domains, such as the vehicle routing problem with different objectives, constraints, and/or graph topology. On one hand, different heuristics are required for different problem domains. On the other hand, the knowledge learned from solving previous related problem domains can be helpful for solving the current one. Most existing studies solve different problem domains in isolation, and train/evolve the heuristic for each of them from scratch. In this chapter, we investigate different mechanisms to improve the effectiveness and efficiency of the heuristic retraining by employing *knowledge transfer*. Specifically, in the context of GPHH, we explored the following two transfer strategies: (1) useful subtrees and (2) importance of terminals, and verified their effectiveness in a case study of the uncertain capacitated arc routing problem.

9.1 Introduction

Due to its advantage of flexible representation, Genetic Programming (GP) has been successfully employed as a hyper-heuristic approach for *automatic heuristic design* for a variety of complex combinatorial optimisation problems such as production scheduling [2] and vehicle routing [19], especially in a dynamic or uncertain environment, where the preplanned solution has to be adjusted in an online fashion to react to the environment change. In these situations, the traditional solution

Y. Mei (✉) · M. A. Ardeh · M. Zhang
Victoria University of Wellington, Wellington, New Zealand
e-mail: yi.mei@ecs.vuw.ac.nz

M. A. Ardeh
e-mail: mazhar.ansariardeh@ecs.vuw.ac.nz

M. Zhang
e-mail: mengjie.zhang@ecs.vuw.ac.nz

N. Pillay and R. Qu (eds.), *Automated Design of Machine Learning and Search Algorithms*, Natural Computing Series,
https://doi.org/10.1007/978-3-030-72069-8_9

(re-)optimisation approaches (e.g. mathematical programming and genetic algorithms) are often not efficient enough to meet the real-time requirement. A GP-based Hyper-heuristic (GPHH) [3], on the other hand, evolves a heuristic that can make real-time decisions.

In the real world, problems rarely exist in isolation [14]. Instead, related or similar problems can be encountered in a sequential or parallel manner. Examples include supply chain scheduling for different companies and timetabling for different universities, which may have different but related considerations (e.g. objectives and constraints).

Human experts naturally gain knowledge from the previous problem solving and leverage it to solve related problems encountered later on. As a result, an experienced domain expert can develop effective algorithms or heuristics much more efficiently than a novice. On the contrary, in automatic algorithm/heuristic design with computers, such *knowledge transfer* is mostly neglected by the existing hyper-heuristic approaches. To address this issue and to improve the efficiency and effectiveness of GPHH in the context of ongoing problem solving, we propose the *GPHH with Knowledge Transfer (GPHH-KT)* in this chapter.

For knowledge transfer, there are three key issues [36]: (1) *what to transfer*, (2) *how to transfer*, and (3) *when to transfer*. In this chapter, we will focus on addressing these three research issues and investigate a variety of strategies in the context of GPHH. For the investigation, we select the Uncertain Capacitated Arc Routing Problem (UCARP) [27], which has a wide range of real-world applications such as waste collection and winter gritting, as a case study. Our preliminary experimental studies demonstrate a great potential of knowledge transfer in improving both efficiency and effectiveness of GPHH for evolving routing policies for UCARP.

The rest of the chapter is organised as follows. Section 9.2 describes the background, including GPHH and its application to UCARP, and transfer learning and optimisation. Section 9.3 describes the proposed GPHH-KT methods. Section 9.4 shows the experimental studies. Finally, Sect. 9.5 gives the conclusions and future work.

9.2 Background

This section briefly describes the background on GPHH and its application to UCARP and transfer learning and optimisation.

9.2.1 Genetic Programming Hyper-heuristic

According to [4, 5], GPHH is a commonly used heuristic generation methodology, which has been successfully applied to automatically generate heuristics for various challenging combinatorial optimisation problems such as boolean satisfiability [13,

35, 40], production scheduling [2, 21, 31, 46], vehicle routing [19], and orienteering problem [29]. In general, the design of a GPHH approach consists of the following key steps [3]:

1. **Examine currently used heuristics** of the problem at hand to understand the commonality between them. Then derive a *framework* of which each existing heuristic is a special case. Such a framework is usually called the *meta-algorithm* in GPHH literature (e.g. [20, 24]).
2. **Decide the component in the meta-algorithm to be evolved by GP**. Such a component is typically a configurable part of the framework, where the existing heuristics differ from each other. The design of the meta-algorithm can be non-trivial. For example, for bin packing, one can use either the AnyFit-based (i.e. open a new bin only if no current bin has enough space) or the reservation-based (i.e. allow opening a new bin early to reserve space) framework [41], depending on the scenario and objective(s) considered.
3. **Decide the terminal and function sets** of GP. The terminal set generally consists of the features expressing the state of the problem, as well as random constants. The function set is problem-specific and typically includes the basic arithmetic operators and domain-specific operators (e.g. AND and OR for boolean variables or convolutional operators for image processing).
4. **Design a fitness function** of GP. Unlike traditional solution optimisation methods, in which an individual is a candidate solution to the problem and can be directly evaluated, an individual in GPHH is a *heuristic* whose fitness function is not trivially defined. Here one can employ the machine learning paradigm and evaluate the individual based on a set of *training instances*. Specifically, for each training instance, the individual is incorporated into the meta-algorithm to generate a corresponding solution. Then, the fitness function can be defined as the (normalised) average objective value of the solutions. Figure 9.1 illustrates the fitness evaluation process in GPHH.

There have been a number of studies on the design of meta-algorithm (e.g. [22, 23]), terminal set (e.g. [26, 30]), and fitness function (e.g. [17, 32]).

In GPHH, an individual is typically represented as a syntax tree, and the commonly used tree-based crossover and mutation operators can be used to generate offspring. There are also some studies considering other representations such as Gene Expression Programming (GEP) [33, 38].

In the following, we will briefly describe UCARP and how to solve it with GPHH.

9.2.1.1 Uncertain Capacitated Arc Routing Problem (UCARP)

UCARP [27] is defined on a graph $(\mathcal{V}, \mathcal{E})$, where $\mathcal{V}$ and $\mathcal{E}$ are the set of vertices and edges. A subset of edges $\mathcal{E}_R \subseteq \mathcal{E}$ is required to be served. Each required edge $e \in \mathcal{E}_R$ has a *random* demand $D(e) \geq 0$ and a serving time $s(e) \geq 0$. Each edge $e \in \mathcal{E}$ has a *random* traversal (passing without serving) time $T(e) \geq 0$. A set of vehicles with capacity q is located at the depot $v_0 \in \mathcal{V}$ to serve the required edges.

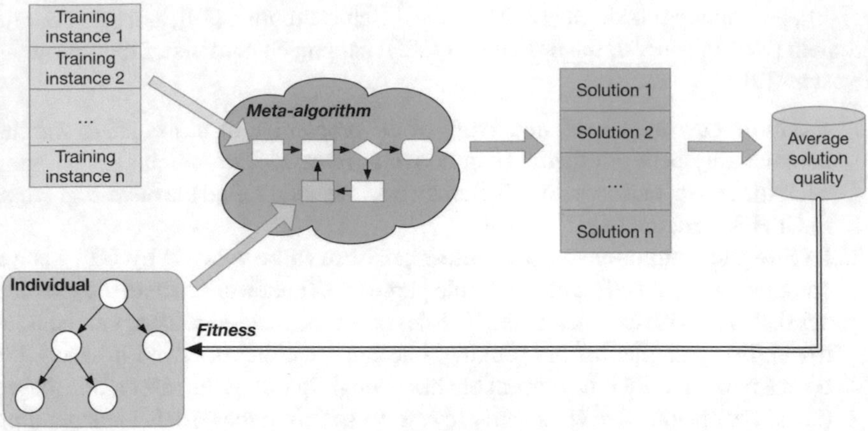

Fig. 9.1 The GPHH fitness evaluation process

A UCARP instance I can have different samples. In a sample I_ξ, each random variable takes a sampled value (i.e. $d_\xi(e), \forall e \in \mathcal{E}_R$ and $t_\xi(e), \forall e \in \mathcal{E}$). The main difference from the deterministic counterparts is that in a sampled UCARP instance, the sampled values of the random variables are unknown until the vehicles have examined them (i.e. completed serving a required edge or traversing an edge).

UCARP is to find a solution to serve all the required edges that minimises the *expected* total travel time across all the possible samples. To guarantee feasibility, each required edge is served exactly once, each vehicle departs from and returns to the depot, and the total demand served by a vehicle cannot exceed its capacity.

Unlike deterministic CARP, *route failures* can occur when executing a solution to UCARP. That is, while serving a required edge, the actual (sampled) demand of the required edge is much larger than expected and thus larger than the current residual capacity of the vehicle. To avoid violating the capacity constraint, the vehicle has to go back to the depot in the middle of the service to replenish. This may induce a large *recourse cost*, making the preplanned solution much worse.

To deal with route failures, studies have considered proactive optimisation [12, 44] so that the solution is robust to the uncertain environment. However, the solutions are not sufficiently flexible if different samples require a significant change in the solution structure. As a reactive approach, routing policy [37] is much more flexible by making online decisions based on the instantaneous information. However, it is hard and time-consuming to manually design effective routing policies. Therefore, in this chapter, we focus on automatically evolving routing policies for UCARP with GPHH.

9.2.1.2 GPHH for UCARP

When solving UCARP with GPHH, a routing policy is represented as a GP tree. To evaluate a routing policy, a set of UCARP training instances is needed. The meta-algorithm is a *decision making simulation* [28]. In the beginning, all the vehicles are at the depot. Then, for the earliest idle vehicle, the routing policy is applied to select its next service (or returning to the depot if no service is applicable). Specifically, for each candidate required edge, the routing policy is applied to calculate its priority value. Then the candidate with the best (lowest) priority value is selected. Route failures are handled in an intuitive way during the simulation. That is, if a vehicle's capacity expires in the middle of a service, then it returns to the depot to replenish and then comes back to the failed service to complete it. The simulation is continued until all the required edges have been served.

The terminal set in the GPHH for UCARP should contain various features related to edges, vehicles, and global information. The commonly used terminals are given in Table 9.1. A typical function set contains $\{+, -, \times, /, \min, \max\}$. For example, a policy "999999 × CFH + CTD" selects the closest candidate to the current location. If there are multiple closest neighbours, the tie is broken by selecting the one closest to the depot.

9.2.2 *Transfer Learning and Optimisation*

Knowledge transfer was first considered in the machine learning community [43], which focuses on the machine learning tasks such as classification and regression. In transfer learning [36], a *domain* $\mathcal{D}$ is defined as a tuple $\mathcal{D} = \langle \mathcal{X}, \{P(X) \mid X \in$

Table 9.1 The commonly used terminals for evolving UCARP routing policies

Notation	Description
`SC`	Serving cost of the candidate
`CFH`	Cost from the current location to the candidate
`CTD`	Cost from the candidate to the depot
`CR`	Cost to refill (from the current location to the depot)
`DEM`	Expected demand of the candidate
`RQ`	Remaining capacity of the vehicle
`FULL`	Fullness (remaining capacity over the total capacity) of the vehicle
`FRT`	Fraction of unserved tasks
`FUT`	Fraction of unassigned tasks
`CFR1`	Cost from the closest alternative route to the candidate
`RQ1`	Remaining capacity of the closest alternative route to the candidate
`CTT1`	Cost from the candidate to its closest unserved neighbour
`DEM1`	Expected demand of the closest unserved neighbour of the candidate

$\mathcal{X}\})$, where $\mathcal{X}$ is the input space, and $\{P(X) \mid X \in \mathcal{X}\}$ is the marginal probability distribution of the inputs. Given a specific domain $\mathcal{D}$, a *task* $\mathcal{T}$ consists of an output space $\mathcal{Y}$ and an objective predictive function $f(\cdot) : \mathcal{X} \rightarrow \mathcal{Y}$, which is the mapping from the inputs to the output. $f(\cdot)$ is unknown and needs to be learned from the training data (X_i, Y_i), where $X_i \in \mathcal{X}, Y_i \in \mathcal{Y}$. Based on the above notation, a formal definition of *transfer learning* with a single source domain and a single target domain is given in [36]:

Definition 9.1 (*Transfer Learning*) [36] Given a source domain $\mathcal{D}_S$, learning task $\mathcal{T}_S$, a target domain $\mathcal{D}_T$, and learning task $\mathcal{T}_T$, transfer learning aims to help improve the learning of the target predictive function $f_T(\cdot)$ in $\mathcal{D}_T$ using the knowledge in $\mathcal{D}_S$ and $\mathcal{T}_S$,where $\mathcal{D}_S \neq \mathcal{D}_T$ or $\mathcal{T}_S \neq \mathcal{T}_T$.

Here, $\mathcal{D}_S \neq \mathcal{D}_T$ means that $\mathcal{X}_S \neq \mathcal{X}_T$ or $P_S(X) \neq P_T(X)$, and $\mathcal{T}_S \neq \mathcal{T}_T$ implies that $\mathcal{Y}_S \neq \mathcal{Y}_T$ or $P(Y_S|X_S) \neq P(Y_T|X_T)$ (or $f_T(\cdot) \neq f_S(\cdot)$).

In machine learning, the outputs y_i's in the training data are also called the *labels*. Depending on the availability of the labels in the source and target domains, transfer learning can be further divided into three categories.

- *Inductive transfer learning*: when the target domain data is labelled.
- *Transductive transfer learning*: when the target domain data is unlabelled, but the source domain data is labelled.
- *Unsupervised transfer learning*: when the data in both source and target domains are unlabelled.

The common transfer approaches are based on (1) instance transfer, (2) feature representation transfer, (3) parameter transfer, and (4) relational-knowledge transfer. Instance-transfer approaches select some source domain data and reuse it in the target domain with some reweighting. Feature-representation-transfer approaches transform the feature spaces in the source and target domains to minimise the divergence between the source and target feature spaces after the transformation. Then, the transformed data can be seen as in the same domain. Parameter-transfer approaches assume that the models in the source and target domains share some hyperparameter (e.g. the prior of a Gaussian process). Finally, the relational-knowledge-transfer approaches identify the relationship among the data in the source domain and transfer it to the target domain. More details can be found in [36].

In addition to regression and classification, transfer learning has also been considered in reinforcement learning [42], and various approaches have been proposed where the transferred knowledge range from the $\langle s, a, r, s' \rangle$ instances to the (partial) policy.

Compared to machine learning tasks, knowledge transfer in the optimisation tasks received much less attention. A general formalisation of **transfer optimisation** is introduced in [14]. The main difference in an optimisation task is that the feature space $\mathcal{X}$ becomes the search space, i.e. the set of all the feasible solutions, and the predictive function $f(\cdot)$ becomes the objective function to be optimised rather than matching a specific label.

So far, transfer optimisation approaches are mainly developed in the context of evolutionary computation, although there are a few works on transfer Bayesian optimisation [45]. Feng et al. [10, 11] proposed an evolutionary transfer optimisation method for the vehicle/arc routing problem domains, which learns the customer assignment as the transferred knowledge. Feng et al. [9] proposed another approach which learns a denoising autoencoder to transfer the populations from the source domain to the target domain by treating the source population as a corrupted data of the target population. Da et al. [7] proposed a mixture model to represent the probabilistic model of the target search space, which is a weighted aggregation of the probabilistic models of the source search space. The weights (indicating the similarities between the source domains and the target domain) are then learned and updated during the evolutionary process.

It is worth noting that transfer learning/optimisation is closely related with multitask learning/optimisation [6, 15], in which the tasks are tackled concurrently rather than sequentially. The knowledge transfer in multitask learning/optimisation is thus omnidirectional.

9.3 Knowledge Transfer in GPHH for UCARP

Knowledge transfer in GPHH is a type of *transfer optimisation*, since the goal of GPHH is to find the optimal heuristic. However, it is different from the conventional transfer optimisation approaches. As a hyper-heuristic method, GPHH searches in the *heuristic space*, while the conventional transfer optimisation approaches search in the *solution space*. Consequently, the existing transfer optimisation methods are not directly applicable for knowledge transfer in GPHH.

So far, the knowledge transfer in GP is mainly focussed on *subtree transfer*. That is, among the GP individuals (trees) examined in the source domain, the reusable subtrees are identified and transferred to the target domain. There are two design issues for subtree transfer: (1) which subtrees to be transferred and (2) how to reuse the transferred subtrees.

For identifying transferable subtrees, the existing studies considered the individuals from the final source population (in terms of source performance [8] or target performance [16]), subtrees of the best individuals in the final source population [8], best individuals in each generation of the source populations [8], common building blocks of the best individuals in the final source population [34], direct children of the trees [18], etc. For knowledge reusing, most existing studies simply add the transferred (sub-)trees into the initial target population (e.g. [8, 16]), treat them as a type of terminal during the tree initialisation in the target domain [18], or add the functional building blocks into the function set [34].

However, the existing studies mainly focussed on GP for machine learning tasks such as symbolic regression and image classification. To the best of our knowledge, no work has been done for knowledge transfer in GPHH for UCARP so far. In this chapter, we have the following three objectives.

1. Investigate the effectiveness of the existing GP transfer methods in the context of GPHH for UCARP.
2. Improve the subtree transfer methods by proposing more accurate measures to identify transferable subtrees.
3. Propose a new GPHH with knowledge transfer, in which the transferred knowledge is represented as *feature importance* rather than subtrees.

9.3.1 Existing GP Transfer Methods

Table 9.2 shows the existing GP transfer methods examined in this study. They perform well on their own problems (symbolic regression or image classification) and are easy to understand/implement. Note that the *FullTree* and *SubTree* methods have a parameter k. In the study, we use $k = 50$, i.e. the top half of the population is selected. We compared different k values (25, 50, 75) in our preliminary studies and found that $k = 50$ yielded the best results.

9.3.2 New GPHH with Biased Subtree Transfer

Intuitively, compared with other subtree transfer methods, the *SubTree* method has a higher potential to identify compact and reusable knowledge with less noise and thus can reduce the likelihood of *negative transfer*. However, randomly selecting a subtree is by no means the best option, as even in the same individual, different subtrees can have very different reusability. In an extreme case, a redundant branch in the best individual will be completely useless after the transfer. To address this issue, we propose two measures to guide a more biased subtree selection than purely

Table 9.2 The existing GP transfer methods examined in this study

Name	What to transfer?	How to transfer?
FullTree [8]	$k\%$ best individuals in the final source population	Add the transferred individuals into the initial target population
SubTree [8]	A random subtree of each $k\%$ best individual in the final source population	Add the transferred individuals into the initial target population
BestGen [8]	Best individuals in each generation of the source populations	Add the transferred individuals into the initial target population
TLGPCriptor [18]	Subtrees of the roots of the good individuals in the final source population, which are no worse than the average of the population	Used as an extended terminal set during initialisation and mutation

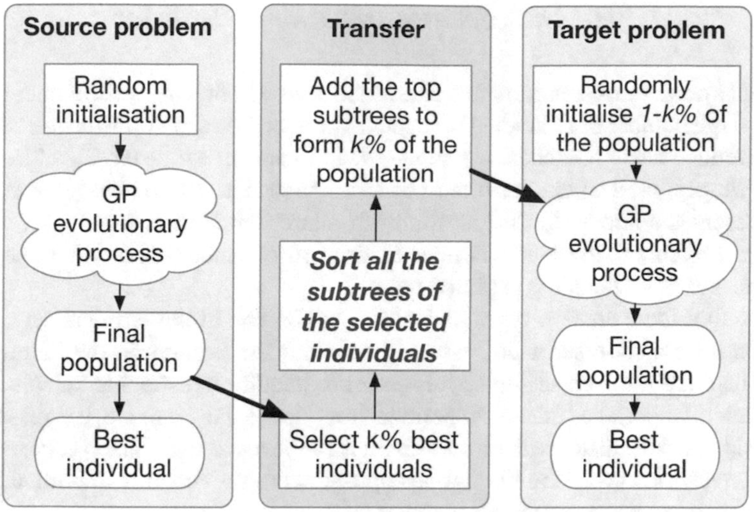

Fig. 9.2 The new GPHH with biased subtree transfer

random. The first measure is based on *frequency* and the second one is based on *contribution*. The newly proposed biased subtree transfer method is illustrated in Fig. 9.2. During the transfer stage, the new method considers all the subtrees of the top $k\%$ best individuals in the source population, sorts them by frequency or contribution, and adds the top subtrees to form $k\%$ of the initial target population.

The frequency and contribution measures to sort the subtrees are described as follows.

- *Frequency*: simply count the number of occurrences of a subtree in all the selected individuals. Note that a subtree can occur multiple times in the same individual.
- *Contribution*: this measure is based on the idea of the shuffle test. Specifically, the contribution of a subtree to an individual is defined as the fitness gap between the original individual and the shuffled individual in which the subtree is replaced with the constant 1. Then, the overall contribution of a subtree is calculated as the weighted sum of its contributions to the selected individuals, where the weights are the normalised fitness of the individuals. Note that a subtree can occur at different places of an individual. In this case, the shuffle test is conducted on each occurrence, and the contribution to the individual is the sum of the fitness gaps obtained by all the shuffle tests. More details of the contribution-based measure can be found in [1].

9.3.3 New GPHH with Feature Importance Transfer

It is well known that GP suffers from the bloat issue, and the evolved GP trees tend to have a large number of redundant branches. Therefore, directly transferring subtrees can introduce noisy branches, which may lead to negative transfer. To address this issue, we proposed to extract more abstract knowledge. In this case, we propose to represent the knowledge in the form of feature importance. Intuitively, a more important feature in the source domain tends to still be more important in the target domain, and thus should be explored more.

Note that there are two types of features in GP, one in the terminal set and the other in the function set. Here, we only consider the features in the terminal set rather than the function set, since it is easier to identify transferable knowledge on the terminal importance than the functional importance. For example, it is reasonable to consider that the distance from the current location to the candidate (i.e. *a terminal*) is important. However, it might not be appropriate to say that it is important to add (i.e. *a function*) any two subtrees together.

Based on the above considerations, we propose a new GPHH with feature importance transfer, which is described in Fig. 9.3. First, the importance of each terminal is calculated based on the top $k\%$ individuals in the source domain. The importance is calculated based on the shuffle test [30] (i.e. fitness gap by replacing the terminal by 1). Then, the feature importance is used in the initialisation of the target population, so that the more important features are more likely to be sampled during the tree generation. Specifically, for sampling each terminal node, the concrete terminal is sampled from the terminal set by the roulette wheel selection based on the importance of the terminals.

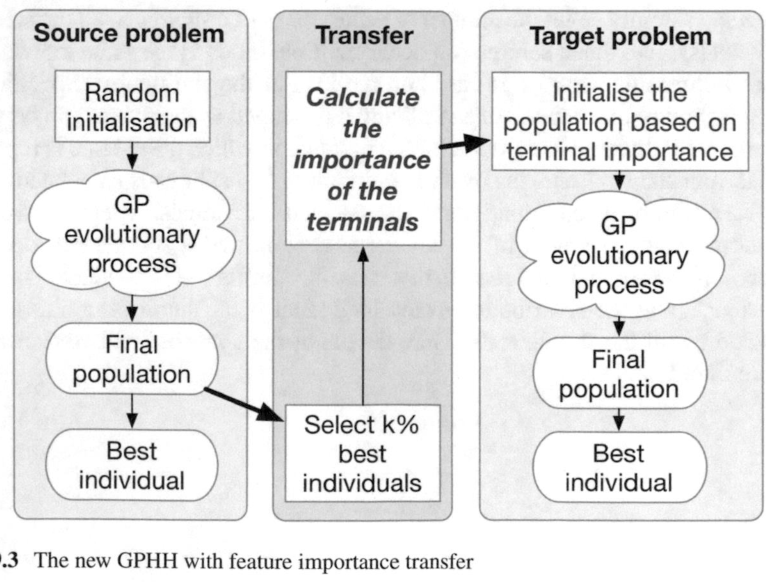

Fig. 9.3 The new GPHH with feature importance transfer

9.4 Experimental Studies

The experimental studies contain three parts: (1) investigate the effectiveness of the existing GP transfer methods; (2) verify the effectiveness of the new GPHH-KT with biased subtree transfer; and (3) verify the effectiveness of the new GPHH-KT with feature importance.

9.4.1 Transfer Scenarios

As a preliminary study, we consider a simple transfer scenario in this work. The source and target domains share the same graph (including the graph topology and the distribution of the random variables), but only different in the number of vehicles. This is motivated by the real-world scenarios where the company may purchase new vehicles, or some existing vehicles may break down. We have demonstrated that the effectiveness of the routing policy can dramatically deteriorate if the number of vehicles changes [28]. On the other hand, the two scenarios are very similar, and it is reasonable to believe that there exists some knowledge gained from the source domain that can be leveraged to help the retraining of the routing policy in the target domain. Therefore, we design such transfer scenarios in our experimental studies.

We conducted experiments on the *Ugdb* and *Uval* instances. For each instance, we set the source domain with k vehicles and the target domain with $k-1$ or $k+1$ vehicles, i.e. one vehicle different from the source domain. Due to space limit, we will show the results on (a) *Ugdb*23 from 10 to 9 vehicles and (b) *Uval*9D from 10 to 9 vehicles, and all the other scenarios show similar patterns. The details of the source and target domains of these two scenarios are given in Table 9.3.

In the experiments, we adopt the commonly used parameter settings of GP. The population size is 1000, and the maximal depth is 8. The crossover, mutation, and reproduction rates are 85%, 10%, and 5%, respectively. The top 10 elitists are retained to the next generation. The number of generations is 50. All the compared algorithms were run 30 times independently.

We conducted the Wilcoxon rank sum test with a significance level of 0.05 between each pair of the compared algorithms, in terms of the initial and final solution quality in the target domain.

Table 9.3 The source and target domains of the scenarios discussed in the experimental studies

Scenario	Source domain	Target domain
1	*Ugdb*23 with **10** vehicles	*Ugdb*23 with **9** vehicles
2	*Uval*9D with **10** vehicles	*Uval*9D with **9** vehicles

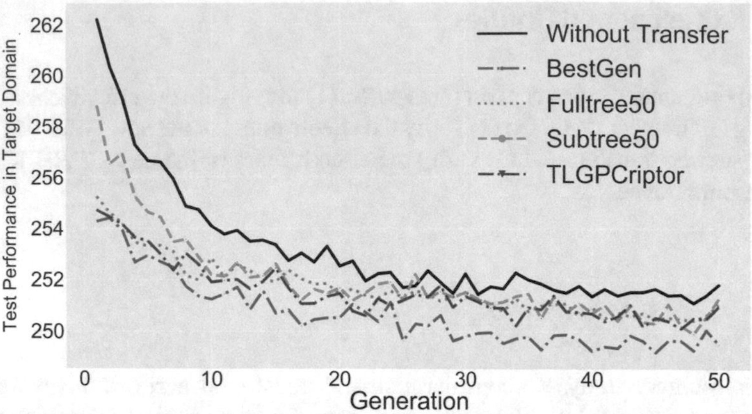

Fig. 9.4 The curves of the test performance of the compared algorithms in *Ugdb*23 from 10 vehicles to 9 vehicles

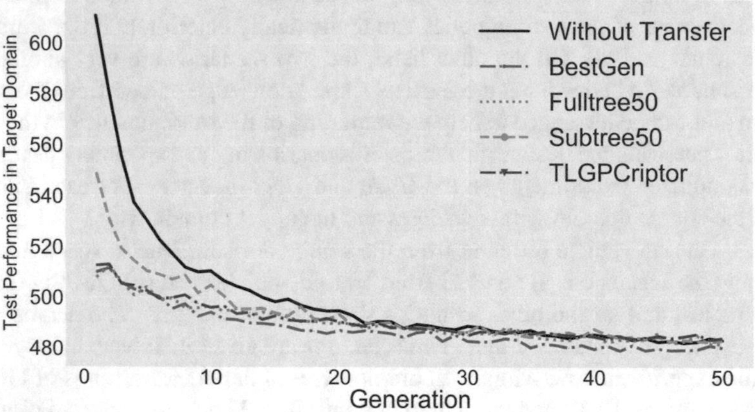

Fig. 9.5 The curves of the test performance of the compared algorithms in *Uval*9D from 10 vehicles to 9 vehicles

9.4.2 Effectiveness of Existing GP Transfer Methods

To investigate the effectiveness of the existing GP transfer methods, we compared the *FullTree*, *SubTree*, *BestGen*, and *TLGPCriptor* with the vanilla GP without transfer. We selected the top 50% individuals for FullTree and SubTree and denoted them as FullTree50 and SubTree50. The results are shown in Figs. 9.4 and 9.5.

From the figures, we can clearly see that all the existing GP transfer methods outperformed the GP without transfer. All of them offered a much better starting point for the population, and their curves are almost always below that of the GP without transfer.

From Tables 9.4 and 9.5 in Sect. 9.4.5, the initial solution quality of most transfer methods are significantly better than the GP without transfer.

In summary, the knowledge transfer can help reaching better routing policies in the target domain, no matter when to stop the training.

Among the transfer methods, BestGen seems to be slightly better than the others, and Subtree50 performed the worst in terms of initial solution quality. An important reason is that the subtrees are randomly selected, making it possible to lose the truly important branches in the promising individuals. The advantage of BestGen over Fulltree50 is partly because the promising individuals in the final population are too similar to each other. By choosing individuals from all the generations, one may extract more diverse and useful knowledge.

9.4.3 Effectiveness of GPHH with Biased Subtree Transfer

To verify the effectiveness of the GPHH with Biased Subtree Transfer (GPHH-BST), we compared the two versions with frequency and contribution, denoted as GPHH-BST-Freq and GPHH-BST-Contrib, respectively, with Subtree50 and the GP without transfer. In other words, we compared the following three ways of selecting the subtrees from the final source population to transfer.

1. Randomly from the top 50% individuals (Subtree50);
2. The most frequent subtrees from the top 50% individuals (GPHH-BST-Freq);
3. The most contributing subtrees to the top 50% individuals (GPHH-BST-Contrib).

The results are shown in Figs. 9.6 and 9.7. From the figures, we have some interesting observations.

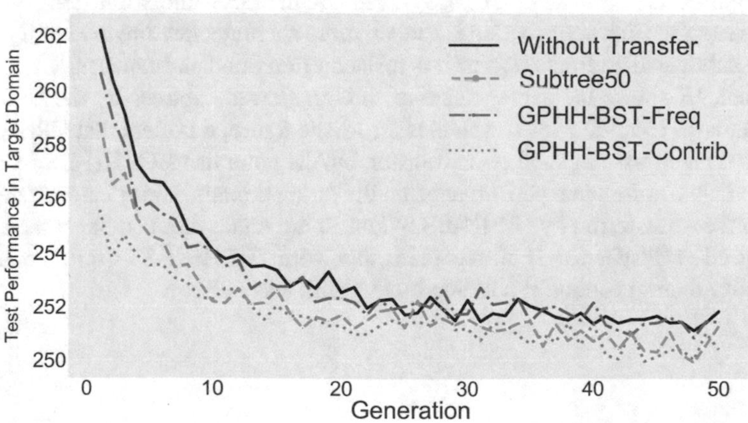

Fig. 9.6 The curves of the test performance of the compared algorithms in *Ugdb*23 from 10 vehicles to 9 vehicles

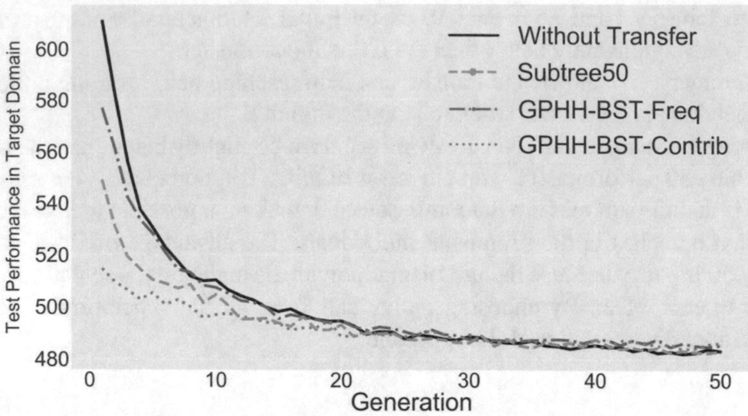

Fig. 9.7 The curves of the test performance of the compared algorithms in *Uval*9D from 10 vehicles to 9 vehicles

First, again we see all the transfer methods outperformed the GP without transfer by providing a better starting point and no statistically significantly worse test performance throughout the training process. On the other hand, when looking into the biased tree transfer strategies, we observed very different performance between the frequency-based and contribution-based measures. GPHH-BST-Contrib showed much better performance than both GPHH-BST-Freq and Subtree50. This indicates that the contribution is an effective measure to identify useful and transferable subtrees. In fact, we can see that GPHH-BST-Contrib can achieve almost the same performance curve as the other existing transfer methods that transfer the full trees.

Tables 9.4 and 9.5 in Sect. 9.4.5 show that in terms of initial solution quality, GPHH-BST-Contrib significantly outperformed the GP without transfer, while there is no significance between GPHH-BST-Freq and the GP without transfer.

This suggests that contribution is a much more accurate measure to identify transferable subtrees than frequency, as it is resistant to redundant branches.

Figure 9.8 shows the average size of the transferred subtrees by the compared algorithms on *Uval*9D with 10 vehicles. From the figure, it is clear that GPHH-BST identified much smaller subtrees to transfer. On the other hand, GPHH-BST-Contrib obtained almost the same performance on the target domain. This demonstrates that the subtrees transferred by GPHH-BST-Contrib are much more compact than those transferred by BestGen and Fulltree50. In other words, GPHH-BST-Contrib managed to identify more meaningful building blocks with less noise.

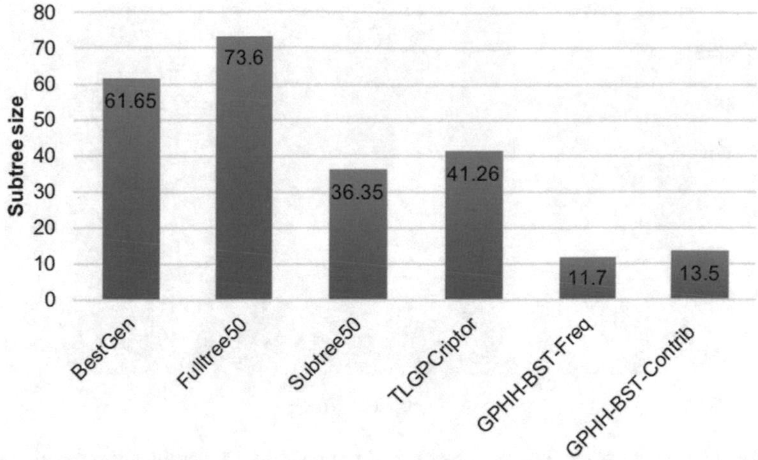

Fig. 9.8 The average size of the transferred subtrees by the compared algorithms on *Uval*9D with 10 vehicles

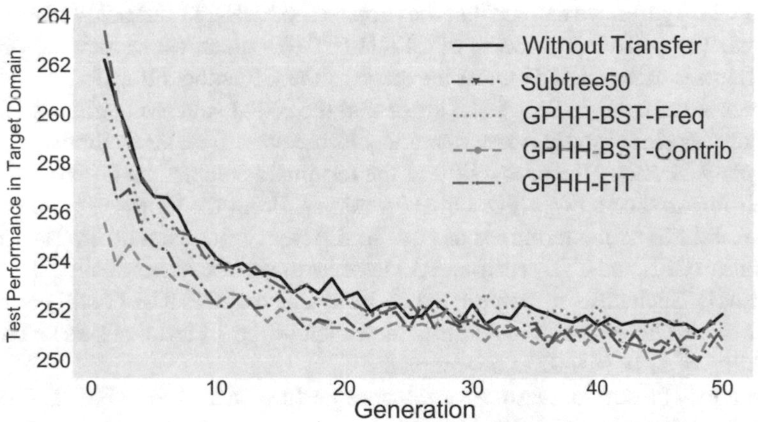

Fig. 9.9 The curves of the test performance of the compared algorithms in *Ugdb*23 from 10 vehicles to 9 vehicles

9.4.4 Effectiveness of GPHH with Feature Importance Transfer

To investigate the effectiveness of the proposed feature importance transfer, we compared the GPHH with Feature Importance Transfer (GPHH-FIT) and the subtree-based transfer methods as well as the GP without transfer. The results are shown in Figs. 9.9 and 9.10.

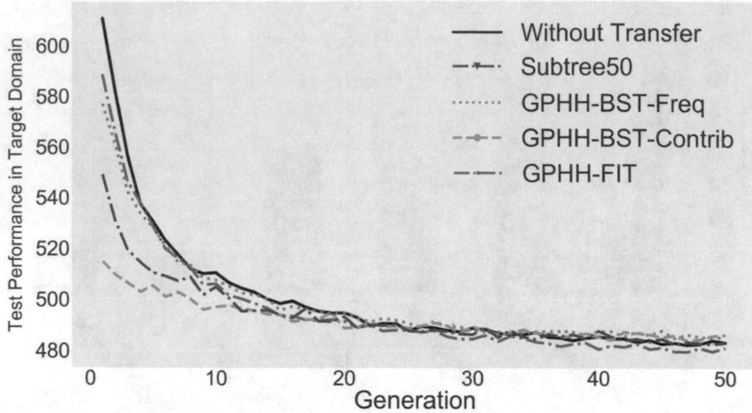

Fig. 9.10 The curves of the test performance of the compared algorithms in *Uval*9D from 10 vehicles to 9 vehicles

From the figures, we can see that the proposed GPHH-FIT did not perform as we expected. The performance curve of GPHH-FIT was much worse than the subtree-based transfer methods and almost the same as the GP without transfer.

Tables 9.4 and 9.5 in Sect. 9.4.5 show that the initial solution quality of GPHH-BST-FIT was significantly worse than most of the other transfer methods.

Figure 9.11 shows the probability of the terminals obtained by GPHH-Fit based on their importance on *Uval*9D with 10 vehicles. From the figure, we can see that the probabilities of the terminals are not so different from each other. The highest probability (CFH and CTD) is around 0.11, while the lowest one is about 0.04 (CTT1 and DEM1). Such difference might not be sufficient, and GPHH-FIT still performed similar to the GP without transfer, in which each of the 14 terminals has a uniform probability of $1/14 \approx 0.07$ to be sampled.

There may be several reasons for the poor performance of GPHH-FIT. First, the feature importance is a high-level knowledge compared with subtrees. It only states which terminals are more important than others. However, how the terminals should be combined together (i.e. useful building blocks) is missing in the transferred knowledge. As a result, GPHH-FIT still needs to search (biased by the feature importance) for promising building blocks from scratch. On the other hand, in the subtree-based transfer methods, the useful building blocks, which may be sophisticated combinations of the terminals, can be directly inherited from the transferred subtrees.

Second, the importance measure of the terminals might not be accurate enough. In GPHH-FIT, the importance measure is based on the assumption that a more contributive terminal in the source domain should be more important and sampled more often. This assumption might not be true, and an important terminal may have a rather straightforward relationship with the decision making. For example, to minimise the total cost, the cost from the current location to the candidate (`CFH` in Table 9.1) is an important feature. However, it may be used in a very simple way, i.e. the smaller

Table 9.4 The detailed results of the compared algorithms on scenario 1 (**Ugdb23**)

Initial			Final		
Algorithm	Mean (Std)	Stat. test	Algorithm	Mean (Stdev)	Stat. test
Without transfer	262.2 (3.19)		Without transfer	251.83 (3.49)	
BestGen	254.27 (2.13)	+	BestGen	250.05 (2.54)	+
Fulltree50	255.24 (2.45)	+−	Fulltree50	251.07 (2.58)	==
Subtree50	258.80 (4.36)	+−−	Subtree50	251.28 (3.67)	===
TLGPCriptor	254.72 (2.48)	+==+	TLGPCriptor	250.98 (2.47)	====
GPHH-BST-Freq	260.66 (4.65)	=−−−−	GPHH-BST-Freq	251.43 (2.71)	=====
GPHH-BST-Contrib	255.57 (2.76)	+−=+=+	GPHH-BST-Contrib	250.41 (1.85)	======
GPHH-BST-FIT	262.97 (3.71)	=−−−−−−	GPHH-BST-FIT	251.43 (2.59)	=======

Table 9.5 The detailed results of the compared algorithms on scenario 2 (**Uval9D**)

Initial			Final		
Algorithm	Mean (Std)	Stat. test	Algorithm	Mean (Stdev)	Stat. test
Without transfer	610.67 (28.11)		Without transfer	483.31 (15.15)	
BestGen	508.16 (22.47)	+	BestGen	481.58 (13.18)	=
Fulltree50	507.74 (23.80)	+=	Fulltree50	481.72 (12.81)	==
Subtree50	548.87 (47.40)	+−−	Subtree50	483.15 (11.59)	===
TLGPCriptor	512.50 (21.87)	+=−+	TLGPCriptor	484.04 (14.45)	====
GPHH-BST-Freq	576.82 (37.50)	+−−−−	GPHH-BST-Freq	485.48 (12.44)	=====
GPHH-BST-Contrib	517.85 (29.66)	+==+=+	GPHH-BST-Contrib	484.59 (15.52)	======
GPHH-BST-FIT	588.52 (34.6)	+−−−−−−	GPHH-BST-FIT	481.19 (11.74)	=======

CFH, the better the candidate is. We may need a more accurate important measure to identify the features that become useful only in sophisticated combinations with other features. Sampling such features more frequently can increase the chance to find such good building blocks.

Although GPHH-FIT was not successful in its current version, we expect it to be potentially helpful if combined with the subtree-based transfer methods to reuse the transferred knowledge not only at the initial stage, but also during the training process in the target domain. This will be further investigated in the future.

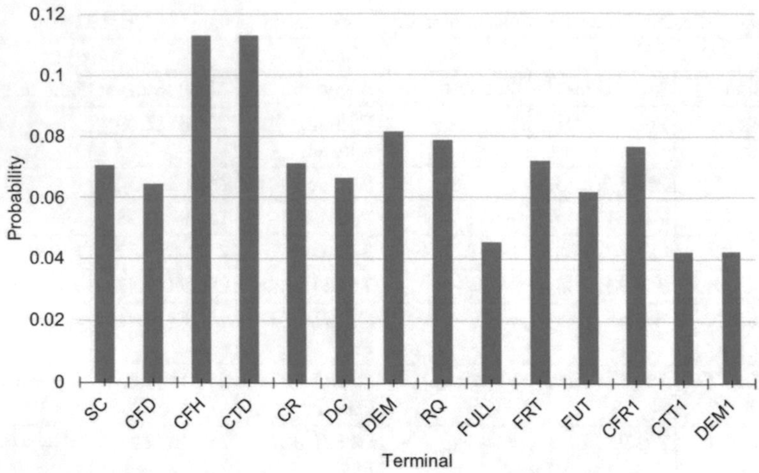

Fig. 9.11 The probabilities of the terminals obtained by GPHH-FIT on *Uval*9D with 10 vehicles

9.4.5 Statistical Significance Test Results

Tables 9.4 and 9.5 show the statistical significance test results on the two transfer scenarios (using the Wilcoxon rank sum test with a significance level of 0.05). In the tables, each row represents a compared algorithm, including the mean and standard deviation of the initial solution quality (generation 0) and the final solution quality (final generation). It also contains the statistical significance test results against all the algorithms above it, where "+", "−", and "=" indicate it is significantly better, significantly worse, and there is no significance, respectively. For example, in Table 9.4, line 3, the statistical significance test results of Fulltree50 under "Initial" is "+−", which indicates that the initial solution quality of Fulltree50 in the target domain is significantly better than the GP without transfer, but significantly worse than BestGen.

From the tables, one can see that in terms of initial solution quality, almost all the transfer methods significantly outperform the GP without transfer. BestGen and Fulltree50 are the two best-performing transfer methods, while GPHH-BST-Freq and GPHH-BST-FIT did not manage to obtain promising initial solution quality.

In terms of the final performance in the target domain, we see no significant difference among all the compared algorithms. This implies that even without transfer, GP can still catch up with the methods with knowledge transfer if given sufficient training time budget. This may be because the target domain in this experiment is not complex enough, and GP is able to achieve promising results even without transfer. We will consider more complex target problem scenarios in our future work to show more advantages of knowledge transfer.

9.5 Conclusions and Future Work

In this chapter, we investigated GPHH with knowledge transfer for evolving heuristics for a series of complex real-world problems. We took the uncertain capacitated arc routing problem as a case study and investigated a number of transfer methods to transfer subtrees and feature importance between different scenarios.

Our experimental studies demonstrate that proper knowledge transfer can greatly improve the efficiency and effectiveness of the retraining of the routing policies, which is consistent with our expectation. In addition, we found that transferring useful subtrees directly can lead to a better performance of the retraining than transferring the feature importance for guiding the search direction. Nevertheless, it is important to identify the useful subtrees to transfer to ensure the superior performance.

Based on the promising outcomes of the preliminary studies, there are a number of potential future directions. First, although the transferred subtrees are useful, it is still hard to understand why they are useful due to many redundant branches (also known as *bloat* in GP) transferred along with the truly useful building blocks. It will be helpful to transform the trees to separate the truly useful building blocks from the noisy branches, so that the transferred subtrees are more reusable and interpretable.

Second, compared with the subtree-based transfer, model-based transfer such as the feature importance is more robust and easier to be adapted to the target domain to reduce *negative transfer*. In addition, it can be combined with subtree-based transfer to further boost the retraining process. In the future, we will propose other more accurate model-based transfer methods (e.g. model-based GP [39] and grammar-guided GP [25]) to capture the reusable knowledge better. We will also explore effective ways to hybridise subtree-based and model-based transfer methods.

References

1. M.A. Ardeh, Y. Mei, M. Zhang, A novel genetic programming algorithm with knowledge transfer for uncertain capacitated arc routing problem, in *Pacific Rim International Conference on Artificial Intelligence* (Springer, 2019), pp. 196–200
2. S.J. Branke, S. Nguyen, C.W. Pickardt, M. Zhang, Automated design of production scheduling heuristics: a review. IEEE Trans. Evol. Comput. **20**(1), 110–124 (2016)
3. E.K. Burke, M.R. Hyde, G. Kendall, G. Ochoa, E. Ozcan, J.R. Woodward, Exploring hyper-heuristic methodologies with genetic programming, in *Computational Intelligence*, vol. 1, ed. by J. Kacprzyk, L.C. Jain, C.L. Mumford, L.C. Jain (Springer, Berlin Heidelberg, 2009), pp. 177–201
4. E.K. Burke, M. Hyde, G. Kendall, G. Ochoa, E. Özcan, J.R. Woodward, A classification of hyper-heuristic approaches, in *Handbook of Metaheuristics*, vol. 146, ed. by M. Gendreau, J.-Y. Potvin (Springer, US, 2010), pp. 449–468
5. E.K. Burke, M.R. Hyde, G. Kendall, G. Ochoa, E. Özcan, J.R. Woodward, A classification of hyper-heuristic approaches: revisited, in *Handbook of Metaheuristics*, vol. 272, ed. by M. Gendreau, J.-Y. Potvin (Springer International Publishing, 2019), pp. 453–477
6. R. Caruana, Multitask learning. Mach. Learn. **28**(1), 41–75 (1997)
7. B. Da, A. Gupta, Y.-S. Ong, Curbing negative influences online for seamless transfer evolutionary optimization, in *IEEE Transactions on Cybernetics* (2018), pp. 1–14

8. T.T.H. Dinh, T.H. Chu, Q.U. Nguyen, Transfer learning in genetic programming, in *2015 IEEE Congress on Evolutionary Computation (CEC)* (IEEE, 2015), pp. 1145–1151
9. L. Feng, Y.-S. Ong, S. Jiang, A. Gupta, Autoencoding evolutionary search with learning across heterogeneous problems. IEEE Trans. Evol. Comput **21**(5), 760–772 (2017)
10. L. Feng, Y.-S. Ong, M.-H. Lim, I.W. Tsang, Memetic search with interdomain learning: a realization between CVRP and CARP. IEEE Trans. Evol. Comput. **19**(5), 644–658 (2015)
11. L. Feng, Y.-S. Ong, I. Wai-Hung Tsang, A.-H. Tan, An evolutionary search paradigm that learns with past experiences, in *2012 IEEE Congress on Evolutionary Computation* (IEEE, 2012), pp. 1–8
12. G. Fleury, P. Lacomme, C. Prins, Evolutionary algorithms for stochastic arc routing problems, in *Applications of Evolutionary Computing*, vol. 3005, ed. by T. Kanade, J. Kittler, J.M. Kleinberg, F. Mattern, J.C. Mitchell, O. Nierstrasz, C. Pandu Rangan, B. Steffen, D. Terzopoulos, D. Tygar, M.Y. Vardi, G.R. Raidl, S. Cagnoni, J. Branke, D.W. Corne, R. Drechsler, Y. Jin, C.G. Johnson, P. Machado, E. Marchiori, F. Rothlauf, G.D. Smith, G. Squillero (Springer Berlin Heidelberg, 2004), pp. 501–512
13. A.S. Fukunaga, Automated discovery of local search heuristics for satisfiability testing. Evol. Comput. **16**(1), 31–61 (2008)
14. A. Gupta, Y.-S. Ong, L. Feng, Insights on transfer optimization: because experience is the best teacher. IEEE Trans. Emerg. Top. Comput. Intell. **2**(1), 51–64 (2018)
15. A. Gupta, Y.-S. Ong, L. Feng, K.C. Tan, Multiobjective multifactorial optimization in evolutionary multitasking. IEEE Trans. Cybern. **47**(7), 1652–1665 (2017)
16. E. Haslam, B. Xue, M. Zhang, Further investigation on genetic programming with transfer learning for symbolic regression, in *2016 IEEE Congress on Evolutionary Computation (CEC)* (IEEE, 2016), pp. 3598–3605
17. T. Hildebrandt, J. Branke, On using surrogates with genetic programming. Evol. Comput. **23**(3), 343–367 (2015)
18. M. Iqbal, B. Xue, H. Al-Sahaf, M. Zhang, Cross-domain reuse of extracted knowledge in genetic programming for image classification. IEEE Trans. Evol. Comput. **21**(4), 569–587 (2017)
19. J. Jacobsen-Grocott, Y. Mei, G. Chen, M. Zhang, Evolving heuristics for dynamic vehicle routing with time windows using genetic programming, in *Proceedings of the IEEE Congress on Evolutionary Computation (CEC)* (IEEE, 2017), pp. 1948–1955
20. M. Jurasević, D. Jakobović, K. Knežević, Adaptive scheduling on unrelated machines with genetic programming. Appl. Soft Comput. **48**, 419–430 (2016)
21. J. Lin, L. Zhu, K. Gao, A genetic programming hyper-heuristic approach for the multi-skill resource constrained project scheduling problem. Expert Syst. Appl. **140** (2020)
22. Y. Liu, Y. Mei, M. Zhang, Z. Zhang, Automated heuristic design using genetic programming hyper-heuristic for uncertain capacitated arc routing problem, in *Proceedings of the Genetic and Evolutionary Computation Conference (GECCO)* (ACM, 2017), pp. 290–297
23. Y. Liu, Y. Mei, M. Zhang, Z. Zhang, A predictive-reactive approach with genetic programming and cooperative co-evolution for uncertain capacitated arc routing problem. Evolutionary Computation (2019)
24. M.A. Martin, D.R. Tauritz, A problem configuration study of the robustness of a black-box search algorithm hyper-heuristic, in *Proceedings of the Companion Publication of the 2014 Annual Conference on Genetic and Evolutionary Computation*, GECCO Comp '14 (ACM, 2014), pp. 1389–1396
25. R.I. McKay, N.X. Hoai, P.A. Whigham, Y. Shan, M. O'Neill, Grammar-based genetic programming: a survey. Genet. Program. Evol. Mach. **11**(3-4), 365–396 (2010)
26. Y. Mei, B. Xue, S. Nguyen, M. Zhang, An efficient feature selection algorithm for evolving job shop scheduling rules with genetic programming. IEEE Trans. Emerg. Topics Comput. Intell. **1**(5), 339–353 (2017)
27. Y. Mei, K. Tang, X. Yao, Capacitated arc routing problem in uncertain environments, in *Proceedings of the IEEE Congress on Evolutionary Computation (CEC)* (IEEE, 2010), pp. 1–8

28. Y. Mei, M. Zhang, Genetic programming hyper-heuristic for multi-vehicle uncertain capacitated arc routing problem, in *Proceedings of the Genetic and Evolutionary Computation Conference Companion (GECCO)* (ACM, 2018), pp. 141–142
29. Y. Mei, M. Zhang, Genetic programming hyper-heuristic for stochastic team orienteering problem with time windows, in *2018 IEEE Congress on Evolutionary Computation (CEC)* (IEEE, 2018), pp. 1–8
30. Y. Mei, M. Zhang, S. Nyugen, Feature selection in evolving job shop dispatching rules with genetic programming, in *Proceedings of the Genetic and Evolutionary Computation Conference (GECCO)* (ACM, 2016), pp. 365–372
31. S. Nguyen, Y. Mei, M. Zhang, Genetic programming for production scheduling: a survey with a unified framework. Complex Intell. Syst. **3**(1), 41–66 (2017)
32. S. Nguyen, M. Zhang, K.C. Tan, Surrogate-assisted genetic programming with simplified models for automated design of dispatching rules. IEEE Trans. Cybern. **47**(9), 2951–2965 (2017)
33. L. Nie, L. Gao, P. Li, X. Li, A GEP-based reactive scheduling policies constructing approach for dynamic flexible job shop scheduling problem with job release dates. J. Intell. Manuf. **24**(4), 763–774 (2013)
34. D. O'Neill, H. Al-Sahaf, B. Xue, M. Zhang, Common subtrees in related problems: a novel transfer learning approach for genetic programming, in *2017 IEEE Congress on Evolutionary Computation (CEC)* (2017), pp. 1287–1294
35. J.C. Ortiz-Bayliss, E. Özcan, A.J. Parkes, H. Terashima-Marín, A genetic programming hyper-heuristic: turning features into heuristics for constraint satisfaction, in *2013 13th UK Workshop on Computational Intelligence (UKCI)* (IEEE, 2013), pp. 183–190
36. S.J. Pan, Q. Yang, A survey on transfer learning. IEEE Trans. Knowl. Data Eng. **22**(10), 1345–1359 (2010)
37. U. Ritzinger, J. Puchinger, R.F. Hartl, A survey on dynamic and stochastic vehicle routing problems. Int. J. Prod. Res. **54**(1), 215–231 (2016)
38. N.R. Sabar, M. Ayob, G. Kendall, Q. Rong, A dynamic multiarmed bandit-gene expression programming hyper-heuristic for combinatorial optimization problems. IEEE Trans. Cybern. **45**(2), 217–228 (2015)
39. Y. Shan, R.I. McKay, D. Essam, H.A. Abbass, A survey of probabilistic model building genetic programming, in *Scalable Optimization via Probabilistic Modeling*, Studies in Computational Intelligence, ed. by M. Pelikan, K. Sastry, E. CantúPaz (Springer, Berlin Heidelberg, 2006), pp. 121–160
40. A. Sosa-Ascencio, G. Ochoa, H. Terashima-Marin, S.E. Conant-Pablos, Grammar-based generation of variable-selection heuristics for constraint satisfaction problems. Genet. Program. Evol. Mach. **17**(2), 119–144 (2016)
41. B. Tan, H. Ma, Y. Mei, A genetic programming hyper-heuristic approach for online resource allocation in container-based clouds, in *Proceedings of the Australasian Joint Conference on Artificial Intelligence (AI)* (Springer, 2018), pp. 146–152
42. M.E. Taylor, P. Stone, Transfer learning for reinforcement learning domains: a survey. J. Mach. Learn. Res. **10**(Jul), 1633–1685 (2009)
43. S. Thrun, L. Pratt, *Learning to Learn* (Springer Science & Business Media, 2012)
44. J. Wang, K. Tang, J.A. Lozano, X. Yao, Estimation of the distribution algorithm with a stochastic local search for uncertain capacitated arc routing problems. IEEE Trans. Evol. Comput. **20**(1), 96–109 (2016)
45. D. Yogatama, G. Mann, Efficient transfer learning method for automatic hyperparameter tuning, in *Artificial Intelligence and Statistics* (2014), pp. 1077–1085
46. F. Zhang, Y. Mei, M. Zhang, A two-stage genetic programming hyper-heuristic approach with feature selection for dynamic flexible job shop scheduling, in *Proceedings of the Genetic and Evolutionary Computation Conference* (2019), pp. 347–355

Chapter 10
Automated Design of Classification Algorithms

Nelishia Pillay and Thambo Nyathi

Abstract Data classification provides effective solutions to various real-world problems in areas such as disease diagnosis, network intrusion detection, and financial forecasting, among others. Classification algorithms such as induction algorithms, e.g., ID3, and genetic programming are used to produce classifiers. The design of these classification algorithms is time-consuming, requiring many person hours, and is an optimization problem. This chapter examines the automated design of genetic programming as a classification algorithm. The study compares the performance of genetic algorithms and grammatical evolution in automating the design of genetic programming for classifier induction. The performance of the classifiers produced by automated design is compared to that produced by manually designed genetic programming algorithms for binary and multi-class classification in various areas including network intrusion detection and financial forecasting. The automated design required less design time and produced classifiers that performed better than the manually designed classifiers. Grammatical evolution was found to produce better-performing classifiers for binary classification and genetic algorithms for multi-class classification.

10.1 Introduction

There has been a fair amount of research into automated design for data classification. The research in this field can categorized into automated design of the classification pipeline [4, 8], automated design of the classifiers themselves, e.g., [11], and the automated design of the algorithms inducing classifiers, i.e., classification algorithms [2, 7, 12]. This chapter focuses on the automated design of classification algorithms. In

N. Pillay (✉)
University of Pretoria, Pretoria, South Africa
e-mail: nelishia.pillay@up.ac.za

T. Nyathi
National University of Science and Technology, Bulawayo, Zimbabwe
e-mail: vuselani@gmail.com

N. Pillay and R. Qu (eds.), *Automated Design of Machine Learning and Search Algorithms*, Natural Computing Series,
https://doi.org/10.1007/978-3-030-72069-8_10

the study conducted by Vella [12], a hyper-heuristic [10] is used to determine the splitting heuristic to use at each node when applying the ID3 algorithm to induce a decision tree. The heuristic determines which attribute to use. The hyper-heuristic consisted of a set of rules mapping the problem state to the splitting heuristic to use. Barros et al. [1, 2] have used evolutionary algorithms to automate the design of decision tree induction algorithms for binary classification. In this work, the evolutionary algorithm is used to determine the split criterion, split type, the stopping criterion, the stopping parameter, the pruning strategy, the pruning parameter, the missing values split, the missing values distribution, and the missing values classification.

This chapter reports on a study comparing genetic algorithms and grammatical evolution to automate the design of genetic programming algorithms to produce binary and multi-class classifiers [6, 7]. Section 10.2 describes the design decisions that are automated. Both approaches are used to evolve classifiers for selected datasets from the UCI Machine Learning Repository [6], network intrusion detection, and financial forecasting. The genetic algorithm and grammatical evolution approaches employed for the automatic design of the genetic programming algorithm are presented in Sects. 10.3 and 10.4, respectively. Section 10.5 provides details of the experimental setup. The performance of both these approaches in automating the design of the genetic programming algorithm is evaluated in Sect. 10.6.

10.2 Design Decisions

The design decisions automated include the following:

- Parameter values - The parameter values for the genetic programming algorithm, namely, population size, maximum initial tree depth, tournament size, maximum offspring depth, and termination criterion. The options for these parameter values are illustrated in Table 10.1.
- Genetic operators - The decision involves determining which of three genetic operators, namely, grow mutation, shrink mutation, and crossover and creation, and the application rates of the genetic operators should be used. The options for the genetic operators are depicted in Table 10.2.
- Classifier type - The evolved classifier can be an arithmetic tree, logical tree, or decision tree.
- Fitness function - Different classifier performance measures can be used as a fitness function, namely, accuracy, fmeasure, random weighted accuracy, and true positive rate. Fitness function operations include:

  –

$$Accuracy = \frac{t_p + t_n}{t_p + t_n + f_p + f_n} \tag{10.1}$$

Table 10.1 Parameter value ranges

Parameter	Range
Population size	100, 200, or 300
Maximum initial tree depth	Arithmetic trees: [2–15]
	Logical trees: [2–15]
	Decision trees: [2–8]
Tournament size	[2–10]
Maximum offspring depth	Arithmetic trees: [2–15]
	Logical trees: [2–15]
	Decision trees: [2–8]
Mutation depth	[2–6]
Termination criterion	A fitness value of 100%
	Number of generation: [50–200]

where t_p is the number of true positives
t_n is the number of true negatives
f_p is the number of false positives
f_n is the number of false negatives

–

$$f_{measure} = 2 * (\frac{precision * recall}{precision + recall}) \tag{10.2}$$

where

$$precision = \frac{t_p}{t_p + f_p} \tag{10.3}$$

$$recall = \frac{t_p}{t_p + f_n} \tag{10.4}$$

–

$$WeightedAccuracy = 0.5 * Accuracy + 0.5 * f_measure \tag{10.5}$$

–

$$RandomWeightedAccuracy = ran * Accuracy + (1 - ran) * f_{measure} \tag{10.6}$$

where ran is a random number chosen in the range of [0,1]

- Control flow - The standard control flow of a genetic algorithm is illustrated in Algorithm 7. An initial population is firstly created and iteratively refined using genetic operators. In this study, creating a population is defined as the creation operator. The control flow decision can be specified as *fixed* in which case one of the genetic operator combination options in Table 10.2 is applied on all generations

Table 10.2 Genetic operator options

Option	Description
Crossover and mutation	The application rates of crossover and mutation are randomly selected from 0% to 100% to add up to a 100%
100% crossover	The population is created using only crossover
100% mutation	The population is created using only mutation
Preset crossover and mutation rates	The crossover and mutation rate pair is randomly chosen from 9 combinations in multiples of ten, e.g., 10%, 90%
100% mutation and Rand% crossover	The current population is created using mutation. The population of the next generation is created by crossover application rate randomly selected from 0% to 100%
100% crossover and Rand% mutation	The current population is created using crossover. The population of the next generation is created by mutation application rate randomly selected from 0% to 100%
Creation	The entire population is replaced with a new population

to create offspring. Alternatively, if this decision is *random*, one of the genetic operator combinations in Table 10.2 is randomly selected for each generation.

Algorithm 7 Generational genetic programming algorithm [5]

1: Create an initial population
2: **repeat**
3: Evaluate the population
4: Select parents using the selection method
5: Apply genetic operators to the selected parents to produce offspring
6: **until** termination criterion is met

The following section presents the genetic algorithm used for automated design.

10.3 Genetic Algorithm (*autoGA*)

A generation genetic algorithm [3] was employed for automated design. The algorithm terminates when a maximum number of generations is reached. The following sections describe the processes of initial population generation, fitness evaluation, selection, and regeneration. The parameter values used by the genetic algorithm are then presented.

10.3.1 Initial Population Generation

Each chromosome is comprised of 13 genes, with each gene representing one of the following design decisions:

- Gene 0 - Classifier type
- Gene 1 - Population size
- Gene 2 - Method of initial population generation, i.e., full, grow, or ramped half-and-half
- Gene 3 - Initial tree depth
- Gene 4 - Maximum offspring depth
- Gene 5 - Selection method
- Gene 6 - Tournament size
- Gene 7 - Genetic operator rates
- Gene 8 - Mutation type
- Gene 9 - Maximum mutation depth
- Gene 10 - Control flow
- Gene 11 - Operator combination (Table 10.2)
- Gene 12 - Fitness function
- Gene 13 - Number of generations

Each gene is randomly selected from the range of valid options for the corresponding design decision.

10.3.2 Fitness Evaluation

Each chromosome is evaluated by applying the genetic programming algorithm with the design decision options to perform classification. Two phases are conducted, namely, the training phase and the testing phase. The training phase involves performing thirty runs of the genetic programming algorithm to produce a classifier. The best classifier evolved over the thirty runs is applied to the test set during the testing phase. The accuracy of the classifier on the test is assigned as the fitness of the chromosome.

10.3.3 Selection

Fitness proportionate selection is used to select parents to apply genetic operators to produce the offspring of each generation. Elitism is also applied to select a percentage of the fittest individuals in a population across to the next generation.

10.3.4 Regeneration

The population of each generation is created by applying mutation and crossover to the selected parents.

Bit flip mutation is applied. This operator traverses the chromosome gene by gene and decides whether the gene should be mutated. This is decided by randomly selecting a number in the range of 0 to 1. If this number is greater than or equal to the mutation probability, the gene is mutated. The mutation involves randomly selecting a value from the valid options for the design decision represented by the gene. The mutation probability is a genetic algorithm parameter and the most appropriate value to use is problem dependent.

Uniform crossover is employed. Both offsprings are created by using a swapping probability to decide whether the gene in the offspring should be taken from the first or second parent. For each gene, a number in the range of 0 to 1 is randomly selected. If the number is greater than or equal to the swapping probability, the gene is taken from the first parent for the first offspring and from the second parent for the second offspring, otherwise the first gene of the first offspring is taken from the second parent and the first gene of the second offspring is taken from the first parent. This process is applied to obtain each gene for both offspring. The swapping probability is a parameter for the genetic algorithm.

10.3.5 GA Parameter Values

Table 10.3 depicts the parameter values for $autoGA$. These values have been determined empirically by performing trial runs.

Table 10.3 GA parameter values

Parameter	Value
Population size	20
Selection method	Fitness proportionate selection
Uniform crossover rate	80%
Bit mutation rate	10%
Elitism	10%
Maximum number of generation	30/50

10.4 Grammatical Evolution (*autoGE*)

The generational grammatical evolution algorithm [9] is used for the automated design of the genetic algorithm. As in the case of *autoGA*, the termination criterion is the maximum number of generations. The following sections describe the processes of initial population generation, fitness evaluation, selection, regeneration, and parameter selection.

10.4.1 Initial Population Generation

Each element of the population is a randomly created binary string containing 14–16 codons. Each chromosome is mapped to a grammar representing the design decisions described above. The grammar [6] is depicted below: processinlinefigure

10.4.2 Fitness Evaluation

Each chromosome is evaluated by mapping the binary string to the grammar to obtain a configuration for the genetic programming algorithm. The genetic programming algorithm is used with the configuration to produce a classifier. As in the case of *autoGA*, two phases are conducted, the training phase and the testing phase. The training phase involves performing thirty runs of the genetic programming algorithm to produce a classifier. The best classifier evolved over the thirty runs is applied to the test set during the testing phase. The accuracy of the classifier on the test is assigned as the fitness of the chromosome.

10.4.3 Selection

Tournament selection is used to select parents to apply the genetic operators to. Elitism is also applied to select a percentage of the fittest individuals in a population across to the next generation.

10.4.4 Regeneration

Mutation and crossover are used to produce offspring for each generation.

Bit mutation is performed. This operator traverses the chromosome gene by gene and decides whether the gene should be mutated. This is decided by randomly select-

Table 10.4 GE parameter values

Parameter	Value
Population size	20
Tournament size	4
Single point crossover rate	85%
Bit mutation rate	5%
Elitism	10%
Maximum chromosome length	14–16%
Wrapping	Yes
Maximum number of generation	30

ing a number in the range of 0 to 1. If this number is greater than or equal to the mutation probability, the gene is flipped.

Single point crossover is employed. A value in the range of 0 to 1 is randomly selected. If this value is greater than or equal to the crossover probability, the crossover is performed otherwise the parents are copied into the next generation. A crossover point is randomly selected. Both parents are crossed over at this point to produce two offspring.

10.4.5 GE Parameter Values

Table 10.4 depicts the parameter values for $autoGA$. These values have been determined empirically by performing trial runs.

The following section presents the experimental setup for evaluating both $autoGA$ and $autoGP$.

10.5 Experimental Setup

The section describes the experimental setup in terms of the experiments that were performed, statistical tests, the datasets used for evaluation, data preprocessing, and the technical specifications of the machines used to implement algorithms and run simulations in the sections that follow.

10.5.1 Experiments

The following experiments were conducted to evaluate the performance of $autoGA$ and $autoGE$:

1. Manual design of genetic programming to produce arithmetic tree classifiers.
2. Manual design of genetic programming to produce logical tree classifiers.
3. Manual design of genetic programming to produce decision tree classifiers.
4. Automated design of genetic programming using $autoGA$.
5. Automated design of genetic programming using $autoGe$.

For all five experiments, thirty runs were performed during training for each dataset. The best classifier found over the thirty runs was used for testing and the accuracy reported.

The performance of the manual design was compared to that of both automated design approaches. The non-parametric Friedman test [6] was used to determine the statistical significance of the results obtained in the experiments.

10.5.2 Datasets

The following classification problems and datasets werc used to evaluate the performance of $autoGA$ and $autoGE$:

- Binary and multi-class datasets from the UCI Machine Learning Repository [6]. Twenty-two datasets were used from the repository. Details of the datasets used are tabulated in Table 10.5.
- Cybersecurity - Six datasets were created from the NSL-KDD 99+20% benchmark set [6]. Each dataset contains forty-two attributes and five classes, namely, normal, denial of service (dos), probe, user to root (u2r), and root to local (r2l). Each dataset is comprised of 5000 training instances and 2000 test instances.
- Financial forecasting data - Stocks were chosen from the NASDAQ, NYSE, XETRA, and HKSE stock exchanges. Details of the fifteen stocks used are depicted in Table 10.6. The number of training days for all instances is 500 and the number of testing days 100.

Preprocessing was performed on the data. Equal frequency interval [6] is used for discretization. Normalization, namely, min-max normalization [6], is performed on continuous attributes for all datasets. All the algorithms were implemented using Java 1.8.

Table 10.5 UCI machine learning repository datasets

Dataset	No. of attributes	No. of instances	No. of classes
Australian credit data	14	690	2
Appendicitis	7	106	2
Breast cancer (Ljubljana)	9	277	2
Cylinder band	19	365	2
Diabetes (pima)	8	768	2
German credit data	20	1000	2
Heart disease	13	270	2
Hepatitis	19	80	2
Liver disease (Bupa)	6	345	2
Mushroom	22	5644	2
Tictactoe	9	958	2
Balance	4	625	3
Post-operative	8	87	3
Car	6	1728	4
Lymphography	18	148	4
Cleveland	13	297	5
Page-block	10	5472	5
Dermatology	34	358	6
Flare	11	1066	6
Glass	9	214	7
Zoo	16	101	7
Ecoli	7	336	8

10.5.3 Technical Specifications

Simulations were run on the Lengau Cluster of the Center of High-Performance Computing (HPC).

10.6 Results Discussion

This section examines the performance of *autoGA* and *autoGE* compared to the manual designed genetic programming algorithm producing arithmetic tree, logical tree, and decision tree classifiers. The results obtained for each dataset are described in terms of the best accuracy $\pm$ the standard deviation at the 95% percentile confidence interval.

Table 10.6 Financial forecasting stocks

Dataset	Sector	Source
Adobe	Technology	NASDAQ
Amazon	Technology	NASDAQ
American Express	Financial	NYSE
Barclays	Financial	NYSE
Center Point	Energy	NYSE
Dominos Pizza	Food	NYSE
Entergy	Energy	NYSE
Horizon Pharm	Pharmaceutical	NASDAQ
Pfizer	Pharmaceutical	NYSE
McDonalds	Food	NYSE
Microsoft	Software	NASDAQ
SAP	Software	XETRA
Standard Chartered	Financial	HKSE
Time Warner	Entertainment	NYSE
Walt Disney	Entertainment	NYSE

Table 10.7 depicts the results for the manually designed classifiers and $autoGA$ and $autoGE$. Both the $autoGA$ and $autoGE$ have outperformed the manually designed classifiers for both binary and multi-class classification. $autoGE$ appears to perform better than $autoGA$ for binary classification. The Friedman test with a post-hoc Bonferroni–Dunn was conducted to test the statistical significance of these results. The result that $autoGA$ and $autoGE$ perform better than the manually designed classifiers for binary classification was found to be statistically significant. However, no statistically significant difference in the performances of $autoGA$ and $autoGE$ was found. In the case of multi-class classification, $autoGA$ appears to outperform both the manually designed classifiers and $autoGE$, with $autoGE$ performing better than the manually derived classifiers. The result that $autoGA$ outperforms the manually designed classifiers was found to be statistically significant. The result that $autoGA$ performs better than $autoGE$ and that $autoGE$ outperforms the manually derived classifiers was not found to be significant.

Table 10.8 presents the performance of $autoGA$, $autoGE$, and the classifiers produced from the manual design on the network intrusion detection datasets. The $autoGA$ and $autoGE$ appear to perform better than the manually designed classifiers, with $autoGE$ producing the best results. However, these results were not found to be statistically significant.

The performance of the classifiers for financial forecasting is illustrated in Table 10.9. The classifiers produced by $autoGE$ appear to perform better than the other classifiers, with the classifiers produced by automated design producing better results than the manually designed classifiers. The result that $autoGE$ performed better than the manually designed classifiers was found to be statistically significant.

Table 10.7 Testing accuracy for the UCI machine learning repository datasets

Dataset	Arithmetic tree	Logical tree	Decision tree	*autoGA*	*autoGE*
Australian credit	0.83±0.01	0.84±0.01	0.85±0.01	**0.88±0.01**	0.86±0.01
Appendicitis	0.84±0.03	0.78 ±0.03	0.85±0.03	0.91±0.03	**0.94±0.03**
Breast cancer	0.97± 0.02	0.93±0.03	0.90±0.04	0.97±0.02	**0.98±0.02**
Cylinder band	0.66±0.01	0.68±0.01	0.69±0.01	**0.75±0.01**	0.74±0.01
Diabete (pima)	0.64±0.01	**0.75±0.01**	0.69±0.01	0.70±0.07	0.60±0.01
German credit	0.65±0.01	0.65±0.01	0.65±0.01	**0.68±0.01**	0.66±0.05
Heart disease	0.77±0.02	0.64±0.02	0.44±0.01	0.72±0.02	**0.81±0.08**
Hepatitis	0.67±0.03	0.75±0.03	0.75±0.03	0.75±0.03	**0.88±0.02**
Liver disease	0.64±0.01	0.64±0.01	0.44±0.01	**0.71±0.01**	0.65±0.01
Mushroom	0.78±0.00	0.75±0.00	0.66±0.00	**0.81±0.00**	**0.81±0.00**
Tictactoe	0.73±0.01	0.76±0.01	0.65±0.01	0.86±0.01	**0.98±0.01**
Balance	0.81±0.03	0.76±0.03	0.68±0.06	**0.98±0.01**	0.92±0.03
Post-operative	0.61±0.09	0.25±0.09	0.71±0.09	**0.75±0.09**	0.64±0.09
Car	0.40±0.03	0.18±0.03	0.64±0.04	**0.66±0.04**	0.46±0.04
Lymphography	0.73±0.07	0.76±0.07	0.78±0.07	**0.82±0.07**	0.78±0.07
Cleveland	0.53±0.09	0.17±0.07	0.48±0.07	**0.57±0.07**	0.55±0.07
Page-blocks	0.55±0.03	0.57±0.03	0.38±0.03	**0.60±0.03**	0.59±0.03
Dermatology	0.67±0.08	0.38±0.06	0.57±0.08	0.69±0.08	**0.78±0.08**
Flare	0.68±0.05	0.43±0.05	0.67±0.05	0.67±0.04	**0.71±0.04**
Glass	0.24±0.09	0.19±0.09	0.45±0.09	**0.53±0.09**	0.24±0.09
Zoo	**0.81±0.09**	0.56±0.09	0.72±0.09	**0.81±0.09**	**0.81±0.09**
Ecoli	0.61±0.08	0.40±0.08	0.31±0.08	**0.90±0.05**	0.43±0.09

The results that $autoGE$ performed better than $autoGA$ and $autoGA$ produced better results than the manually designed classifiers were not found to be statistically significant.

The automated design was found to reduce the design time. The manual design including parameter tuning and deciding on the classifier type took 50–100 h. The average runtime for $autoGE$ was 26.49 h and for $autoGA$ 30.41 h.

This study has illustrated the effectiveness of the automated design of genetic programming to produce classifiers using evolutionary algorithms. The classifiers produced by the automated design performed better than the manually designed classifiers. $autoGE$ produced better-performing classifiers for binary classification than $autoGA$ and $autoGA$ performed better than $autoGE$ for multi-class classification. However, these results were not found to be statistically significant.

Table 10.8 Performance on the network intrusion detection datasets

Dataset	Arithmetic tree	Logical tree	Decision tree	*autoGA*	*autoGE*
normal	0.97±0.03	0.96±0.03	0.92±0.03	**0.98±0.02**	**0.98±0.02**
dos	**0.99±0.01**	0.97±0.02	0.92±0.04	**0.99±0.01**	**0.99±0.01**
probe	**0.99±0.01**	0.98±0.02	0.91±0.04	0.98±0.02	0.98±0.02
u2r	0.99±0.01	0.99±0.01	0.99±0.01	**1.00±0.00**	0.99±0.01
r2l	0.98±0.02	0.98±0.02	0.98±0.02	0.98±0.02	**0.99±0.01**
multi	0.81±0.02	0.68±0.02	0.59 ±0.02	**0.82±0.02**	0.72 ±0.02

Table 10.9 Performance on the financial forecasting stocks

Dataset	Arithmetic tree	Logical tree	Decision tree	*autoGA*	*autoGE*
Adobe	0.69±0.04	0.66±0.04	0.47±0.04	0.70±0.03	0.69±0.04
Amazon	0.69±0.04	0.52±0.04	0.55±0.04	0.71±0.04	0.66±0.04
American Express	0.62±0.04	0.61±0.04	0.64±0.06	0.66±0.04	0.66±0.04
Barclays	0.70±0.04	0.54±0.04	0.55±0.04	0.80±0.03	0.81±0.03
Center Point	0.77±0.03	0.57±0.03	0.58±0.03	0.80±0.03	0.81±0.03
Dominos Pizza	073.±0.04	0.58±0.04	0.54±0.04	0.77±0.04	0.77±0.04
Entergy	0.54±0.04	0.53±0.04	0.51±0.04	0.54±0.04	0.53±0.04
Horizon Pharmacy	0.48±0.04	0.53±0.04	0.51±0.04	0.53±0.04	0.53±0.04
Pfizer	0.64±0.04	0.56±0.04	0.74±0.04	0.65±0.04	0.65±0.04
McDonalds	0.58±0.04	0.64±0.04	0.60±0.04	0.66±0.04	0.69±0.04
Microsoft	0.69±0.04	0.72±0.03	0.70±0.03	0.65±0.05	0.81±0.03
Sap	0.54±0.04	0.55±0.04	0.58±0.04	0.56±0.04	0.58±0.04
Standard Chartered	0.82±0.03	0.75±0.03	0.57±0.03	0.81±0.02	0.82±0.03
Time Warner	0.41±0.04	0.86±0.04	0.74±0.04	0.89±0.03	0.89±0.03
Walt Disney	0.49±0.03	0.49±0.04	0.51±0.04	0.51±0.04	0.51±0.04

10.7 Conclusion

This chapter has examined the automated design of a classification algorithm, namely, genetic programming, to produce classifiers. The performance of genetic algorithms and grammatical evolution has been compared for the purpose of automating the design of genetic programming for binary and multi-class classification. Genetic algorithms were found to perform better for multi-class classification and grammatical evolution for binary classification. The automated design required less design time than the manual genetic programming design and produced better-performing classifiers.

Future work will study the correlation between search in the design space and solution space in an attempt to better understand the performance of the automated design approaches. Extensions of this research will also investigate the automated design of the approaches that perform the automated design. This study revealed that $autoGA$ performed better for multi-class classification and $autoGE$ better for binary classification. Further analysis revealed that the fitness landscape for the genetic algorithm was smoother for multi-class classification than grammatical evolution. Similarly, grammatical evolution had a smoother fitness landscape for binary classification than a genetic algorithm. Future research will also investigate hybridizing both these approaches for classification.

References

1. R.C. Barros, M.P. Basgalupp, A. Freitas, A.C.P.L.F. de Carvalho, Evolutonary design of decision-tree algorithms tailored to microarray gene expression data sets. IEEE Trans. Evol. Comput. **18**(6), 873–892 (2018)
2. R.C. Barros, A. de Carvalho, A. Freitas, *Automatic Design of Decision-Tree Induction Algorithms* (Springer, 2015)
3. D.E. Goldberg, *Genetic Algorithms in Search, Optimization and Machine Learning* (Addison-Wesley, 1989)
4. B. Komer, J. Bergstra, C. Eliasmith, Hyperopt-sklean, in *Automated Machine Learning-Methods, Systems, Challenges* (Springer, 2019)
5. J. Koza, *Genetic Programming: On the Programming of Computers by Natural Selection* (MIT Press, 1992)
6. T. Nyathi, *Automated Design of Genetic Programming Classification Algorithms using a Genetic Algorithm and Grammatical Evolution*. PhD thesis, School of Mathematics, Statistics and Computer Science (2018)
7. T. Nyathi, N. Pillay, Comparison of a genetic algorithm to grammatical evolution for automated design of genetic programming classification algorithms. Expert Syst. Appl. **104**, 213–334 (2018)
8. J.H. Olson, R.S. anf Moore, Tpot: a tree-based pipeline optimiation tool for automating machine learning, in *Automated Machine Learning-Methods, Systems, Challenges*, ed. by F. Hutter, L. Kotthoff, J. Vanschoren (Springer, 2019)
9. M. O'Neill, C. Ryan, *Grammatical Evolution-Evolutionary Automatic Programming in an Arbitrary Language* (Kluwer Academic Publishers, 2003)
10. N. Pillay, R. Qu, *Hyper-Heuristics: Theory and Applications* (Springer, 2018)
11. N.R. Sabar, X. Yi, A. Song, A bi-objective hyper-heuristic support vector machines for big data cyber-security. IEEE Access **6**, 10421–10431 (2018)
12. A. Vella, *Hyper-Heuristic Decision Tree Induction*. PhD thesis, School of Mathematical and Computer Sciences, Herriot-Watt University (2012)

Chapter 11
Automated Design (AutoDes): Current Trends and Future Research Directions

Nelishia Pillay

Abstract The book has presented current trends and state-of-the-art advancements in the automated design of machine learning and search algorithms. In this context, we define automated design(AutoDes) to include automated algorithm/approach configuration, composition, and selection. This chapter provides a conclusion to the book by bringing together these contributions, highlighting different focus areas, and setting the agenda for future research directions. This is presented in terms of reusability in automated design, explainable automated design, computational costs, theoretical aspects, automated design standardization, and semi-automated design.

11.1 Introduction

As we move into the fourth industrial revolution, the use of machine learning and search algorithms to solve real-world problems is rapidly increasing. There is an urgent need to develop off-the-shelf machine learning and search algorithm tools that can be used by non-experts to solve real-world problems. As can be seen from the research presented in this book, there have been great strides made in the automated design of machine learning search algorithms. However, there is still room for future extensions of this research to further reduce the gap between research and real-world application.

As defined in Chap. 3, automated design (AutoDes) refers to the configuration, composition, and selection of algorithms and approaches and including the following design decisions:

- Parameter and hyper-parameter tuning
- Operator selection
- Heuristic selection
- Operator creation
- Heuristic creation

N. Pillay (✉)
University of Pretoria, Pretoria, South Africa
e-mail: nelishia.pillay@up.ac.za

N. Pillay and R. Qu (eds.), *Automated Design of Machine Learning and Search Algorithms*, Natural Computing Series,
https://doi.org/10.1007/978-3-030-72069-8_11

- Algorithm composition
- Hybridization of algorithms or approaches.

The following sections highlight the current trends in the field and future research directions in terms of reusability in automated design, explainable automated design, computational costs, theoretical aspects, automated design standardization, and semi-automated design.

11.1.1 Reusability in AutoDes

Generally, the research in AutoDes has been done in isolation, with the automation being developed from scratch. Investigations into reusable automation need to be conducted. This will involve generating designs that can possibly be used for other instances of the same problem or other problem domains. The use of transfer learning needs to be examined in this context as well. Certain aspects of the design or configuration may be reusable while other aspects will need to be optimized.

11.1.2 Explainable AutoDes

One of the challenges experienced with some of the approaches that may be used for AutoDes is that these are black-box approaches that do not provide details as to how the particular design was arrived at, which may be necessary for certain instances. An area that requires investigation is the use of explainable artificial intelligence approaches for providing explanations of how design decisions were arrived at.

11.1.3 Computational Cost of Algorithm Automation

High computational time and effort are associated with automated algorithm design, configuration, and selection. Chapter 7 provides an alternative for reducing the computational cost of NAS. Further investigation into techniques such as federated learning needs to be examined with the aim of reducing computational costs for the various approaches performing optimization for design decisions.

11.1.4 Theoretical Aspects

Further research into the theoretical aspects, such as time complexity analysis and fitness landscape analysis, needs to be conducted to better understand AutoDes search spaces. Chapter 6 reports on a study of time complexity for the selection of perturbative hyper-heuristics for the configuration of algorithms solving function optimization problems. In [1], the author performs fitness landscape analysis to examine the design and configuration space for genetic algorithms and grammatical evolution for the automated design and configuration of the genetic programming algorithm to produce classifiers. This study revealed that using genetic algorithms to produce binary classifiers results in a more rugged space than when using grammatical evolution, and hence grammatical evolution was more suitable for exploring the design and configuration space for genetic programming to produce a binary classifier and provided a justification for the experimental results obtained on various datasets, indicating that grammatical evolution produced binary classifiers of superior performance to those produced by genetic algorithms. Such analysis can be used to determine the suitability of different techniques for exploring the design space.

11.1.5 AutoDes Standardization

From the research in the area of algorithm automation, it is evident that these studies are done in isolation which in some instances have led to the replication of work. More rapid advancement of the field can be achieved if previous work can be built on rather than starting the same or similar studies from scratch. This can be achieved by establishing a standardization for the research community and providing a platform for researchers in the field to share initiatives. Chapter 3 presents a starting point that can be built on for developing a standardization for the field. A platform needs to be created to enable researchers in the field to share resources. Such a standardization and platform will also facilitate reproducibility of results, the need for which is highlighted in Chap. 2.

11.1.6 Semi-automated Design

An area that warrants further investigation is the semi-automated design. This would involve a tool in which optimization is used for AutoDes with guidance from a researcher. It is hypothesized that this would be effective for new areas and domains where AutoDes is based on simulations of the environment that it would be employed, for example, the design of robot swarms presented in Chap. 5. This can also be used as a means of the approach employed for AutoDes learning from the researcher.

Reference

1. T. Nyathi, *Automated Design of Genetic Programming Classification Algorithms*. Ph.D. thesis, School of Mathematics, Statistics and Computer Science, December (2018)

Printed in the United States
by Baker & Taylor Publisher Services